ATTACKING THE ZONE DEFENSES

Del Harris
Ken Shields

CHAMPIONSHIP Productions

2730 Graham Street
Ames, Iowa 50010
1-800-873-2730

www.ChampionshipProductions.com.

Published by:

Championship Productions, Inc.
2730 Graham Street
Ames, Iowa 50010
1-800-873-2730
www.ChampionshipProductions.com

Attacking the Zone Defenses

DEDICATION

"There are very few grand masters of basketball, but Rick was one of the best in the game of basketball's chess match. His love for the game, his players and his friends was a gift to those who worked and competed with or against him. The times together, the moments shared and the dedication to friendship is one of the most valued blessings of my life."
- George Karl, Sacramento Kings Head coach

"Rick Majerus was well-known for the thoroughness of his game preparations. This book gives the reader a look into his thinking when preparing to face a zone defense. He was a masterful coach in all phases of the game."
- Don Donoher, former University of Dayton Head Coach;
Distinguished member of the National Collegiate Basketball Hall of Fame

"If there ever were a mind meant for basketball, it was the one "Coach" had. There has never been a better teacher of the game or someone who respected the game more than he. The game and I are better off having been part of it with him."
- Alex Jensen, Utah Jazz Assistant Coach,
played for Coach Rick Majerus at Utah (1998 NCAA Runner-Up)

ACKNOWLEDGEMENTS

First of all we want to recognize the game of basketball that has become our life work and has afforded us a way to make a living doing something we both love. We are thankful for our families for standing with us in this endeavor as well. It may have helped that both our wives were basketball coaches. We respect the game for the values that can be developed in players and coaches when this great team game is played and taught well and for the multitude of enduring relationships that result in the process. Thanks to all the players and fellow coaches who have contributed to our success. We are happy to acknowledge so many that have been important to us in the production of this book that we are dedicating to the memory of our beloved friend, Rick Majerus.

We appreciate the staff at Championship Productions, which has been the leader in publishing written and video materials that have upgraded the coaching and playing levels of various sports, but particularly basketball in our estimation, for four decades at the time of this writing. Thanks to Thom McDonald and Nate Landas for believing we had a worthy project and to Chad Bauman for the yeoman work he did in the everyday process of helping us get through the process of putting together a 300-plus tome on the singular important subject of Zone Offense.

While we have gained much from the coaching world at large in our combined coaching years that total nearly 100 years that involved many years of double seasons, coaching the winter season in North America and summers in FIBA basketball around the world in many major international events including various World Championships and Olympics. But here we want to express appreciation particularly to the great coaches who answered our request to make a token contribution to our endeavor (in alphabetical order); Steve Alford, John Calipari, Mike Krzyzewski, Sean Miller, Lorenzo Romar, Bo Ryan and Bill Self — an all-star cast. Thanks also to works we lifted from watching the work of Tom Izzo and Jamie Dixon as well as to the amazing FIBA coaches we worked against. While there are many top coaches in the world outside the USA borders, we chose these with whom we have competed against most recently as representative of the great group of international coaches — Dave Blatt, Sergio Hernandez, Jonas Kaslauskas, Ruben Magnano, and Zeljiko Obradovic.

Many thanks to Rick's friend and former assistant coach Paul Biancardi, now of ESPN, for writing the thoughtful foreword, as well as to Coach Fran Fraschilla of ESPN. A special thanks to others who were among Rick's closest friends that we believed had to be included in the honoring process — George Karl, Don Donoher, and Alex Jensen. Rick had a profound affect on so many of us, from high school coaches like Tommy Thomas to NBA Hall of Famer, Don Nelson.

Ken and Del have the utmost respect for Women's Basketball and for the tremendous growth and improvement in the quality of play that has taken place over the last 20 years. Ken's first coaching job was the Women's Team at UBC that won the Canadian National Championships in 1969-70. He and his wife Kathy won a total of 15 Canadian University National Championships and over 20 of their players went on to represent Canada on the Senior National Teams. They coached the Canadian Men's and Women's National Basketball Teams for a combined total of 9 years with each finishing 7th in the World Championships in 1994. Ken went on to assist Women's Teams in Japan and was the lead assistant with the British Women's National Team in their successful drive to qualify for and compete in the London Olympics. Ironically, Del's first coaching job was as a middle school boy's and girl's coach. We certainly apologize to any woman who feels slighted as we have been limited to using the masculine terms and we offer our ideas on zone offense to women with an equal level of honor and respect, as we do for all the men who coach and play this wonderful game.

All play and drill diagrams were made in FastDraw® play diagramming software made by FastModel Sports®. A big thank you to Ross Comerford, CEO of our trusted partner FastModel Sports, for empowering coaches with FastDraw, and to Brett Hartig and Matt Marlow for their diligent work. This is the best preparation tool in the game, saving coaching staffs countless hours of preparation time, allowing us to focus on what really matters: developing our players and winning games. Visit www.fastmodelsports.com to learn more and get FastDraw for yourself.

FOREWORD

BY PAUL BIANCARDI

I had the honor and the privilege to be part of Rick Majerus' original staff at Saint Louis University. I first met Coach Majerus when I was the head coach at Wright State University. The legendary coach of the Dayton Flyers, Don Donoher, had put us together through his son, Brian, who was a member of my coaching staff at WSU. Brian was a sharp and diligent basketball coach who knew I loved the history of the game and always wanted to learn from other coaches. He mentioned to me that Rick Majerus was coming to Dayton and wanted to know if I would want him to watch our team's practice.

As all coaches who want to grow in the profession, I jumped at the opportunity to have someone with Coach Majerus' history and success in the game. Having such a person watch, give feedback to me, and to speak to our team was priceless. Our relationship grew naturally from that point on as the love of basketball was the common thread.

Our conversations took place late in the evenings during and after dinners quite often. That is when "Coach" would like to talk ball. We discussed how the game should be taught, the value of skill work, academics, as well as coaching philosophies and strategies of recruiting. He was in love with the game and the game was his life. As a 17-year Division 1 collegiate basketball coach, I felt very confident in my coaching abilities. But once I became a part of his staff, I realized what a great teacher of the game he was and what one ought to be. He was as close to brilliant as one could hope to find.

His passion and respect for the game was unparalleled. This is a man who held our pre-season coaching staff meetings at an outdoor playground in Milwaukee near his house. We walked through all his offensive and defensive concepts on a cement court that had major cracks and weeds protruding through the cement. It didn't matter to Rick. It was a basketball court.

During that first season at Saint Louis, Porter Moser and I begged him to put in a zone defense because we were grossly under-manned. I'll never forget his response: "I never played a minute of zone defense in my life, only a triangle and two (which won the game for Utah against

Arizona to advance to the NCAA Championship game against Kentucky in 1996). I only know how to attack a zone. I don't know how to teach a zone defense. You and Porter put in the zone defense you want and you guys can teach it!"

How appropriate that two of his very best friends, Del Harris and Ken Shields, whom he would talk about on a daily basis would write a book on zone offense and dedicate it to him! Let's face it; zone offense is way behind man-to-man offense in today's game. The high school game is saturated with zone defense, while the college game is going to a 30-second shot clock that will increase zone play. Even NBA teams play a morphed zone defense at times with their 3-second defense rule in effect for the last several years. And most teams struggle against the smart zones. That's why this book is invaluable with the contributions of some of the nation's top collegiate coaches also contributing zone ideas as a tribute to a coaching legend.

Del Harris and Ken Shields contribute their vast basketball acumen, which they shared with Coach Rick Majerus throughout his coaching career. This book also presents clearly some of Rick's many outstanding zone plays and concepts that could beat any defense, when augmented in his own unique style. The one thing I know is that Del Harris and Ken Shields would never write a book on zone defense and dedicate it to Coach Majerus because he never played a minute of zone defense!

Regardless of the level that you coach from beginner to the NBA, this book will enhance your knowledge of zone offense and help you become a better zone coach!

Paul Biancardi
ESPN Basketball
National Recruiting Director

INTRODUCTION

The relationship we have that has led to our collaboration for this book began back in 1993 when our close mutual friend and great coach, Rick Majerus, told Ken that he would not be able to help him prepare his Canadian National basketball team for the impending 1994 World Championships to be hosted in Toronto. Rick suggested Ken contact Del, who was in between being head coach of the Milwaukee Bucks and Los Angeles Lakers, whom Rick had worked with one season when both were assistant coaches at the Bucks.

We immediately became friends who respected our mutual commitment to excellence in the great game of basketball combined with a deep concern for our players. We had a very successful run in those World Games with our 19-year old point guard who became one of the game's great players, Steve Nash and a young small forward who became a championship player with the Lakers years later, Rick Fox. Canadians still recall a questionable call or two in the game against Russia that may well have kept them from winning a medal as hosts of those games.

We maintained that friendship over the years and collaborated in the 2004 Olympics in Athens when Del needed help from Ken in preparing his Chinese National Team for those games. Del was handicapped by not having the same film library on the opponents that the rest of the teams had nor the film editing equipment. Ken was assistant coach of the Australian National Team for those Olympics and, by Australia being in the opposite pool from China, was able to have Del come to the Aussies' headquarters to get some good scouting on the teams China would be playing in the preliminary rounds. Del believes that his team would not have been able to have qualified for the medal round in those Olympic Games without that assist from Ken and the Australian staff.

Having stayed in contact over the ensuing years, we shared our grief together at the funeral mass of our great friend, Rick, in December of 2012. The following Spring, after watching so many teams stumble over the zone defenses various teams threw at teams in the 2012-13 season, Ken suggested that Del have a re-do of his successful book, *Coaching Basketball's Zone Offenses*, written in 1975. He suggested adding anything learned in the intervening years from watching others and from having to attack NBA zones since zone defenses were allowed several years ago. Del rejected the idea initially, having just endured writing his book on team building, *On Point, 4 Steps to Better Life-Teams*.

However, after giving it more thought, Del called Ken with a proposition: Ken could utilize any of the book he liked and contribute his expertise to start the new book. Then, when he felt comfortable that he had something going on it, we would get together and finish it off. In addition we decided we would add some ideas from some top NCAA coaches as well as from FIBA coaches that we had coached against. At that point we agreed that it would be fitting to dedicate the book to the memory of our friend, Rick. It made sense at that point to add some of Coach Majerus's zone offense attacks that we were both familiar with due to our close relationship that resulted from our mutual sharing of ideas over the years.

Why are Zone Defenses so Problematic in Today's Game? First of all, this is not a new issue. Zone offense has always lagged behind the other technical aspects of the game. There are a lot of reasons for this, but we will point out some of the obvious ones:

1) at the higher levels of the game where innovations occur — high school, college and professional — the majority of teams play man-to-man as their primary defense. Therefore, teams spend much more time preparing for that type of defense.

2) Consequently, coaches teach more man-to-man offense techniques and employ more of such sets than the zone offense counterparts.

3) Most coaches will still have a zone defense they will throw out on the court to have one or two types to practice against, but perhaps as a potential momentum or game changer. However, they most often **have only two or three main offensive sets against the zone defenses.**

4) Even if the team has more zone offense options at their disposal, the players will not have been schooled in those sets enough to read for subtle defense adjustments like they normally have been taught in their man-to-man sets.

5) **Perhaps the biggest reason** is that coaches who use zone defenses as their principle defense and master the various adjustments that zones can make are able to study what the upcoming opponent tends to do against zones and find a way to adjust to about any move that will be

thrown at them. That may sound fanciful, but it is true because they will normally be facing very few moves that they don't already know exactly how they are to move/slide/rotate to defend.

If this is the case, why doesn't everyone play zone defense all the time? There are a lot of reasons for that, but this is not an essay on the reasons coaches do what they do. We are here to talk about zone offense. So, let it be enough to say that it is mandatory that players be skilled at man-to-man play on both ends of the court, regardless of what defensive type is used. **A good man-to-man defense will employ sound zone principles, particularly on the weak side; and a good zone defense must execute good man-to-man technique, especially on the strong side.** Apart from that, traditionally, it has been regarded more macho to go man-to-man and it has been considered to be the defense of the over-dog. That is, a team with superior players physically and technically should be able to beat the opponent on a man-to-man basis is the concept. Zone defenses are generally regarded as an equalizer for the lesser talented team and a default to go to when being overpowered by a better team.

These points are arguable, but it is certainly true that some teams with great players have decided to use zone as their main defense and have had great success — Temple University and Syracuse University being two of the best-known examples. But there have been many other such examples with the lesser publicized programs in high school and college for that matter. It is likely that the most successful of those teams played good individual man-to-man techniques within their zone defense and that many used some concepts that relate to the principles of **matching up defenders to players in their specific area at the time, i.e. using man-to-man principles in a zone format.**

Having said this, we began this writing with full respect for zone defenses. When we describe a play by saying that it will work against any zone formation such as 2-3 or 1-2-2 or a match-up, we know that the adept zone coach can quickly say, "Oh yeah, not if I rotate here or overplay there or trap or blah, blah, blah!" And he will be correct. **Every play action in basketball, theoretically, can be hindered; and yet any excellent defensive maneuver can still end up with the defensive team having to take the ball out of the net. There are no shutouts beyond the Biddy level.** Our point is that if you have more than just 2-3 plays, and if you have taught and drilled a team to be able to read and react to most of the tactics a zone can employ, the team can expect to be able to get a decent look at a shot most of the time.

If there were one perfect offensive play set against any defense, it would already have been seen and all the coaches would be copying it. We don't guarantee that here, despite all our positive statements. So, until that happens, we think that the best way to be able to expect success against the zones is to study what we have included here and select those items that fit your team and what you believe you can teach. The points we make are an amalgamation of principles, concepts, rules, plays, and actions that have proven to be successful for many coaches and ourselves in our long journey. No individual coach has used all of these strategies and never could. But when you have looked through our presentation, you will know more about zone offense than you do at this moment. That is our promise, with thanks to those who have one way or another contributed to our being able to present these things to the coaching world at large.

Finally, let us say at the start that we know that coaches tend to want only "tricky plays" and drills from clinics they attend and books they read. We will supply both. But we are obligated to write about some of the fundamental aspects of zone offense relative to our collective philosophy of offense and the necessary attention to various teaching aspects that are required. As indicated at the start, we believe that zone offense has trailed all the rest of the various aspects of basketball historically, and continues to do so. Coaches often skip over the part that we will present early on that lays the foundation for a successful zone attack in our opinion and skip right into the "real stuff" of set plays and drills. Our recommendation to all coaches of every level is to study what we consider foundational details essential to success. We attest that the best coaches we have known over our dual careers, covering nearly 100 years on the bench, were ones who focused on the details. As in all of life's endeavors, we think that it is important to start with the basics when building something of significance.

We are not arrogant to think that what we put down on these pages is the last word in zone offense. In fact we think one of the under-recognized beauties of the game is that it continues to evolve. We have heard many times that the game hasn't changed, that it is a simple game, that it is not rocket science. While there are elements of truth in each of these statements, anyone who has spent a lot of in-depth time in teaching/coaching the game knows how hard it is to win a competitive game of basketball when played at the highest levels. Every year and every game present unique challenges. The coach who understands this and seeks to learn and improve all the time will have the best chance to have an extended career in a highly competitive endeavor. As for ourselves, we continue to seek better concepts to learn and to teach, as we share what we have to give on these pages.

.

—————————— **CHAPTER 1** ——————————

CONSTRUCTING A ZONE OFFENSE INSIDE-OUT WITH SPACING

PHILOSOPHY OF OFFENSE

Play it inside out! There are many ways to play the game of basketball successfully. One very important fundamental tenet of the game, which applies equally to both man-to-man and zone offenses, has emerged over the years. It is clear that the team that gets **the most high percentage shots** in the lane will usually win the game, the addition of the 3- point shot notwithstanding. Even the most skilled shooting teams find it extremely difficult to maintain a high perimeter shooting percentage for the duration of a game. Thus, evolution of the **inside-out philosophy of offense** continues. Even teams who win at "Small Ball" will draft or trade for the next Moses Malone, Hakeem Olajuwon, Shaquille O'Neal, Bill Russell, and so on when one becomes available. The NBA's lust for Dwight Howard for several years in hopes he might be like one of those is proof enough of the point.

Even the proponents of volume 3-point shots per game being the wave of the future in basketball admit the best of those attempts come either from inside penetration of one kind or another or in transition. Certainly the **uncontested** layup is the highest percentage shot; therefore, a **fast break** that yields a layup is the optimal element and an important component of any successful offense. If we can attack any kind of defense in transition for a high percentage shot before the defense gets set, we will be happy.

In the half court, if the rim is threatened, either by the drive or by a pass inside, the defense will be forced to rotate or stunt to prevent an easy high percentage scoring opportunity. If the ball is **quickly kicked out** to an open perimeter player, this player will have an open shot or an opportunity to attack a recovering defender, one of defense's greatest challenges. So, if all of our early actions make the defense guard **inside-out** first, the opportunities for open shots from 3-point range will be available more frequently; consequently, the offense will have more opportunities to attack the recovering defender whose job it is to take away the 3-point shot.

John Wooden taught that "what you did before you got the ball, determines what you can do after you get it." In other words, if we can get an advantage on a defender close to the basket, **usually by sealing or ducking in,** and can get that player the ball, we will usually have a good chance for a very high percentage shot. We may even draw a foul in the process. We must, therefore, teach our players to constantly look for opportunities to attack an unprepared defender to gain an advantage close to the rim. Of course, a critical element of this approach involves teaching the posted players to create passing lanes to themselves and teaching the passer **the art of post feeds** by taking into consideration the positioning of the player guarding the ball, the player guarding the post, and the weak side defender's positioning.

Having an **inside-out** approach comes with several important caveats. We do not generally recommend forcing first side attacks. Even weak defenses are usually set on the first side of the attack, which gives them an advantage both defensively and in the rebounding game. For the offense to attack on the first side, we prefer to have a 75% or higher opportunity to score. For example, a perimeter player may have a very open shot or a short driving lane to the rim; or a post player has an advantage on his defender when the ball is caught before defensive help can arrive. The initial side of the offensive attack is **the shift side,** as the offense makes the defense commit to a strong side. The point is that this is when defenders can usually position themselves in the best position to contain the offense, so it is not normally the best situation for the offense to attack.

When the ball is rotated to the opposite, or second side, we refer to it as the **"attack side."** From this point on, as the ball is moved in combination with player movement and proper spacing, the team should be in attack mode, seeking options to penetrate the zone through passing or dribble penetration. An eye is always kept on getting an easy inside pass for a shot, or to collapse the defense in order to pass it back out to an open player for a shot or drive. This kind of approach will break down a defense that is forced to move from side to side most of the time. **"Swing and attack"** is a common mantra among knowledgeable coaches in planning to beat the zone defenses. The **inside-out** attack approach thus has many facets.

An exception to the **inside-out** approach can occur when a high percentage 3-point shooter has an open shot in transition, or on the first side of the attack early in the shot clock. We believe that a **Three-Point Shot License,** first observed by Ken at the Australian Institute of Sport, can be awarded to players who have successfully maintained a 40% 3-point shooting percentage (charted in practice). These players may shoot on the first side, or early in the shot clock, if they are afforded an on-balanced, uncontested opportunity. Of course, this is relative to time and score situations, plus the coach reserves the right to **suspend** the Three-Point Shot License if game 3-point shooting percentages for a player drop below a certain percentage level.

Obviously, a successful coach will have had good players that he will have taught the **"What, How and Why"** aspects of the game. That third element is integral to players' development of their basketball IQ factor, not to be overlooked as a plus. The master coach will help his players excel by taking time to teach through film and drilling the final step in player maturity — the **"When"** aspect of the various components of the game. This involves **timing and decision-making** that are necessary for quality execution, and players who combine these aspects separate themselves from the pack.

Coaches have many responsibilities, but teaching and leading should be the main priorities. Volumes are written on each of these topics and are worthy of study. Through high quality teaching and leadership, coaches must strive for the development of trusted, confident, and competitively tough young men and women — ones who can be trusted to have a high degree of competence and integrity. Confidence can thus be earned and developed through many trials, featuring both success and failure. Through our book, we hope to assist coaches in their ability to develop players who will light up with confidence, when they are confronted with any type of zone defense, because they will know that they are prepared and competent to the task.

RECOGNIZE THE VARIOUS TYPES AND STYLES OF ZONES TO PLAY AGAINST

There is no single definition of a zone defense. It is not enough to identify the simple fact that they are not playing a man-to-man defense. Players need to know the alignment of the zone and which of the styles they must attack: containing, laning, matching or trapping. Players must align themselves in such a way as to create the biggest problems for the zone defenders. One of the simplest starts to this is for the perimeter players to line up right in the seams or gaps in the zone to make the defenders have to decide who will defend each of them initially.

It is essential that players understand the basic coverage area responsibility of the players in the various types of zones, and where the natural seams in the zone are located. This may not be easy since many teams that use zones will match up against the offensive alignment that is presented, right out of transition. Other coaches start in their particular alignment regardless of the offensive alignment and adjust with designated keys.

Diagrams 1-3 following indicate the gaps in three of the most common zone defensive alignments that players may choose to line up in to make the defense decide who they will match with them when one of them gets the ball or to block out when a shot goes up.

TYPES OF ZONES IN TERMS OF VARYING ALIGNMENTS

2-Guard Fronts: 2-3 or 2-1- 2 Zones

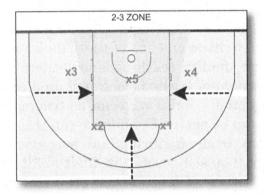

1-Guard Fronts: 3-2, 1-2-2 or 1-3-1 Zones:

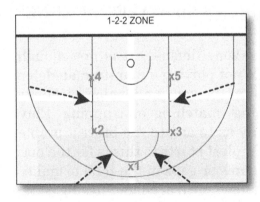
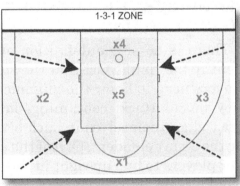

STYLES — How the various types may be utilized

Containing

The standard zone types first used in basketball were the basic 2-3 and 1-2-2 formations, which dictated that each player cover a defined area in a containing, sagging manner within the 18-20 foot area. The idea was to keep the ball out of the middle and force the outside shot. Shooting was generally a 33% proposition until the 1960s, including all shots from the field. Percentages beyond 20 feet shooting fell below 20% in most cases. Even with today's outstanding shooting, there is a place for the hard-hustling, quick-moving containing zone defense. It is still effective against poor shooting teams and late in games at times when the opponent is reluctant to shoot outside. It is amazing to chart the **true outside shooting percentages** of even today's teams and find that many shooters struggle to shoot higher than 33% beyond 19 feet, if they are pressured at all. Therefore, each team must be prepared to defeat the containing style of defense, whether it be zone or man-to-man.

Fundamentally, it is important to know that the containing zones thrive on the quick outside shot and poor ball and player movement. Furthermore, with the addition of the 3-point line and the shot clock, some teams now decide to use a 3-point shooting attack as the primary weapon against all defenses, and forego the inside game. To be effective, the offense must avoid this pitfall with an inside-out focus first with good spacing. If this is not done, the reason this old technique still helps win games becomes quite clear.

Laning

The laning style of defense popped up in the late 1950s in response to teams that were moving the ball so well that they were beating the standard containing zones and shooting was getting better than it had been previously. The first laning concept was to encourage the ball to be thrown to a corner and then to have the defender on the wing get out into the passing lane from the corner back to the wing. This simple move stymied the ball movement necessary to make the zone shift. This then caused players to realize they needed to cut to hurt the zones as opposed to standing in formation and moving the ball rapidly.

From that adjustment coaches broadened the laning concept to include having **every player adjacent to the ball handler** leave his containing position (ball-you-basket) in favor of extending his defensive perimeter by **getting at least a hand into the adjacent passing lane** (ball-you-next man). The net effect was to disturb the easy flow of passing that the containing zones allowed. Turnovers resulted as defenses upset the opponent's entire passing and cutting rhythm.

The 1-2-2 and 1-3-1 formations lent themselves to laning more than did the 2-3. Coaches soon found that the middle was vulnerable when the 1-2-2 extended into the lanes and so the 1-3-1 emerged as the formation of choice for teams that chose to do a lot of lane-playing. The middle man with long arms and an active body wreaked havoc against teams trying to get the ball inside.

Matching Up From Any Alignment

As a means for out-manned or underdog teams to confuse offenses when standard man-to-man and zone defenses proved to be inadequate, defensive strategists became interested in finding a different compromise to man-to-man defenses and the aforementioned types of zones. The result was the gradual development of the **Match-up Zone Defense** style beginning in the 1960s. The concept in this defense is to play a zone defense while using many man-to-man principles that can be initiated out of any of the alignment types, 1-front or 2-front. The match-up has grown over the years and there are many adaptations of it. It can be set in motion as the ball crosses into the front court or after a specific cut or pass by the offense. It can involve only a few man-to-man rules or a long list of rules. The operative word here is "rule." Teams that play effective zones of any style will always be guided by some set of guidelines or rules to cover situations including specific cuts, overload formations, baseline rovers, two men in a zone, no men in a zone, screens on and off of the ball and other contingencies.

Effective scouting becomes important against teams that execute their ruled defenses. This is especially true in the case of the match-up zone team. Unless the offense knows how to identify and attack the match up correctly, it can spend all evening with a defense matched up *right in their face*. To compound the problem, the defense has the advantage in the scouting game, if the offensive team only has two or three things that they do to attack the zone. A good match-up team will be able to set rules to cover those moves and make it difficult for the offense to get open, unchallenged looks at the goal. Beating the best match-up zones, as well as the traditional zones that combine hard hustle and good rotations, remain major challenges at all levels of the game.

Trapping

There are many variations that may be employed in the scoring area to utilize trapping with the zone defenses. The defense may be all-out trapping, or it may be one that traps only in certain areas such as in the corners, or in the low post, or the short corner. It could be that the defense will trap only one time and be done, or it may continue to chase the ball the entire possession. However it is ruled, the defense can cause problems and confusion, if the offense is not prepared. It is important for the offense to know proper escape techniques when faced with a trap.

In summary it is important to understand how the different styles of zones work in order to make an effective game plan. If one sees all defenses broken into just man-to-man, zone and trapping and fails to see the subtle nuances in each, he will find frustration waiting for him coming out of the opponent's locker room.

COMBINATION DEFENSES
Triangle and 2 and a Box and 1

A much simpler approach to combining man-to-man and zone than the match-up is broadly called using combination defenses. In the 1960s the **Triangle and Two** and the **Box and 1** surfaced as trick defenses to help the underdog teams or to attack the teams that had one or two outstanding players but little help from their teammates. These adjustments and other combinations, which allow certain players to play man-to-man while others play zone, became popular again in the 1990s and still show up frequently. It becomes incumbent upon the coach to know how to free up his key player/players or maximize the other players when faced with these attacks.

THE GEOMETRY OF THE GAME

Basketball is based on several sciences. Among them are kinesiology, physics and **geometry**. After all, the ball is a sphere that is projected elliptically toward a circle in the form of a net-enclosed cylinder. That cylinder, or goal, is mounted on a rectangle and the court is yet another rectangle lined with segments, arcs, and more circles. Many angles come into play as one considers the aspects of passing, cutting, and defending. Well, there is a lot more to it than that, of course.

The Line of 45 Degrees

First of all, the point filled by the posted man is of utmost significance. He should assume a position well above the painted block. Many posted people hear the term, "get to the blocks" and go literally to a position on the painted block or even below. By doing either one, the player sets up too low and limits the ability to go either right or left when receiving a pass. However, setting up well above the block, basically straddling the first hash mark above the block puts the player in an approximate 45-degree angle from the basket relative to the baseline and the general top of the free throw circle. The posted player can catch and make a move to the baseline or penetrate into the middle, since he is at the optimal 45-degree angle.

The concept of the **line of 45** is a fundamental principle of **post play.** When the ball is above the line of 45, the post defender must play on the high side. When the ball goes from above the line of 45 to below it, the defender must shift his position to the baseline side of the low post.

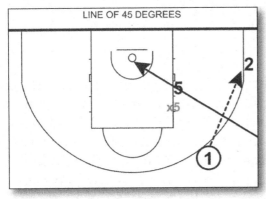

Diagram 1

Every time the ball crosses the line of 45 in either direction the offensive post player has a chance to **angle off his defender and seal him,** which will create an easy scoring opportunity at the optimal scoring angle of 45 degrees. This principle, as vital as it is to inside scoring, has been largely lost in today's game at virtually all levels. (Diagram 1).

The 3-In-A-Row Line

Diagram 2 shows a common occurrence that inhibits the ability of the wing man to feed the ball inside. Even though the post man is in perfect position on the line of 45, the wing man 1 and his defender form

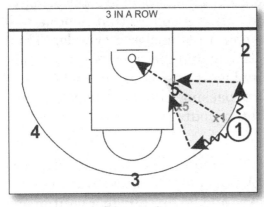

Diagram 2

a straight 3-in-a-row line with the posted man 5. Player 5's defender will have at least his hand in the passing lane, and perhaps half to all of his body, to make it even harder to feed the post man. The diagram shows that if all the offensive players have observed proper spacing rules, ball handler 1 will have room to bounce the ball once to the right or left to break the straight 3-in-a-row line.

Player 1 can then stretch low, thereby creating a better angle to help provide a clearer passing lane to 5 – especially when he sees that Player

5 uses his body to angle off his defender by sealing him to allow himself an improved opening to receive the pass. Of course he has to hold position as opposed to allowing himself to be pushed in the same direction the ball handler is moving to create the better passing angle. We have seen too many post men either be pushed or to decide to slide in the same direction as the dribbler — either move negating the possibility of creating a better pass angle to him.

The Low Post Triangle

Also, in the diagrams below observe that Player 2 in the corner is on an angle that **puts him below the line of the posted man.** Most players pay no attention to this detail and line up in a general area indicated by the broken lines in Diagram 4. However, if the corner man is able to keep lower (closer to the baseline) than the posted man, he has a better passing angle to the inside. For example the defender on posted man 5 will be playing on the high side opposite the baseline when wing player 1 has the ball.

As Player 1 passes down to 2 in the corner, 5 can use his body to lock his defender on top of him, **sealing him off** and allowing him easier access to the pass from 2. The sealing technique is a fundamental that must be taught and practiced just as with all other fundamentals. Bill Self of Kansas teaches what he calls a "leg-whip" as the aggressive movement a post player must make to seal his man. Player 2's deeper angle will allow him to feed the ball inside under the defense, plus afford him the cutting lane to score.

Again, when Player 5 posts up too deep (close to the baseline) his defender can often muscle him down even deeper and effectively shut down any good passing angle from both the wing and the corner, considered as two triangles with the wing man (1) a common point to the two triangles, seen in Diagrams 3 and 4 below.

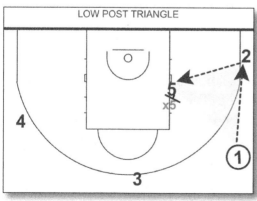

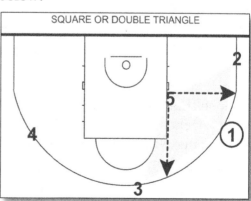

Diagram 3   Diagram 4

Easy to hinder offensive spacing through carelessness. Players 1-2-5 have a good triangle set in Diagram 5, but by looking closely to Player 3's position we can see that 3 can foul up the geometry by being just a step or two inside the vertical line from post man 5. He limits his passing angles for successful passing inside as well as to the weak side to Player 4, if he lines up directly above 5. By Player 3 keeping well spaced above 5 and positioned on or near the direct split line to the basket, he will have a better passing angle to 5 down low when the

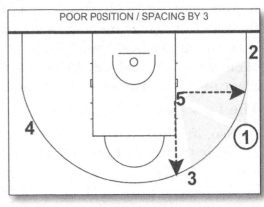

POOR POSITION / SPACING BY 3

Diagram 5

ball is reversed. He will also have a better slot for dribble penetration to the reverse side (his left) plus a shorter and better passing angle to Player 4 on the weak side.

As per Coach Wooden's theory of preparing before catching the ball, players in spots 3 and 2 must be taught the importance one or two steps can make in these passing angles. This can be taught through both drilling and video. Proper spacing is more complex than many think. It is not accomplished by simply yelling out, **"spread out"** or **"spacing"** from time to time.

"Spacing is Offense and Offense is Spacing" (Rick Majerus). Of course, Rick was trying to make a point as opposed to diminishing the value of other aspects. However, in fact it is hard to over-emphasize the **proper 15-plus feet spacing** in the geometry of the game. Contrary to what many think, the concept of "spacing" was not invented by coaches in the last 10 or 20 years, all due respect to the success San Antonio has had with this old school approach. It was always a vital fundamental of the game going back to the theories of great coaches of the game — Bee, Rupp, Hinkle of the great Butler system, the Drake Shuffle, Wooden Smith and many, many others. It is the essence of the so-called "Triangle" offense that started out under the name of "Triple Post." Most of the winning coaches over the last 70 years thrived on three aspects of the game — spacing with ball and player movement. These are not new concepts and will never go away.

Players must think in big triangles and squares in order to get the spacing correct. **Keeping the wings wide and initiating the offense from a high point position** will improve pass angles and open the middle for penetration, essentials to successful offense. **The more spread the scoring area becomes, the more territory the defense has to cover.** Obviously, if we took it to ridiculous lengths and had all five offensive players try to play in the area of the free throw lane, one could readily see that it is impossible to play in such a limited space. However, many players constantly **do the defense a favor** by crowding in closer to the goal, the longer the possession lasts. We call that "the Incredible Shrinking Offense."

The reason spacing is a problem is likely due to each player's subconscious desire to get himself into the easiest shooting range; therefore, he creeps in from the weak side or mashes down from the top of the circle. While this may seem to carry the player into a better range, it actually does **three things to limit his team's offensive potential:**

- it allows his man to sag in on the inside players and render the inside game less effective;
- it gives the weak side defender a shorter run back to his assigned man when the ball is reversed, actually making the player less open by moving in;
- it compacts the cutting and driving lanes, making it much more difficult to penetrate the compacted defense with dribble penetration or good cuts for catches.

One obvious problem posed by proper spacing concerns the perimeter player who has limited shooting range. Defenders will not respect this player's shooting range so will sag off him anyway and take a chance on the outside shot. However, by being well spaced, he may become a better ball mover as a quick relay man, and can look for opportunities as a cutter and/or a screener. Still, if he has the ability to do so, he may be able to catch out wide and then back his way into a scoring or playmaking situation closer to the goal. Or, he may be able to attack a man seeking to close him out with a dribble penetration.

Spacing-conscious coaches find themselves constantly saying "stay high at the top and wide on the weak side if you are open, but cut or screen if you are covered." Players who insist on taking up the slack between themselves and their defenders just to get closer to the goal are the "enemies within."

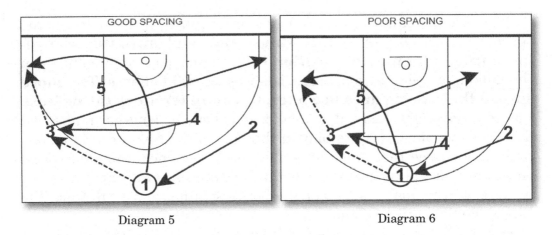

Diagram 5   Diagram 6

Stay High at the Top and Wide on the Weak Side. Diagrams 5 and 6 show the difference that good spacing makes. It is easy to see that the defense must guard more hardwood in Diagram 5 than in Diagram 6.

Starting out wide in an offensive set does not guarantee that an offense will stay spread. Besides the subtle creeping in that players tend to do, **the biggest reason that offenses shrink as the ball is rotated is that players do not complete their cuts into the 3-point area to create pass lanes.** Observe that Players 3 and 2 are both guilty of shortening their cuts in Diagram 6. An offense may begin in tight, as some box (1-2-2 formation) and 1-4 offenses do. However, to begin the offensive action, someone has to break out of the formation to create spacing. Thereafter, the subsequent cuts must tend to open up the offense. The point is that an offense may start either wide or tight, but good spacing must be observed as the ball is moved.

Whether it is fatigue, carelessness, ignorance or selfishness, most players quit on their cutting routes and that creates a shriveled up offense with congested passing, cutting or driving lanes. Most players are reluctant to go beyond their range because they want to shoot the next time they get the ball. **Players must be educated on the concept that it is important to present themselves as passing outlets out of their shooting range when necessary for ball movement.** When players see the importance of creating the spread offense and believe that they will still get their fair share if everyone plays correctly, a team has a fighting chance for an effective offense that can exploit a defense through posting, quick cutting, penetrating and intelligent passing in a well-spaced offense.

Read the Defensive Positioning to Determine the Next Pass.
As a player learns to see the court to prepare for his next move, he will
know first of all where the defender responsible for guarding him is located, even before he receives a pass. Therefore, he will know quickly
whether to shoot or drive as he catches the ball. In addition, if he uses
proper vision, he will locate his teammates and observe the other rel-
evant defenders **before he receives the ball.** All perimeter players
must concentrate their vision on the middle of the floor prior to receiving
a pass. This will allow the receiver to know in advance where the low
post defender is, as well as all other perimeter defenders. Many commentators used to mention how players such as Magic Johnson, Larry
Bird and Jason Kidd *seemed* to know where all the players were located
on the court. They actually did.

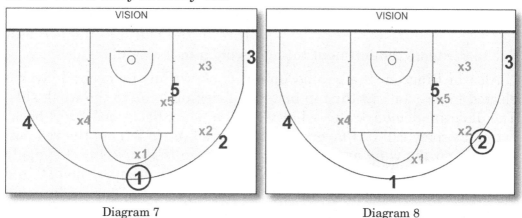

Diagram 7   Diagram 8

See Diagrams 7 and 8 and quickly read what Player 2's options will
be. Player 2 in the diagrams can tell that he may be able to lob to 5 since
X4 is not in a sag, or that he can swing it on to 3 in the corner who may
be able to catch and shoot or slip the ball underneath to 5, if 5 can seal
off X5 playing on top of him His decision-making time will be reduced,
since he will not have to receive the pass, then turn and see who is open
inside or in the corner below him. He will be able to **relay the pass** to
an open player quickly because he already knows he is open. If he waits
to face up and read the defense, the moves may be gone.

Seeing the court and reading it will help prevent players from passing
without any purpose in mind. All players should be reading to find holes
in the defense on the ball side and **to see how the defense is setting
up to defend the low post and weak side of the court.**

Lastly, it is important that players understand the importance of using "pass fakes" versus the zone. Crisp pass fakes can be valuable tools
to move defenders on the perimeter and freeze defenders inside before

actually making a pass.

In Diagram 9 the red arrows indicate fake passes and the actual pass

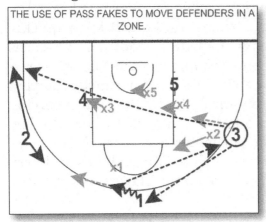

is in the normal black broken lines. A pass fake to Player 4 can help keep X3 inside and facilitate a hard skip pass to Player 2. This results from a good weak side read by Player 3. Since the weak side defender X3 is sagging far off the wing man 2, ball handler 3 sees the opportunity for a skip-pass directly to 2, and especially so, if 4 should screen X3. It would have been a terrible decision to have thrown the ball into the low post

Diagram 9

due to the team commitment to sag deeply into the paint.

Also in Diagram 9 a second option is shown in the event Player 3 elected to pass to 1 at the top instead of risking a lob to the weak side. The diagram demonstrates what we call a "snap-back" or "throw-back" option as some call it. Player 1 made a pass fake to 2 (note the red dotted line) on the wing or even took a bounce in that direction (squiggly line), which would likely influence X2 to commit to dropping off of 3 into a proper weak side position. If Player 2 were open in the corner, he could make that play to him. If not, Player 1 would snap it back quickly to 3 who could shoot or penetrate the gap toward the baseline.

Critical low post reading situations are shown below in Diagrams 10 and 11. In Diagram 10, Player 1 reads that X5 is fronting 5 and that X3 has his back in a deep sag, so he can pass fake to 5 to freeze X3 and throw the skip pass to 3.

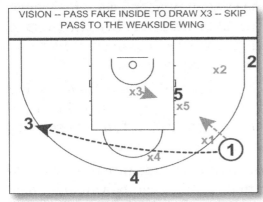

Diagram 10

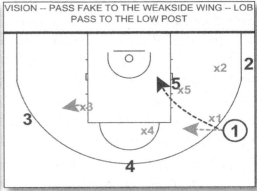

Diagram 11

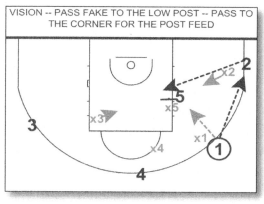

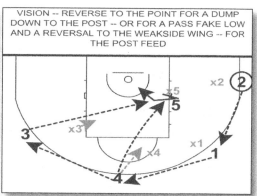

Diagram 12   Diagram 13

In the situation in Diagram 11 the defender X5 on Player 5 is fronting 5 and the weak side defender is cheating up on 3, likely a good 3-point shooter. Player 1 could fake a pass to 3 to freeze X3 to set up the lob to 5.

Another low post read is shown in Diagram 12. Player 1 reads that X5 is on the high side of 5 and so a fake pass to 5 may entice X2 to stunt a little toward 5 and allow a pass to 2 in the corner. Player 5 would lock and seal 5 with the leg-whip action for an easy drop-step to the goal, or 2 could possibly put it down and make a play. However, it is **not wise to bury the ball in the corner** if there is no high potential play action.

Diagram 13 is a continuation of Diagram 12 and shows that player 2 had no catch and shoot option and X5 was able to get to the baseline side of 5 to shut off the pass angle from 2. Player 2 reverses the ball to 1, who reads X5 on the baseline side as 5 spreads out and seals his man on the base line side. If Player 1 has read it early, he knows he can quickly swing the pass to the top of the box to 4, who may be able to insert the ball down low to 5 quickly, or he can fake the pass inside to freeze X3 and swing to 3 for a shot or feed to 5. Had Player 5's man been directly behind 5, Player 1 could have tried the direct feed himself. Smart players are thinking of these things during the action. As explained earlier, in order to create safer passing, it is essential to have the proper angles from the top to the low post and weak side. And as simple as this all sounds, not many players are this engaged in this kind of action at any level because it is not taught adequately. These are some of the small things in zone offense that are more important than the "tricky plays." Trust it!

The Weak Side is the Attack Side When there is Good Spacing. As noted in the segment on offensive philosophy, when facing a set defense at half court, it is a general truth that the first pass or two are made to key the offense to force the defense into motion. "Stir it up" is the mantra.

A static offense is the defense's best friend. Quick shots and passes for scores against most good defensive teams will not come easily, particularly on the entry side. As noted before, we believe it is good strategy to teach that if you do not have a 75% scoring chance on the first side, it is better to reverse it! Get it from the first or **"shift side"** to the **second** or **"attack side"** quickly. As the ball continues to move with intelligent player movement, the attack gets even better after that. The point is: how many errors can a defensive team make, if they only have to defend one side of the floor and only one pass or less in the process?

Good ball and player movement give the defense an opportunity to make mistakes. Obviously, careless passing gives the defense an opportunity for steals and not all players are excellent passers. Know your team and its capabilities. The best teams are good passing teams — check it out! This is far from a new concept, of course. In our years of coaching at every level, we have rarely seen a good team that lacked this skill, and the willingness to utilize it unselfishly. Isolation and one-on-one can take a team just so far. The Miami Heat became a champion after improving its ball movement. The San Antonio Spurs are consistently noted for their ball movement. Excellent ball movement identified the great Celtics and Lakers that have been champions in multiple eras, almost as much as did their star players. The same is true for outstanding college and high school teams through the years too numerous to mention.

Naturally, it makes sense to exploit the first easy opening and the offense must be constantly probing; however, **we are talking about preparing for the very good teams, and good teams do not yield on the first side.** Teams with poor passers can adjust by using a lot of dribble entries, but they should work to develop that skill, as they will still be best served by looking to attack on the second side rather than on the initial side of entry.

It can be defended that the most important pass a player can make is the first reversal pass. There is no statistic to give credit for this action, but it can be the catalyst for creating a breakdown in the defense that allows a player receiving the ball two or three passes later to get a good shot. It is easy to understand that all five players must move in the defense when the ball is swung from one side to the other on just one reversal. One may make a mistake. If the ball is moved a second time, the odds of a defensive lapse increase. Good teams don't let the ball get stuck on the first side

CHAPTER 2

FOCUSING ON POST PLAY THEORY

Importance of Focusing on Post Play Spacing

It is Difficult to Overemphasize the Importance of Avoiding to Jam the Middle. There are over-riding reasons why this basic spacing fundamental should be understood and exercised. After the first entry pass to any area, it is counterproductive to have three offensive players in the middle lane. Let us clarify what we think is one of the least understood concepts of spacing in zone offense:

- It jams the lane and prevents cutting routes to the middle as this puts six players in the middle lane;
- That same jamming constricts the ability to penetrate to make a play;
- It leaves only two players on the perimeter that are good outlets for a pass from the post to set up open shots, penetration, or further ball movement.

Diagram 1 defines the middle lane and shows the **value of having only two players in the middle lane when possible after the ball is fed to the high post from the top or even the wing.** In the end, it is important to cut to a corner or drift to either side outside the middle lane while keeping basic spacing with the post man and the wing. Perhaps the most obvious reason to clear out the point guard is that this generally takes away the defensive player from behind the post who may come from behind and knock the ball away. Unless he traps immediately, he must adjust to the movement of the player from the top.

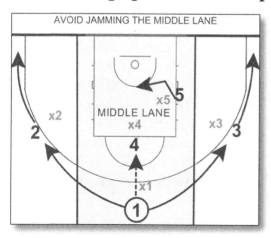

Diagram 1

By looking at the diagram, one can see that high post man 4 can dump the ball low to Player 5, his first look, or can pass to 2, 3 or 1. Passer 1 should move to a high wing slot right or left, preferably to the area further spread from Player 4 for the best spacing. This puts all three players in scoring-threat positions. If Player 1 stays behind 4, not only can X1 harass 4, Player 1 is totally out of the play action. **Players should be geared to making themselves an option on offense at all times.**

This **"open middle lane"** principle is worth the price of the book and it sets up a second vital element in the zone attack that follows — **the importance of the high post attack.**

Attack Through the High Post as a Principle of Attack. As in any offense, attacking in the high and low post will put extreme pressure on the defense. Therefore, it is one of the foundations of **inside-out play.** Regardless of the style of zone being attacked, it is essential to get the ball to the high post. As a matter of fact, it can be said that any time a player is open in the High Post Attack Area he should receive a pass. At the very least the posts should handle the ball every third or fourth pass. This is true of combating zones in general but it is **most difficult to beat a laning style of zone or to respond to trapping without utilizing this weapon.**

The high post player must go as high as he has to go to catch, even out to the 3-point line or higher, if he is not open easily, whether he is a 3-point shooter or not. Posts must be aggressive on their movements in the high post area to catch the ball in an open spot and quickly turn toward the basket to focus on attacking with a shot, drive or pass. If there is nothing quickly, he becomes a swing man, a ball mover in this case — especially true vs. a sagging defense — or he could pass and cut, set a pick and roll or use a dribble handoff move. This entire colored area is his attack area shown in Diagram 2.

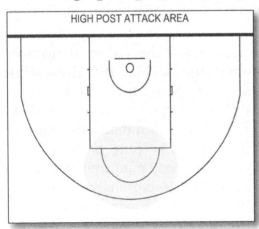

HIGH POST ATTACK AREA

Diagram 2

It would be difficult to overemphasize the absolute fundamental offensive concept that the high post receiver turns immedi-

ately to face the basket with vision of the rim and both corners of the court. At this point, he may have a shot himself. He is also in the best driving spot on the court, so he must be alert for opportunities to quickly drive the ball to the rim. And he is in the best position to feed the low post, or to pass to a player on a wing or corner who can.

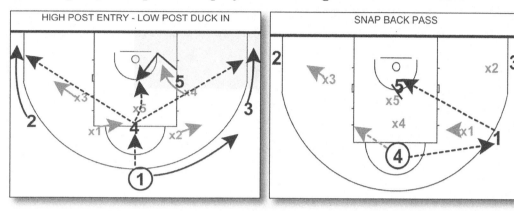

Diagram 3   Diagram 4

Diagram 3 shows the excellent pass opportunities available to high post man 4 if he squares to the basket on his catch and sees both corners of the court. Low post man 5 **will automatically do his best to present himself as a big target by ducking in and sealing off the defender, or crossing under the defender to the opposite block to post, whenever he sees the ball go to the high post.**

Diagram 4 illustrates what can happen if Player 5 does not receive the ball on his duck-in because his defender X5 gets to a high position to deny the pass. Player 4 can read that X5 is in a high ¾ position, ideal for sealing off and can make a fake reverse pass, a misdirection action, to set up a **"Snap Back"** pass to Player 1, who had drifted to a wing angle after his pass to 4. Player 1 has a very good passing angle to 5, if 5 gets a good seal on X5.

The rule for the perimeter players is that the **wings move toward the corners on a pass to the high post.** This allows room for the point man above the wings to fill a spot and still have spacing. It opens the court and puts their defenders in a position where they cannot help on a duck-in at the front of the rim, or a drive by the high post man without risking giving up an open corner shot. **Diagram 3 also shows X5 defending the high post and how taking one defender (X4) to the edge of his coverage area in the low post, while filling the other end of his coverage area in the corner with a wing player, is a concept zones find difficult to defend.**

Diagram 5 shows that, alternatively, if Player 5 does not get open on his duck-in, he can clear to the weak side for a possible paint catch or to post. Player 4's second look is weak side to 2, who should put pressure on the opponent's weak side defense by cutting to the corner area. He may be open for a shot or to make a relay pass inside to Player 5.

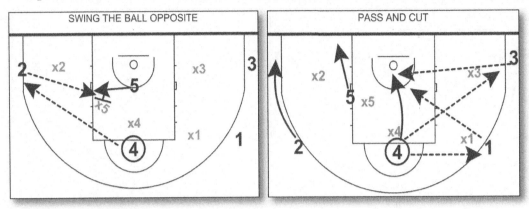

Diagram 5   Diagram 6

If the ball is not passed to Player 2, 5 clears out to the short corner. In this case X5 cannot play him and still help out on Player 4 adequately, if he attacks the rim on the dribble. Also, Diagram 6 shows more space for Player 4 to cut into, if he were to pass to 1 or 3 and then cut to the basket. In that case, **Player 5 can bust a cut up into the now open high post area and all options are renewed.**

The High Post is the Lynchpin to Attacking Zones.

Therefore, we feel that anyone in the high post attack area should receive the ball any time one is open. At the very least, he becomes a "ball mover," which is an under-appreciated function in offense. **Make the defense shift.** The ball mover has many options that can be used against any defense. When he looks low, and then weak side and nothing is open, he can:

- Pass to any of the open men and cut,
- Make a dribble move to handoff/pitchout to a perimeter,
- Set a screen and roll

Remember the mantra when getting the ball in the middle: ***Look for your own, look low, look opposite, move the ball.*** (See diagrams 7 and 8 on the following page).

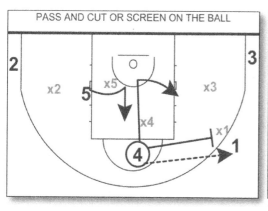

Diagram 7

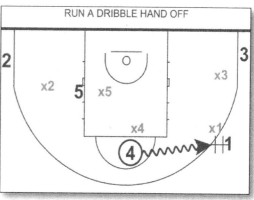

Diagram 8

Attacking in the Low Post is Essential vs. Zones — Key is Correct Spacing

Don't start firing away from the perimeter as soon as you see a zone. Diagram 9 illustrates attacking in the low post with a wing feed. Player 1's move should be to drift to the corner, to drag his man down or to force a back man to come out to cover him. If the corner

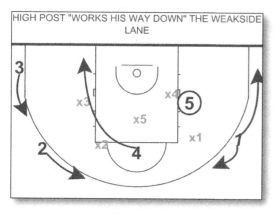

Diagram 9

is filled by a teammate he can make a "short high drift." It is very important that Player 1 does not stand in the same spot after passing and that he **not drift past the vertical line of the ball above 5, unless he makes a complete exchange with another player.** In the short high drift Player 1 comes back into a better pass angle once the post starts to make a move or is doubled. If all four players are ever on the strong side of the vertical ball line, that places nine men behind the ball. This is a huge favor to the defense whether man-to-man or zone as it jams the lane and makes any rotation shorter, if the defense decides to trap the low post.

On a low post catch, unless Player 5 has a quick scoring move to the middle or a drop step to the basket, his next option is his post partner, Player 4. Player 4 can dive to get a rim catch to score, if he has a clear path due to his man doubling, or if he takes his eye off of him to look at the ball. If he cuts and does not get the pass, he can exit to the weak side short corner as in Diagram 10. As Player 5 looks at his partner, he looks to the weak side for any player whose man may be sagging to help on 4's cut. This pass must be clearly open, as it is a difficult one to make. All perimeter play-

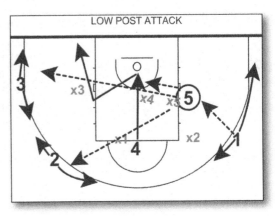

Diagram 10

ers must move to **create a pass lane to themselves — become an option!**

Each player must try to get to a position whereby **"the ball can see them."** In other words **"get yourself into vision and always make yourself a threat."** The post will have an easier outlet pass in front of him, so the strong side player(s) must present themselves to be open if possible, Player 1 in this case. The post should be encouraged to make the easiest play. Turnovers out of the post lead to bad things quickly at the other end of the court.

High post 4 can "work his way down" as an option. When the ball is the low post, a cut to the rim by Player 4 is good, **if it is clearly open.** However, if he cuts to the rim routinely, as soon as the low post gets the ball, the posted man will never have a chance to move to the middle for a jump hook. When the post is making a move, or there is no easy cut to the goal, the high post should loop slowly down the weak side of the lane to give room for Player 5 to make his move.

To clarify, Player 4 makes this cut when the low post man has received a catch from the wing area, and the man defending him in the high post stays up with him. Instead having Player 4 take his man down into the low post man's potential middle move, **he will wait to read Player 5's move and drift down wide to the weak side** rebound area to the short corner just behind the corner of the board, to allow space; or **he may dive to the rim any time that X4 decides to attack Player 5 late.**

The point is not to bring a defender into the paint unnecessarily, and thus help the opponent to defend Player 5 in the low post. Player 4 needs to read the situation and to react accordingly. This concept allows Play-

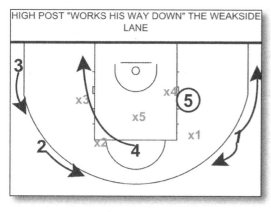

Diagram 11

er 4 to avoid being a bystander, a non-factor to score or rebound. Obviously, these principles are all calculated to maintain the best spacing possible in the post attack game. Player 4 being active also opens the area for another player to cut into vision in the **diagonal catch angle** as Player 2 does in Diagram 11, maybe even as close as the elbow.

Note: It is sound fundamental zone offense to have a diagonal pass option whether the ball is high on a wing with a diagonal toward the weak side corner, or from a ball down below the foul line up to the weak side diagonal high wing area, as in this case here where Player 2 has gotten to the **high diagonal outlet** for Player 5. Looking back at Diagram 10 one can see how Player 3 has gotten to the **down diagonal angle** from ball handler 1, who passed the ball inside to Player 5 instead of making the cross court diagonal pass. Players need to be taught and drilled on the advantages of **habitually presenting themselves in these angles when they are on the weak side.**

Attack Under the Zone

If coaches study the films of any team that knows how to play an effective zone defense, one of the characteristics they will find is that the defense sets up high on the baseline. In other words, the baseline defenders will assume positions well in front of the basket, as opposed to being flatter and close to the baseline. To be competent, the baseline people must play in the higher positions to **shut down the middle** to cutting and penetration routes. High positioning also makes it harder to make direct low post feeds from any angle.

A good comparison or analogy would be that of a baseball outfield that has the speed and ability to play in shallow positions. By closing the gap between the infield and the outfield, it becomes more difficult for hitters to make the singles and doubles that are the bread and butter of any baseball offense. They are challenged to hit the ball over the outfielders' heads.

The basketball offense that is challenged by a high-playing, tight-in-the-middle zone defense should have as a concept the idea of flattening down the zone by attacking under/behind the zone along the baseline as part of what they do often. It was this basic concept that led to the development of the **short corner option** in zone offense action about 40 years ago that we will note as we go along. It also caused the **lateral dribble rotation moves** to become so popular, after many years of coaches warning not to dribble against the zones.

In addition to flattening down the defense to open the middle, attacking behind the zone also causes the defenders on the back line of the defense to have to keep turning their heads to check the action behind them. In doing that, they often make mistakes that allow cutters to break open in front of them. Or, they may allow a pass to get over the top for an easy play. Diagram 12 shows in simple terms how players 5 and 2 can exert more pressure on the defense by slipping in behind the defenders.

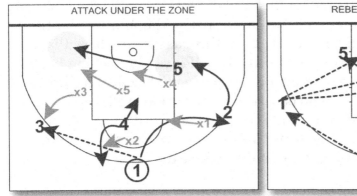 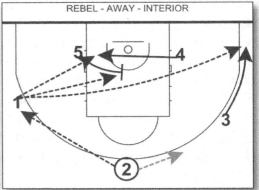

Diagram 12   Diagram 13

Diagram 13 illustrates a Majerus play that attacks under the defense. After Player 1 has dribble rotated the defense down he has passed to 2 at the top. Player 2 fakes a pass to 3 and snaps the ball back to 1. Player 5 sets a screen on 4, who cuts low, while 3 seeks to get to a deep weak side spot diagonally from the ball. Of course, Player 5 will seal and pop back to look for a catch in the mid post area or will move on up to the high post. It is easy to see how the threat low opens up the middle for cuts.

Diagram 14 (next page), shows a common fundamental high-low post action that features a classic attack on the back line. We will present this action as one of what we call **The Five Basic Elements** for zone attack. Ball handler 1 dribble-pulls **to create space and a good pass angle, a normal key for Player 4 to pop up to catch.** The key attack actions are done by 2-3-5 as they put immediate pressure on the baseline people by dropping to the flat baseline area when Player 4 catches. Player 1 slides into a spaced, shooting or driving position on the high wing.

High post 4 can pass to any one of the three who have flattened the defense down and helped to open up the middle. Player 5 has the option

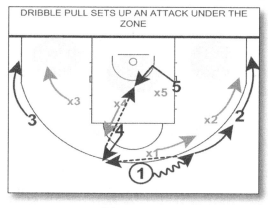

DRIBBLE PULL SETS UP AN ATTACK UNDER THE ZONE

Diagram 14

to seal off his defender or to cross underneath him to the weak side block to seal and post. If Player 5 gets the ball, he can score it. If Player 2 or 3 receives a pass, they may have a shot or a pass to 5 as he seals off his defender. By drifting to the open hole opposite his pass, Player 1 will be able to make a play if he gets a pass from 4 or 2. A key phrase that good zone offense coaches will repeat often is, **"when you catch the ball in the high post, quickly turn and look under and then opposite."** This simple act creates havoc against all formations of zone defense, and is central to attacking inside of a zone defense.

POST PLAYERS MUST PLAY AS A TWO-MAN TEAM. They need to be a tandem operation, always looking to help create space for one another and trying to help the other to be open. They need to be comrades in arms when it comes to accepting the challenges of rebounding and of protecting the paint by defending their own assignments, but also by helping perimeter teammates as needed. The posts must play as a two-man team, using synchronized moves timed with the movement of the ball and the perimeter players. Previously, we outlined how the posts look for their post partner when they catch the ball, if they do not have an immediate scoring opportunity themselves. In addition they play off each other's penetration out of the low post. To be effective they must communicate with, watch and help one another in any way they can, since they are a team within a team. At all costs, they must avoid standing in the same position or drifting aimlessly back and forth across the lane as the ball is moved around the perimeter. Post men must be **active,** a key word for them, but they **should not always be chasing the ball.** If a player moves in total sync with the ball, the defender on him can keep track of the ball and the post player simultaneously quite easily. Timing on cuts will vary as they read the best moment to break to the ball or to seal off for a post up. Ultimately, they need to keep their spacing between one another, and **when one of them moves, it normally dictates a complimentary move by the other.** If the talent allows it, the posts should change positions every three or four passes. They may mix up how they do this by letting the high post initiate movement, or they may use another key.

The posts may screen for one another, with the picker normally sealing and cutting back to the ball in the opposite direction from which his partner cut. That is, if the cutter went low under the pick, the screener would then seal and step back high to the ball to maintain spacing with his partner. Naturally, if the cutter went high over the top, the picker would step back low and present himself for a catch or move to the short corner.

There are four basic types of cuts the posts can make: straight line, flash, circle and the most threatening X-cut. The simple **straight line cuts** are the most common ones traditionally, but as suggested, they should be done on an **intelligently timed basis** as the ball is swung from one side of the court to the other. That is, the low post will move from one block to the other and the high post may move from one elbow to the other. This can be effective when timed properly, but usually quite ineffective if the posts simply move by chasing the ball.

Sometimes a quick straight line cut is in order, if the nearest defender is in a bad position or loses sight of the post by ball-watching only, especially in the low post. But often, it is **better to wait until the ball is actually caught on the weak side and then to read** for an opening for a catch. One or both posts may hang back and serve as a picker for a weak side perimeter player who is cutting to a diagonal position for a possible skip-pass. Or, they can wait to be in position to rebound, or to pop into an open slot, if there is a penetration by a weak side player. **All of these options are positive moves, whereas just floating around the post begging for a ball is not.**

Flash cutting is particularly effective when the offense starts out in a low double post formation, usually with the two posts starting behind the zone and then moving into high/low positions once the actual offense starts. One post will flash up into the mid or high post to look for a catch and the other will then move to post up or cross under, as we have mentioned already at the start of this chapter. They may even flash cut from the opposite post and if not open, continue on out to set a pick and roll on a perimeter player

They may **Circle Rotate** by cutting in a circular motion as in Diagrams 15 and 16. The Circle Rotate cut can be initiated in two ways, to an open low post or a filled one. In Diagram 15, Player 4 cuts to the open low post as the pass goes from 1 to 3. He may catch his defender sleeping and get an easy catch, but normally, the move helps Player 5 get open as he will follow immediately with a flash cut, usually putting his body on defender X5 in this case and trying to get a catch in front of the goal, or in the paint.

In any event, Player 4 will be ready to circle on over to the weak side area when 5 catches so that 5 may have an opportunity to catch and make a move to the goal. If Player 5 does not have that, he will turn to look at 4 sealing off or will pass to the weak side corner area where 2 should be sliding for a shot or a dump down into 4.

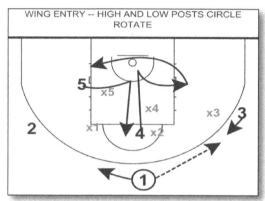

Diagram 15

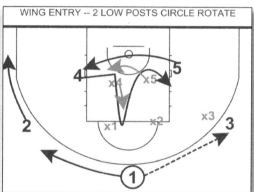

Diagram 16

Diagram 16 shows a variation of the circle cut action that occurs more often when there is a double low post alignment to start. Post 5 is covered in the low post but initiates movement by clearing to the weak side block, keying Post 4 to flash to the goal and up into the paint for a catch. In the circle action, if Post 4 does not get an easy catch, he continues on down to the strong side block and 5 steps into the lane to get a catch and moves up into the high post, if he does not get one deep. Again, Post 4 circles under to the weak side block as shown in Diagram 15. This gives Player 5 a chance to drive to the open block or to possibly pass to 4, but more likely to swing the ball for a shot by 2 in the corner or a dump down into 4 on the weak side block. If the ball cannot be inserted safely into the low or high post after the two cuts, Player 5 will step out as high as it takes to catch and move the ball to the weak side where play will continue.

Posts X-Cuts on Reversal. On ball reversal, probably the strongest option for the posts to perform is the **X-cut** shown in Diagrams 17 and 18 (next page). This action is **most effective when the post man passes the ball out to a wing or corner and makes a hard dive to the basket.**

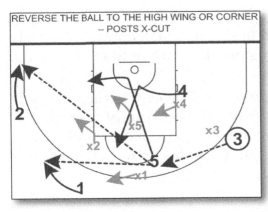

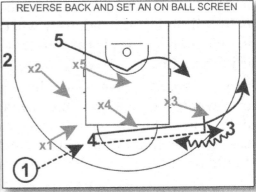

Diagram 17   Diagram 18

In Diagram 17, the ball has been passed from Player 1 to 3 and 1 has drifted opposite his pass to open up the high post area. Post 5 was not able to get an easy catch, so he fill cuts to the top as a swing man and passes to Player 1 or 2 and dives to the goal, seeking a pass from 1 or 2. When he cuts, Player 4 reads that and cuts off of 5's tail into the goal area for a deep catch and on up into the high post, if he cannot get the ball in the paint. This is a prime move for a high post player and he has this option anytime, as well as the **freedom to read differently and set a pick/roll/pop on the wing, or even to turn and set a down pick on the other post man.**

In Diagram 18 we see a continuation that can occur in X-action. Post 5 did not get the ball on his cut to the goal and moved on out to the short corner as is usual in X-cutting, though he could rotate on through to the weak side as in a circle cut, his call. Weak side Post 4 has cut up into the lane and on to the high post without having a scoring move, so in this case, he swings it to Player 3 and could continue to X-cut and dive to the block or he can **set the pick and roll on 3 as in Diagram 18.** On the penetration Player 3 has 1 and 2 sitting in front of him into an open lane. If Player 4 pops, 5 can duck in and if 4 rolls, 5 can roll up behind him, always a great high/low action with pick and roll.

These post actions are free options, unless a set play has been called. In proper X-cutting we teach that the high post passes out and **dives first in the paint toward the rim** looking for a catch and score. If he does not catch, he **proceeds to the block and preferably to the short corner area,** opening up the lane for his partner's cut into the paint for a catch and on up into any open slot he reads in the high post area. At that point the basic principles take over, whether it becomes a high/low game, a continuing X-cut option, a pick and roll, a dribble pull move, etc. As we go further, the possible options will become obvious.

Critical elements of post movements. All of their cuts should ideally start with movement into the paint instead of going directly to a low block or a high elbow. Generally speaking, this involves bodying up on a defender first and then cutting. The defense may not let one go directly to the basket, but it is important to make a threatening cut to the goal when possible. If the post is not successful in getting a catch at the front of the rim or in the paint, then he vacates to the block and perhaps to the short corner, or into the high post. An exception to bodying up would be when a low post sees a defender out of position or with his head turned that gives an opening slot in the mid or high post. While that is not goal threatening, it is a scoring threat to break down the defense nonetheless.

Through 2-on-2 drilling the posts learn when these options are available and how to work together to execute them effectively. These cuts are all pretty organic to a player who is thinking the game, reading the defense and communicating with this tandem teammate.

Dribble Pull to "Pop the Post" to Help Post Penetration

When the offense is having trouble passing to the posts because the defense is moving and matching up on the posts movements, the ball handler can still get the ball to one of the posts by executing a quick "dribble pull" exercise with one of the posts. In Diagram 19, Player 1 takes two quick dribbles away from 4. As Player 1 makes that move, 4 takes two quick steps out and away from X2. Point 1 passes to 4, and all the sequences of our high post entry occur. Post 5 flashes to the front of the rim or clears to the other side under X5. Wings 2 and 3 drop to the corners, and 1 spaces away from 4. Post 5 and the three perimeter players now become passing targets.

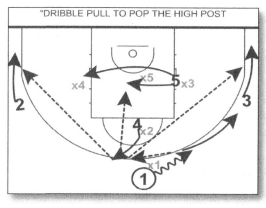

Diagram 19   Diagram 20

Diagram 20 represents an action that will work against virtually every zone since **all zones become 2-3's when the ball is in the corner,** or low wing as well in many cases. Player 3 takes two dribbles up from the baseline into the seam between the X3 and X1. If Player 3 dribbles too far up in the wing area, he takes himself right into X1's zone and the play is negated. This signals Player 5 to pop to the short corner or wider, depending on his range. Player 3 may pass to 5, if he is open, or pass fake to him to ensure that X5 guards him. As space opens in the middle of the lane due to X5 moving towards Player 5, 4 dives to the front of the rim. The pass to Player 4 may come from 3 or 5. Player 2 drifts to the diagonal pass angle behind 4 where the ball can see him. If the weak side wing sags to cover Player 4, 2 will be open for a skip pass. Player 1 also drifts into an open lane depending on what X2 does. Player 3's looks are **strong side post, weak side post, skip pass, or reverse it.**

Note: Player 2 gets to the low diagonal pass angle toward the corner from 3 when 3 dribbles up toward the wing area, but moves to a high wing diagonal angle if the ball is in 5's hands, as shown by the dotted passing lines.

Never Underestimate the Value of the Inside Fill-Cut Replace Action

High post fill cut at the top, the swing spot. The most commonly used method of fill cutting is to allow the perimeter players to do all the fill cutting, often called a replacement cut, to replace a player who has cut through the defense in order to have a reverse passing route to the other side. It is not generally the most effective way to fill cut. Particularly in a high/low offense, the preferred method involves fill cutting from the inside man, the high post, as illustrated in Diagrams 21 and 22.

In Diagram 21, Player 1 passes to 2 and cuts to the strong side corner. The fill cut is made from inside man 4 this time. To make it the traditional way would force Player 3 to come from the weak side, eliminating him as a diagonal pass threat from 2 or a swing pass option from 4 and would jam the middle lane with six players — three defenders and three offensive players. This concept of inside fill cutting, or **replacing the top from the high post accomplishes three things:**

- Opens up the free throw lane for the high-low game by creating space for the high/low 2-on-2 game that is quite difficult when the middle lane has three offensive players and three defenders.

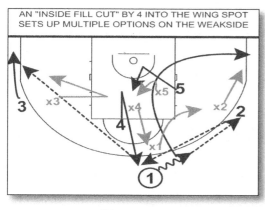

Diagram 21

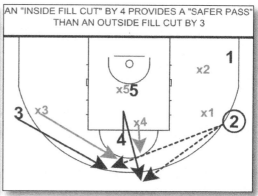

Diagram 22

- It allows for a better angle to catch the pass from wing man 2 on the reverse. If wing man 3 cuts to the top spot, he comes from a flat angle, which is favorable for a steal. The inside man's angle is a <u>shorter</u> and <u>sharper</u> one and harder to defend as shown in Diagram 22 above.

- Player 4 can swing the ball easily to 3 on the weak side. Player 3 is probably a scoring threat from outside; therefore, the better outside shooters will get more shot opportunities this way than by going to the top for a swing pass, even if the high post is popped out to the weak side wing, **which is an option for a special play when Player 4 is a good shooter that Tom Izzo often utilizes at Michigan State.**

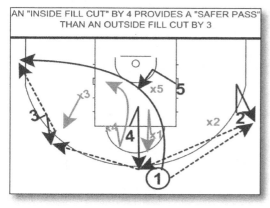

Diagram 23

If player 1 cuts to the weak side corner, as he does in Diagram 23, instead of to the ball side corner as in Diagram 21, Player 4 has not only the option of dumping into 5 down low, but may also pass to 3 and 1 on the weak side. Both Player 3 and 1 are likely scoring threats.

Unless an inside player is in the strong side low post, he should look for every opportunity to fill cut to the top when that area is vacated and the ball is on the wing. Thus, a high post player or even a weak side low post man in a 1-2-2 set can look for opportunities to cut up to the top to catch.

The Inside Wing Fill Cut option. In addition, a high post player can put pressure on the defense if he fill cuts to the wing on occasion when a wing player cuts through to the weak side. Diagram 24 illustrates a set play action whereby Player 1 "dribble rotated" to the wing, pushing 2 to the corner and pulling 3 up to the top in an overload. This flattened the zone and will put any starting zone formation into a 2-3 that can now be attacked easily. Player 1 passed to 2 in the corner, then cut through to the opposite wing since the wing was vacant, thus opening up the strong side wing.

High post man 4 makes an inside wing fill cut, giving Player 2 a quicker outlet to swing the ball than if he had waited for 3 to come from the top, after having left the weak side wing. This really opens the middle up as well. As the ball is reversed to Player 3 in the swing spot, he may be able to make his own move as an active wing man, or to slip a pass down to 5 in the low post. Or, he can complete the swing of the ball as Player 2 has roved the base. (Diagram 24).

In Diagram 25 this play action has gotten the "low wing out" — a strategic move that must always be recognized that we will deal with many times when we describe zone play action. Note that big defender X4 has had to move up from his baseline position in Diagram 24 to cover Player 1 on the wing in Diagram 25 while Player 2 has roved the base on the swing of the ball, filling the open corner.

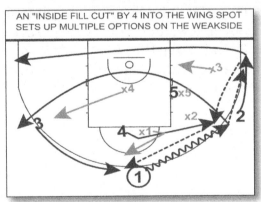

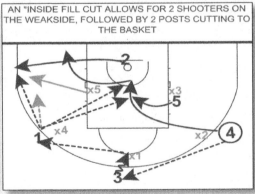

Diagram 24   Diagram 25

Regardless of what the defense does, **Player 4 is now a key player.** He **could get a high pass** near the basket if **X3 roved** with Player 2, or is locked up **defending 5. And if they made the bump down to Player 2** with X1 and X4, **Player 4 can still flash into the gap** in the lane. (Diagram 25)

The inside fill at the top or on the wing can be very useful with an active 4 player, especially if he can shoot reasonably well. This tends to put more shooters in scoring-threat situations. The best option is to force the zone to adjust to three scoring threats rather than two.

—————— CHAPTER 3 ——————

ESTABLISHING A FREELANCE SYSTEM

UTILIZING THE BASIC FIVE ELEMENTS OF ZONE OFFENSE, AUTOMATIC RESPONSE GUIDELINES AND THE PRINCIPLES OF PENETRATION

In this book we will present a lot of zone plays that can be used against the various zone defenses from the standard formations to the match ups to the combination man and zone trick defenses. However, we want to continue with the establishing of certain principles that work universally against the zones. We have already expressed some of those basic principles as we see them in the opening chapters relative to geometry, spacing, playing it inside-out, and so on. In this chapter we will set forth the **three aspects that can allow a team to execute what amounts to a passing game type of attack** similar to how one can go against man defenses by knowing basic principles of passing, cutting, and screening. The players will gradually learn to be able to read and react to the zone defenders and to be able to go for long stretches of time without having to call a set play, once it is learned. We have both had this experience with our teams. These are not untried theories. No, we didn't win every game in case you had that thought in mind. But our teams did not fear the zone.

Most passing game coaches still combine set plays to get the ball to certain players in special spots on the floor at propitious times during the game. Certainly, this has been the case with us with our zone offense tactics as well. Though we have slightly different ways of affecting this concept, we both agree that we have had great success by following the premise we present here. What you will see is a combination of our thinking, which we agree can be used in a free flowing system against zones when presented and drilled properly.

We will start with the **Basic Five Elements** that we think all will agree are fundamental to offense, and we will combine these with a set of **Automatic Guidelines,** which are responses that can be made after certain key actions. We will then set forth certain **Principles of Penetration,** often called bailout rules for short, that go together to form a **menu for a motion game** kind of concept for zone offense. It may best be described as **freelance** or **read and react** moves that can be used with any offensive formation against any style or type of zone.

Since these moves are components of virtually every set play used against zones, having a knowledge of them will serve to help players execute any play that is set before them as well. Our proposition is that they can be taught in such a way that they can be used not only as parts of the sets, but that the players can learn to use these as **"default actions"** spontaneously in any combination, depending upon what they read in the defense to give them the best advantage. **In other words they have something to use as a base for free lance actions versus zones that will allow them to attack on their own much of the time eventually.**

We will elaborate extensively as we progress through the book, but following are the thumbnail sketches for the Basic Five Elements, the Automatics and the Principles of Penetration.

1. Attack the High and Low Posts — "High/Low it!"

The High/Low Game. As noted earlier, the high post is the single most important attack area in the zone since it is the best passing/shooting/driving spot on the court against the zone. A catch in the high post by a good passer yields a potential deep catch by the low post, or quick passes to corner shooters, as well the start of great post movement if the ball is passed to the perimeter.

Similarly using the **triangle principles of Chapter One** affords opportunities for scores versus a post defender who is beaten even before the offensive post has the ball. If the low post does not have an immediate scoring opportunity, there may well be a quick rim attack from his partner, in coordination with movement on the weak side perimeter players designed to attack the defender who sags to protect the basket against the posts. Finally we have the two-man game between the posts who play off each other's catches and dribble attacks.

2. Player Movement — "Cut it!"

The Cutting or Player Movement Game. Players must cut quickly with score-threatening cuts, while moving to open areas in the zone. When done in a coordinated fashion with their perimeter partners while spreading the zone to the 3-point line with good spacing are difficult for zones to guard.

When they are complemented by posts who cut quickly in concert with the perimeter players and their partner posts, the synchronized movement create serious difficulties for all zones by maximizing the space that must be covered by the five defenders. Recognizing when the zone is matched up, reading for holes in the zone, and proper timing of the subsequent cuts are often more effective than plays with movements that can be scouted far more readily.

3. Penetrate the Gaps — "Punch it!"

The Penetration Game. The ball handler is constantly looking for gaps between his defender and adjacent defenders in the zone and safe entry passes to the low post. A quick bounce or two to draw the extra defender to the ball, combined with simultaneous movement by his four teammates, will create passing lanes fundamental to attacking zones, especially the aggressive and laning style zones. Low posts players have options of passing to the weak side perimeter, and their post partner. Quick penetrating dribbles followed by sharp passes ideally to four players who move to open angles are difficult for any defense to handle.

4. Use Screens as in Man to Man — "Screen it!"

The Screening Game. Screens on and off the ball can be as effective against zones as they are man-to-man, especially if they are random and come within the flow of the offense. Ball screens whether at the top, the elbows, or the high wings bring challenges to zones similar to those experienced by man defenses. Screens that pin the zone in for good shooters to attack the space behind the screener can be devastating for zones. Just as the screeners become viable scoring targets versus man-to-man, they also have a role by sealing in for deep catches, or cross screening for post players, and then showing back for shots.

5. Use Dribble Pull Moves — "Pull it!"

Positive Dribble Game using non-penetrating dribbles. This differs from Punching in point 3 above. For decades in basketball history, the common mantra when going up against zone defenses was to keep the ball off of the floor. Coaches insisted on constant rapid ball movement and eschewed even the penetrating punch, ironically, for a long time. But that was before players became so adept in ball skills and jump shots. Still, even the use of lateral dribbles to change passing angles to an inside man or to shorten a pass to a perimeter player to avoid a turnover was slow to be recognized as a positive.

Slower yet has been the utilization of the dribble to **rotate a defender up or down** by dribbling to the edge of his coverage, or even into the area of an adjacent zone defender, to **distort the zone** formation and to make a **realignment** on the offense by flattening it.

Dribble rotating a zone from one perimeter spot to another, be it from point to wing, wing to point, wing to corner, or corner to wing, can distort and confuse the zone. When combined with complementary cutting, it poses difficulty for virtually all zones. A **Dribble Pull** at the top, accompanied by the high post popping out, creates instant pressure on the low post defense as mentioned in the discussion on post play. A **Dribble Rotate** that takes a point defender to a wing can change a point defense into a two-front defense instantly and may draw out a low wing defender in a 2-3 zone to come up off the baseline, thus weakening the inside defense or the 3-point defense.

The **Dribble Pull Up** move out of the corner is an effective tool in the zone attack to pull a defender up off the baseline and expose the corner to a cutting offensive player. As will be shown later, players can learn to react automatically to it when they see a teammate do it in a game, if they have drilled it, or it may be a called set play action.

Summary on the Basic Five Elements

The **5 Basic Elements** themselves comprise the fundamental components that go to make up about every zone set offense. When combined with the Automatics and the Penetration game, they form a free flowing system for free lance play and provide the basis for about every set play a team will run. It can be an especially effective offense since the players are able to simply **"play against the defense"** by reading the coverage and attacking with intelligence with no predictable prescription that can be scouted or anticipated accurately. Players love the freedom and grow in confidence as they meet success through their own initiatives on the court.

The Short Corner concept. What could be added here is the subtle use of the **"Short Corner"** principle in attacking zones that has been alluded to in the discussion on post movements. It is not quite in the class of the **Basic Five,** but that is arguable, so we will note here that the posts should rely on this action as one of the "tools" in their box.

When unable to catch in the normal low post area, it is smart to extend the post cut at times to the 16 foot area along the baseline and face out to see the entire floor with his back to the baseline and his body position actually below the level of the backboard. While this may seem "out of position," he is actually accomplishing at least three major things:

1) he is opening up space for the other post man or any cutter into the paint,

2) he can see from this vantage spot when and where he may make the best next move to get open and,

3) if he catches the ball, he is in great position to make the **low/high pass**, as well as the **weak side diagonal** pass to an open shooter. That is, he can pass to his cutting post partner, or to any other flash cutter to the middle, and is in position to make a strong outlet pass to any of the perimeter players.

As we go forward in the book we will present a multitude of play options against zone defenses, but each will borrow from some aspect of the Basic Five Elements, the Automatics and the Penetration responses that follow. These concepts lay the groundwork for our overall understanding of Zone Offense.

ZONE OFFENSE AUTOMATICS
Actions to Complement Any Action or Set Play

Regardless of the starting formation, these **Automatics** can be used as a part of the **motion game concept** against zones, or can be used in combination with most set zone plays. These Automatics should be regarded more as guidelines than strict rules, but are effective moves that can be used in most contexts.

1. High/Low Post Automatic Action. We have already established this action in the Post Play presentations. It is so integral to zone attack that we will only reiterate briefly certain principles:

- Throw the ball into the high post as often as is possible, basically to break down the zones.
- On the catch the high post man must immediately turn and face the basket and his routine is to:
  1) look for his quick open shot or drive,
  2) **see if he can pass to the low post who must seal his man immediately, or cross under the basket to the opposite block,**
  3) **look** weak side to pass to an open teammate.

- His **rapid fire thought process** is said more briefly: "**my move, pass low, pass opposite.**" Those are the options that will be open only for a short moment. If he has none of those he has time to calculate his next move relative to what the defense allows.
- If there is no easy play to make at this point, he may find the strong side corner man open or he can **pass** to any open perimeter man and **cut** to the goal, or go set a **pick and roll** on him.
- The high post player may also elect to dribble over to a perimeter player to execute a **dribble handoff** move.
- If the post player elects to pass it right back to the player who passed to him, or to swing to another perimeter player, his cut to the goal will key a response from his post partner to cut into the middle and replace him in the high post in an **X-Cut option**.

Summary on the high/low game.

1. We have noted that the low post man moves to free up immediately when the ball goes to the high post.
2. The wings quickly get to the corner areas.
3. There must be no players directly behind the high post at this point.
4. All three perimeter players should put themselves in shooting threat positions, spaced from one another and have hands and feet ready to catch and shoot, or to make a play off the dribble or pass.

2. The Corner Pass Automatic. When a wing area player passes to the corner, our guideline (not a hard, fast rule understand) as an automatic response the largest percent of the time is for the **wing player to cut to the goal, looking for a return pass.** If he does not get the ball he continues out to the corner beyond the 3-point line on the weak side, or to the wing if no one is occupying that spot (Diagram 1).

- The man in the corner with the ball can give a quick return give and go pass to the cutter, but if he is not open for a catch in the first couple of steps, the new ball handler looks to penetrate right into the gap created by the wing man's cut.

- If the corner man penetrates, the strong side post man will pop to the baseline opposite the penetration and open up with hands and feet ready for a catch and shoot 14-17 footer or to swing the ball outside. (Diagram 1)

- The high post player will read his defense and present himself for an elbow area catch, or he may drift down to the weak side block to be in position to rebound, or to catch a high pass if his man leaves him. (Diagram 2)

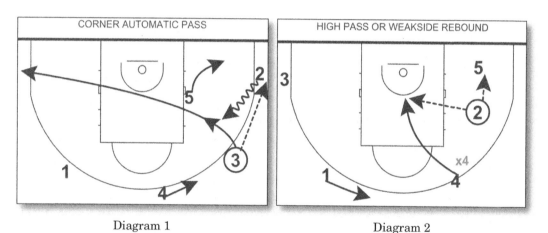

Diagram 1   Diagram 2

3. The Baseline Rover Automatic. In Diagram 3 on the following page Player 1 can fake a pass to 3 to key his start to cut to the weak side. He reverses the ball to Player 4 popping from the high post.

- The corner player 3 **may choose to rove the baseline** even if Player 1 does not key him with the fake, especially if he reads that a low wing will have to cover 2 on the weak wing. This cut puts pressure on the back line to make serious adjustments. If Player 4 had been down low in a double low post set and did not pop up, 2 would have to move to the top as the swing man, a weaker move.

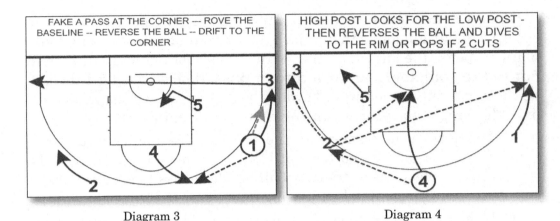

Diagram 3   Diagram 4

- **But the play works best with Player 4 popping up** and looking to pass low to 5 first or swing to 2 on the wing. Post 5 should clear the lane to the weak side, if he does not get a pass from 4. This presents many options for the offense. Player 4 may pass to 2 because X5 is guarding 5 hard on the high side creating an open gap as a result. Post 4 can dive quickly into the space in that event. Player 1 has cut to the now open diagonal corner angle for a pass from 2 (Diagram 4). At this point, if there is no shot or penetration and Player 2 still has the ball, he could pass to 3 and run the Corner Pass Automatic.

- **Note that point 1, who reversed the ball** should drift toward the now-empty corner area after passing and be ready to read to make his next move. This is called "passing and replacing oneself," and puts him in the favorable diagonal angle from Player 2. We don't like for anyone to pass and stand. Pass and cut or pass and drift up or down are options for movement, but avoid passing and standing still. Backtracking or counter flow is another good option when Player 4 got the initial pass. That is, Player 4 could fake a pass or take a freeze bounce toward the weak side and snap the pass back to 1, who can pass low to 5 or penetrate. Play the game! This is the power of automatics with options.

4. The Dribble Rotate Automatic. Players in front and behind the dribbler must rotate in the direction of the dribble when a perimeter player drag dribbles over laterally out front, down vertically on the wing or up from the corner. This is not a penetrating punch, but a rotating of the offense.

- The player who is in front of the ball must move ahead a slot to maintain spacing, even if that means that he crosses under to the weak side, certainly when a wing player dribbles down toward a filled corner. A player immediately ahead of the ball being rotate dribbled in his direction always has the option to spot up, back cut to the goal to post up, or clear out to the weak side. A player behind the dribbler needs to fill cut into the slot vacated by the dribbler.

• In Diagrams 5 and 6 below, Player 1 drag dribbles toward 3 to pull X1 to the edge of his coverage. At this point, Player 4 could pop up to fill in for 1 and 2 can hold on the wing. Another option is for Player 2 to follow 1 to fill in for him and have 4 pop out to the weak wing, a good move if 4 is a shooter. As mentioned, Michigan State uses this pulling technique often in their sets. Mixing up on reads tends to make X4 and X2 have to decide who they are going to cover.

• X3 will stay with Player 3 on his move to the corner so he will not be open there. Player 3 will do best by roving on the baseline, usually.

• This Dribble Rotate Down that drags X1 to the wing, **brings X2 to the top and thus exposes X4 on the weak side when the ball is reversed quickly.** That is the advantage of dragging a guard to the wing and then roving the base with Player 3.

• X4 will not be able to do a great job of covering Player 2 on the wing and still get to 3 in the corner. This forces a rotation and can cause a mistake by the defense. Player 1 should read that and reverse the ball quickly. (Diagram 6)

• Diagram 6 shows a bump down rotation by X2 to X4 to try to get X4 to Player 3 in the corner. A defensive rotation must take place if X4 is to cover 3 in the new corner or else X5 exposes the goal by covering the corner. Still another option is for X3 to chase Player 3 man-to-man and further distort the defense.

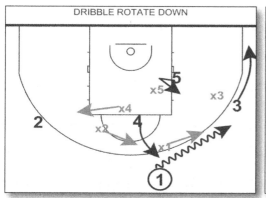

Diagram 5

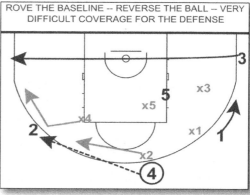

Diagram 6

- The **Automatics** continue from here, depending on what Player 2's next move is with the ball. He could pass to Player 3 and cut. He could pass to Player 4 if he dived in an X-cut or to 5 flashing into the lane after 4's dive. Or he could pass to Player 5 in the low post, if he ran a straight line cut to post.

- The point is that **the defense doesn't know what is coming next, but the players can read each other and the defense.**

- Remember that the player who fill cuts into the spot vacated by the drag dribbler will generally be the high post who jumps out to the top as **Player 4 does in Diagram 5.** In a double low post set, it would be the weak wing man.

- If wing 3 comes to the top and there is a high post player, that man should replace Player 3 on the weak side wing to keep there from being three offensive players in the middle lane. Someone must always make replacement cuts so that the ball can be swung back quickly opposite the direction of the dribbler. **This keeps good spacing and sets up the option for misdirection, always a good ploy.**

The Dribble Rotate Up move. Note that a dribble move in any direction demands corresponding moves to fill the spot vacated by the dribbler and to provide an immediate pass option in various directions.

- In **Diagram 7** either the coach or Player 1 has called for a **"cut back"** move from a Dribble Up. Player 1 takes two or three steps as if he is going to cut on through as usual, but then cuts back to the open corner.

- X3 will have followed Player 3 on the Dribble Up, exposing the corner where 1 may have a shot. If X5 pulls out to cover Player 1, this leaves 5 open in the post.

- If X4 covers Player 5, the weak side is totally open on the skip-pass to 4 at the short diagonal angle from 1 in the corner shown in Diagram 7.

- In **Diagram 8 no "cutback" was called,** so Player 1 passes to the corner and cuts on through on the Automatic Corner Pass, but when 5 sees that 3 either cannot penetrate, or that he simply decides on his own to use the Dribble Up move, it keys 5 to move on out further than the short corner, his natural move on this penetration angle. It is his cue to pull further out. If Player 5 has 3-point range, then he can go out past the 3-point line.

- **Note that post 4 will dive right to the goal** as a scoring cut or post up option.
- **Player 1 should be open at a weak side diagonal angle** on the wing from 5, if X4 drops down to help defend 4's cut. (Diagram 8)

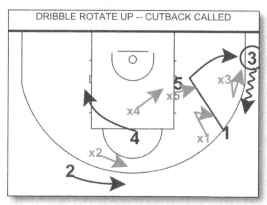

Diagram 7

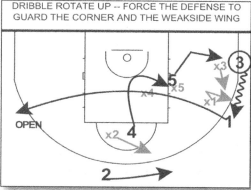

Diagram 8

Using a Dribble Rotate Across move: in Diagrams 9-11 on the following page, the offense lines up in a two-front set and Player 1 runs a lateral **Dribble Pull move** across the top to distort the coverage of the perimeter players in what is a counterflow, misdirection move. The defense must adjust across the top or else either Player 2 or 4 will be able to drift away into an open shot or move. There are various ways the play may proceed.

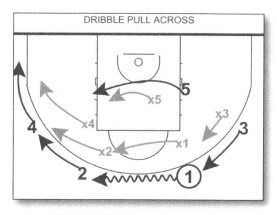

Diagram 9

- Player 1 can pass ahead to 2, who will fake a pass to 4 in the corner and pass back to Player 1. (Diagram 10)
- Player 4 knows he must rove the base as soon as he gets to the baseline, if the ball is reversed.

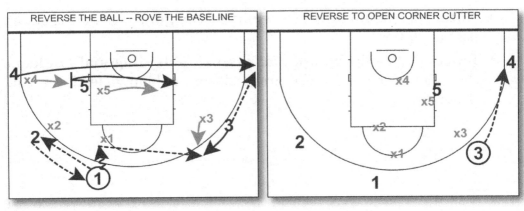

Diagram 10   Diagram 11

- Player 1 may have to freeze dribble a bounce or two to engage X1 to help with 4's timing, and to keep X3 close to 3, but the ball will be reversed to 3 and then on to 4 in the corner normally. (Diagram 10)
- **Player 5 will post up after setting a bother pick on X4, if he tries to go man-to-man with 4 on the cut.**
- **Note that X3 has no chance to get to Player 4 in the corner, so X5 or X4 must make an adjustment that could open up the basket or the weak side for a skip-pass from 4 to 2 or 1. (Diagram 11)**

If no shots are available, the play will proceed with the use of one of the **Basic 5** moves or **Automatics. Understand that these dribble moves are not penetrating punches, but pulling actions.**

5. The Front Inside Fill Automatic from a High/low set. When a **point guard cuts from the front** after passing to a wing, or if he makes a **quick drag dribble or two** to the right or left, the **high post player should pop out to fill the slot** vacated. The guard may pass to the wing or post and then cut to either the **strong side or weak side corner** if both are open. If only one is open, he will fill that one (Diagrams 12-15). **This applies to a 1-3-1 set and high double post sets like a 1-2-2 or a high 1-4.**

When a low wing player in the 2-3 covers the wing pass:

- Diagram 12 shows Player 1 engaging X2 and passing to 3 moving up for a catch just above the foul line so that X4 is drawn to him. If Player 3 comes too high, X2 will easily slide over. Since X4 came up here, Player 1 cuts to his corner forcing an adjustment by the defense to cover him there. Post 4 pops as the swing man.

- Diagram 13 has Player 3 passing to 1 to force X2 to bump X4 down or to draw X5 out to the corner.

- Wing 3 could fake a pass to Player 1 and pass to 4 in the swing spot, as 1 roves the base in a Rover Automatic. In that case it would put X3 in a bind on the weak side to cover the pass to Player 2 who would come up to a high wing for a catch from 4 and still get to 1 in the new corner.

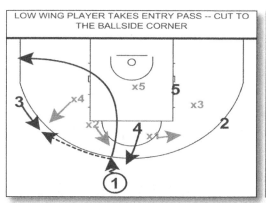

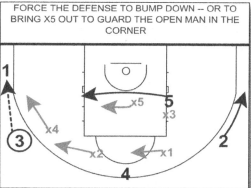

| Diagram 12 | Diagram 13 |

When a front defender covers the wing pass in a 2-3.

- Diagram 14 illustrates a different possession as Player 1 passes to Wing 2 coming up for a high wing catch so that X1 moves to cover him. This leaves X2 at the top to defend Player 4 on the pop up so Point 1 reads to cut to the weak side corner, <u>knowing that X4 will have to come out to defend 3</u> on the high wing when the ball is reversed to him.

- Diagram 15 depicts the difficult situation X4 will have to cover the high wing catch of a good shooter at the high wing and still be able to get bumped down to cover Player 1 in the corner.

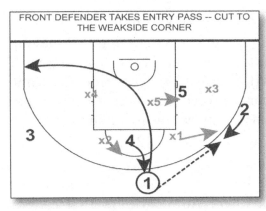

Diagram 14

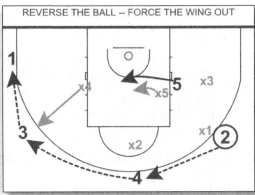

Diagram 15

Key Note: The point of this is that it is to the advantage for players to understand that they can **pull a bigger defender/rebounder type away from the goal by getting him to come out to defend a wing shooter, called "getting the low wing out" most often in this book.** If the back line wing player in a 2-3 has to come up off the baseline to defend, the offense should react **to fill and attack that corner** immediately.

If X4 has to cover a wing up above the foul line extended, it is difficult to get to the corner in a bump down rotation. If he can't make it, the defense will be forced to have X5 to come out for an emergency corner coverage and expose the goal, or for another player to break the zone and go man-to-man with a corner cutter, which distorts the defense and still gets the bigger player up off the back line.

This read is easier to see on the initial wing pass to start the offense, but an **experienced team that understands this concept can adjust and cut a player to the corner any time that they read a back man has been pulled up to the wing.** It may be even a post player with shooting range that makes the cut. Remember that any zone can be forced into a 2-3 formation when the ball is on the low wing or corner.

This theme of getting the bigger back men up off the baseline will occur quite often in this book along with the advantages of distorting the original formation of the zone defense. Players must learn the reads that enable this to happen whether it involves the proper cut, a dribble rotate move or a tactic called a "freeze dribble" that Ken has perfected that is designed to engage a specific defender for a brief moment to facilitate open shots.

Remember: it is important that the fill cut be made by the high post man when it is possible. However, if there is **no high post play-**

er as in the **1-2-2 low/low post and 4-out/1 in sets,** the next perimeter player behind the cutter will run the replacement cut. **But the "getting the low wing out" is equally effective, particularly when the X4 is a bigger inside presence than is the X3.**

6. Low post to High Post Automatic. The low post man looks first to see if he can pass to the high post man when the ball is passed to the short corner or at times even into the low post. **However, he has the first move — if there is no quick scoring move available of his own.** In Diagram 16 below Player 5 gets the ball in the short corner and looks for 4 at the elbow or on the dive to the rim. If there is no play from low to high, then he will seek to make the next best play.

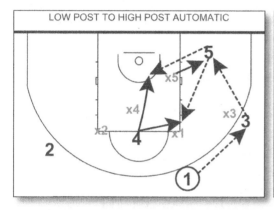
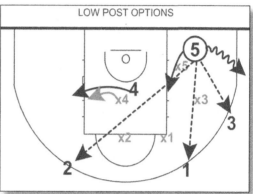

Diagram 16   Diagram 17

- In Diagram 17, Player 4 was not open so he cut to the other block. Player 2 seeks to get open at the high diagonal angle, as the defense will normally collapse at this point. Player 2 may even see a slot he can cut into for a nice high post or paint catch. When Player 5 passes the ball outside, he may look to **re-post, if he passes back out to the strong side,** but will generally read the situation with his other post man, if he passes to the top or weak side.

- If there is no quick outside shot, he will work opposite the other post man. That is, if his post partner is low, he will cut high and vice-versa. **Automatics and Basic 5** can continue until a good shot is found.

- If there is no easy play at all from the short corner, Player 5 can execute a **Dribble Pull to the corner or a little higher** to get an angle to pass safely to one of the options. One of those being the option to pass inside to Player 4 down low or to 3, if he back cuts to the goal when Player 5 is dribbling out. Player 1 would replace cut for 3 in that case to be 5's outlet to swing the ball to 2.

- **This is the least occurring Automatic,** except for teams that rely heavily on the short corner attack, but it is good to know that there is not only **high/low** but also a **low/high** option.

PRINCIPLES OF PENETRATION
THE BAILOUTS

Dribble Penetration — Spacing and Five-player Movement are Essential. While there are not as many 1-on-1 driving opportunities against zone defenses as against man-to-man, there are more than one imagines. This is especially true when it becomes a priority to look for these situations to develop. The key is for the perimeter and high post offensive people to be educated to the fact that they can find these quick-opening opportunities to attack the goal directly off the dribble, if they are aware of them immediately upon catching the ball. Often, the defense will shift too slowly to react to a quick 1-on-1 move. Players with the ball handling skill and quickness to make this play would be well-advised to take the driving option right away upon receiving the ball on the perimeter, since they should know where the defenders are by **looking at the middle of the floor prior to the actual catch.**

Dribble Drive is Not Only Redundant, it is Not New and is Essential to Zone Offense. Obviously, the only way to drive the ball in basketball is to dribble it. Any penetration without dribbling is called, "travel!" True, it has been an effective catch phrase and has been developed into an entire offense by several outstanding coaches. Our point here, while attempting a bit of levity, is to note that the penetration into the gaps of a zone, whether for just a bounce or two or all the way to the rim is a must for effective attacking. It is hard to imagine in retrospect how coaches traditionally said the team had to keep the ball off of the floor when facing the zones. But, while many things stay basic, the game is quite dynamic and coaching must be as well. While never designing an elaborate offense around the driving game, for several decades we have followed certain principles of what was most often called one of various descriptive names: Penetrate and Pass, Draw and Kick, Drive and Kick, etc. What many have failed to teach is how or where the four other teammates should move each time there is a penetration, whether just a punching into a gap or a full-blown drive to the hole.

The focus on spacing is far from a nuance in the 21st Century game, contrary to what some would deduct from listening to most talking heads on TV broadcasts. Many of the outstanding coaches' offenses by the 1960s were set up for that very purpose. What is now called the Triangle Offense had its origins over a half century ago and was called the Triple Post Offense. It was and is based upon the principles of **spacing with ball and player movement.** There were many others that were designed with the same purpose in mind, such as the "System" of Hall of Fame Coach Tony Hinkle, the 50-year coach at Butler University, and the West Coast flex action developed by several California college coaches a principle one being Hall of Fame coach Pete Newell. We could go on and talk of the Drake Shuffle and the offenses of various great coaches we have known in our long history in the game that emphasized spacing with ball and player movement.

While there have been times when it was fashionable to focus on mismatches, as there are in certain moments of most games today as well, there was a brief time in the NBA when there were so many bizarre defense rules that isolation ball was totally in vogue. The reason was that for a few years in the 1980s and early '90s, if a team placed one or two players out above the 3-point line in the outside lane, their defenders had to play well out of the lane as well and above the foul line. As a result in order to beat the rule, many coaches would isolate their two or three best offensive players on the other side to go 2-on-2 or 3-on-3. And guess why! It was because they had enforced spacing. Spacing has always been a premium in offense. The rules were an attempt to open the middle of the court, but with these rules they eliminated what must complement spacing and that is ball and player movement. There was little of that in the "iso" game. The change in rules and the addition of so many players, including a lot of foreign born ones who could shoot outside, has opened the game up again and dull, low-scoring games are no longer an issue.

The Bailout Concept of Movement. But for the most part basketball has been a 5-on-5 game, as when the ball moves, all the other offensive players move, not just the defenders. When a player penetrates with the ball, it is vital that the other four offensive players move into positions whereby at least three can be outlet options and, hopefully, all four. Nothing is more upsetting to a player to have a penetration jam up and have no one presenting himself as an outlet.

We **define four general penetration angles** with guidelines as to how the other players should move when there is a punch or a drive to the goal from each one. These are the same moves that are a part of the "Dribble Drive" concept, but we are not talking about a full offense to be learned with multiple play calls. These are common sense moves and, therefore, quite easy to learn, especially if the shooting drills utilize these movements to create habits, as will be shown in the chapter on drills. It is amazing how many teams fail to exercise them, however.

Know your players and define roles and their values. It may sound pretty risky to give specific advice for some individuals to look more aggressively to drive the ball instead of others on the team, but a **coach needs to define roles.** He should also inform good rebounding or defensive (but poor-shooting) players that it is best for them to look to pass and cut when catching the ball out of shooting range. The concept here is that it is important to make it clear to players that, for the most part, **shooters look to shoot, drivers look to penetrate, and others look largely to cut.** They must understand their strengths and stay away from their weaknesses. While some coaches and players resist this method of defining roles, it has proven to be pretty effective when done in a positive way.

It takes all kinds of talent to make up a winning team. We are not saying a poor shooter should never shoot. On the contrary, they should shoot those shots that are open and in their rhythm and range. They should not be volume shooters, however, ones who expect 15-20 shots a night while shooting 30%. But players can still contribute appropriately on offense while concentrating on their better contributions, whether that is defense, rebounding, setting picks or moving the ball and cutting. These are all significant parts that make up the whole of a good team. **And of course, we like to remind the shooters that they should get a rebound and guard someone every chance they get.**

Get to the foul line even against the zones. The problem with teams that forego the aggressive look for the drive is that they often find it difficult to get to the foul line. Without adequate free throws, a team must score a lot of field goals to win games. Having *designated drivers* is one way to help get to the foul line without overdoing this particular tactic. However one does it, a coach should inculcate the driving game into all his offenses, while avoiding forcing it when it is not there. Forced drives and passes are worse than forced shots in reality — the shot might go in, the others have no chance.

As penetration to gaps is important, the movement of the other players is more important in keeping proper spacing and outlet options. Remember that "Punching it" is a part of the

Basic 5. The four basic angles of penetration that demand a response are shown in Diagram 18:

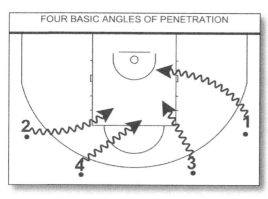

1. Wing penetration toward the baseline.

2. Wing penetration into the middle.

3. Front penetration toward the goal.

4. Front penetration across the front, at an angle to the weak side of the goal.

Diagram 18

Wing Penetrations — attacking the baseline and the middle when a gap allows. In Diagram 19, wing man 3 penetrates to the baseline side and all four players respond in a way that we will elaborate more on in this chapter. For now note that the posted players must move opposite the penetration to set up an easy short pass, if their defender helps to stop the driver. Player 1 behind the ball should follow up as a safety outlet so that the ball can be reversed quickly, if the penetration is stopped. Player 4 is giving a baseline drift release pass and 2 provides a high diagonal outlet pass lane in Diagram 19.

In Diagram 20, Player 3 penetrates into the middle of the defense in the gap between X1 and X5. Again, 1 provides a safety release while post man 5 moves opposite the drive ready to catch and shoot, if X5 helps toward the ball. Player 2 once again finds a slot at the high elbow/wing angle and moves to a spot where X2 is not in the pass lane to the ball. Player 4 cuts to the low diagonal pass angle, putting himself in position to see the ball and let the ball see him.

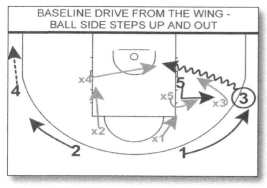

Diagram 19

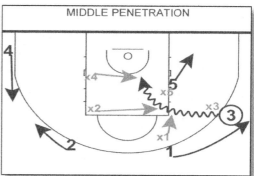

Diagram 20

Front Penetrations — the direct drive at the low post man and the diagonal cross-penetration. When the ball handler is able to penetrate directly down toward the low post, Player 5 needs to re-locate to the opposite side of the goal, or to pull out wide if he sees the action too late. Player 2 will read the wing defender and usually get to a diagonal angle in front of the ball. Player 3 in front of the ball will move up if he is in the corner, but will usually drift down as in the Diagram 21, if he is up on the wing when the penetration begins. Player 4 in the high post will move behind the penetration to follow

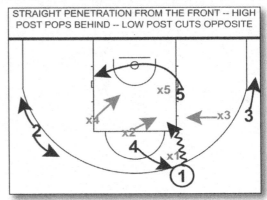

Diagram 21

up for safety and be ready as a swing man if Player 1 gets stopped. Regardless of the formation, when a ball handler comes down from the top directly toward a posted man, the post's best move is to relocate to the weak side and his alternative is to spread out to give room for the drive. Either way he needs to be ready to catch and shoot.

In Diagram 22 we see a penetration that occurs more often vs. man-to-man play than vs. zones, the cross penetration. Still, it can happen in zone play as Player 1 executes a penetration toward the weak side elbow right at the man defending 2. Too often in this action Player 2 will drift away from the ball in the direction of the penetration, thus keeping the defender in line to steal a pass from Player 1 to 2 that leads to a fast break layup. In Diagram 23, Player 1 pitches back to 2 and 2 could make a second penetration down toward 3, nor-

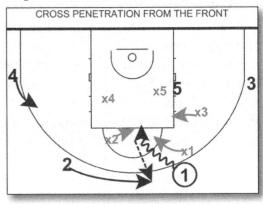

Diagram 22

mally a strong move. Player 1's pitch is best made when 2 has gotten even with the ball or a little past him in order to prevent the defender on 1 from switching out hard. Player 4 gets to a position to create an open pass lane from the ball.

BAILOUT DRIBBLE GUIDELINES

Perimeter player's movements — following is a more in-depth look as to where the other four players go when there is a penetrating punch or drive, <u>whether vs. zone or man-to-man.</u>

A player in front of penetration should move a step or two toward the ball handler, against the direction of the penetration. So that if his defender drops to help on the ball, he can create an open pass lane to the ball handler, as opposed to drifting in the same flow as the ball handler. **This one is generally violated by players at all levels as they drift in the direction of the ball,** putting the off-ball defender in a great position to help on the penetrator and still stay directly in line with the pass to the drifting player. (Diagram 23)

Moving up breaks the three-in-a-row alignment as when the off-ball defender is in position between the passer and the receiver. Such movement allows the player in front of the ball to move with rhythm into a catch and shoot, or to make a second penetration. Note that Player 1 continues on to a position behind 3 who is in position to penetrate into the gap between X3 and X1. (Diagram 23)

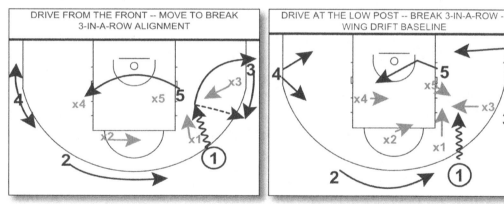

| DRIVE FROM THE FRONT -- MOVE TO BREAK 3-IN-A-ROW ALIGNMENT | DRIVE AT THE LOW POST -- BREAK 3-IN-A-ROW -- WING DRIFT BASELINE |

Diagram 23   Diagram 24

Caveat: if you are on the wing area generally foul line extended, play your defender, in this case your best drift may be to the open corner. (Diagram 24)

Notes:

1. **Second penetration** will often create something more positive than the first, especially if the **passer curls up behind his pass as in Diagram 23.**

2. **Defensive balance is key.** If the ball handler shoots or dishes off inside, the player coming toward the ball is already in a better position for **defensive balance** than is one who drifts away in the same direction as the penetration.

3. **Corner shooters, when both corners are filled upon a penetration, both should move up** a step or two, when there is penetration from the front, to make themselves perimeter targets and putting them in positions to be back on defense.

Alert: be ready to back cut. In the case where the defender on the man in front of the ball does not open or drop to commit to give help to the ball, but maintains visual and /or body contact with the front man, the rule can be broken, **if** the player thinks he can make a good back cut to the goal. He should **continue the cut on through to the 3-point line on the weak side,** if he does not get the ball. (Diagram 24)

Players behind the ball on penetration must rotate to follow in the direction of the penetration.

1. If a player is on the perimeter and the ball is dribbled away from him, he should fill cut in behind the penetrator in order to provide a safety outlet pass in the event he cannot get to the goal and gets stuck. Ideally, he should pull up for a jumper, or pass to any of the other three players on his team. Mainly, he provides a safe angle outlet pass whereby he can catch and swing the ball, while being in a **safety position** on defense.

2. In the case of a baseline penetration, it is especially vital that the nearest perimeter player follow the penetration since the best defensive teams will attack the ball at the baseline, **cutting off clear passing angles** in front. See Diagram 25.

3. The **penetrator knows he can stop and reverse pivot then get the ball out of the problem** when he has the player in the safety position behind him.

4. **The follow up man will be open for a catch and shoot or an easy penetration or reversal** because the defender on the player following up the penetration will normally drop down toward the help area.

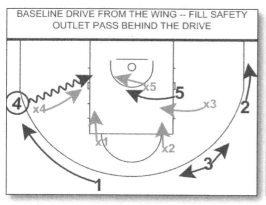

Diagram 25

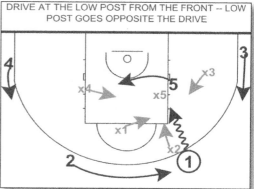

Diagram 26

5. **Create four targets.** Making this cut also **opens up the floor** for the penetrator, as he will **have four targets** — the safety, the post who moves, and the other two perimeter players will all be in good positions. (Diagram 25)

6. If the play started from the front with **both corners filled,** the corners move up a couple steps. This puts Player 4 in the diagonal down angle and 3 in a position to catch to rhythm up or penetrate a second time. Player 2 is the safety and the post 5 has relocated. (Diagram 26)

Post Players Movements — go opposite the penetration

1. **Baseline drive from wing**. If a player is on the **strong side post,** he quickly takes a position a couple steps up the lane and out a step or two and opens up to the ball, ready to catch and shoot. The **other three players** put selves in position to have a safety and to be outlets to the ball. (Diagram 27)

    a. If a post man is on the weak side block, he should **loop to the middle in front of the rim.**

2. **Middle Drive from wing.** When the drive comes into the middle the low post again moves opposite the direction of the penetration. **This time Player 5 pops out on the baseline two or three quick steps** and opens up with hands and feet ready to catch and shoot the 14-17 foot shot, assuming he has that range. If not, he may back his way in closer or simply move the ball to an open man and get back into the post. The **other three players** put themselves in positions as outlets with a safety. (Diagram 28)

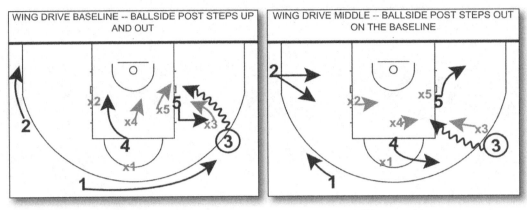

Diagram 27   Diagram 28

Weak Side Player's Guidelines on Penetration — the object is to make oneself an option at all times.

Post Players. We have already covered the movements of the post player when on the weak side and there is either baseline or middle penetration from the wing, whether as a single post man or as a part of a low double post tandem setup.

1. **On a drive from the front when there is a double low post,** it is generally better for the **strong side post to spread out** to the short corner area as Player 4 does, ready to catch and shoot or make an appropriate play. For him to relocate to the other side would put him right in his post teammate's lap, obviously. (Diagram 29)

2. **The weak side post man will have more options** than that of the strong side player. He reads his nearest defender's action and goes accordingly. He may be able to slip in behind him or even seal him off for a high pass or lob; he may be able to move straight up a step or two from his position for an 8-10 foot catch, or he may read that spreading out to the baseline to allow more space in the lane for the ball is the best move. Post 5's options are shown in Diagram 29.

Perimeter Players. If a player is on the weak side wing area and the penetration is going toward the base line opposite, he quickly drifts to the corner to be an outlet along the baseline in the **baseline drive, baseline drift.**

1. **Come out of the corners.** However, if a player is already in the **weak side corner** and there is a **middle penetration from the wing** or **from the top,** he should **move up a step or two out of the corner.** That way, if his nearest defender moves into the lane area to jam the middle, he creates an easy pass lane from the ball handler for a catch and shoot or a catch and second penetration.

2. **Follow the penetration.** As been noted, if a player is the first one behind the penetration, he will follow it, getting spaced behind him to serve as an outlet in case the driver gets stopped and has no positive passing options. See Player 3 following 1 in Diagram 29.

3. **Inside fill possible.** Occasionally, a high post man can pop out to be the safety for a penetration, in an inside fill cut from the wing as well as from the top as shown before. (Diagram 30)

4. **The weak side high diagonal outlet.** On penetrations this spot can often be filled. On an inside fill from the high post, this often leaves two perimeter players in the weak side area, a real advantage. In any case when there are two players on the perimeter on the weak side, this puts a player in the high diagonal spot and one in the corner as players 1 and 2 demonstrate. These are excellent spots for shooters and the inside fill sets it up. (Diagram 30)

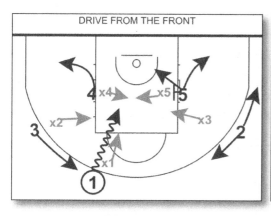

Diagram 29

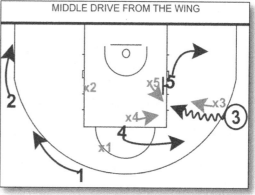

Diagram 30

Benefits of Knowing the Bailout Guidelines

Purpose. The guidelines are to help players know **how to respond in general to the various penetration possibilities,** with the overriding concept being to try to put oneself in a position to be a receiver, to be a part of the play, even if your number were not called. The axiom that goes, "if you can't see the ball, the ball can't see you" applies to much of this area of the game.

Eliminates guesswork and lends organization to a free lance situation. When there is penetration, it usually indicates that a set play has been broken or that good ball/player movement has put a ball handler in a position in which he can go on his own to punch into a gap in the defense. In other words, the defense makes a mistake, offering a breach into which a player can go on his own to attack.

A knowledge of the items we have covered in the **Basic 5, the Automatics and now the Bailouts** puts players in a position whereby not only does the ball handler have an idea of what to do, but his teammates can make a read relative to the situation as well.

While this summary is redundant to a degree, this is the third of the three steps that go together to make for a team that can attack a zone on their own from time to time. But more than that, they will know the ingredients of most set plays and how to finish them off once the first two or three options fail to produce the desired shot.

From this point we will go into a lot more specific zone sets and quick-hitters that will utilize the principles and guidelines presented thus far, but **first we present a detailed look at how the dribble may be used in so many ways to counteract the zones.**

─────── **CHAPTER 4** ───────

ELABORATING ON THE POSITIVE USE OF THE DRIBBLE

Using the Dribble Positively to Attack the Basket, Middle Space, and to Create More Space

We believe that a team must be aggressive to score against the zone by attacking full court before the zone can set up and that requires a lot of mental and physical commitment, as well as a mind set to push the ball and attack the basket. This requires excellence in two basic basketball skills, passing and driving the ball toward the basket in a full court approach when possible. At the half court, it requires the same mindset: attack the basket through the passing or driving the ball inside, or at least attack the space in the middle of the defense through passing or smart dribble penetration called "punching into the gaps or seams, i.e., the space in the defense. The passing and the penetration not only attack either the goal or the space in the zone, but each action creates more space on the perimeter by drawing the defense to compress toward the ball, leaving space that was originally defended uncovered for open shots.

As mentioned previously, for decades coaches had shown utter disdain for using the dribble against zone defenses. By the time laning and matchup zoning styles came into vogue, it became very difficult for teams handicapped with the "no-dribble rule" to get a good shot against those defenses. Admittedly, dribbling is a temptation that most players will tend to overuse considerably, if left to their own devices. However, the positive use of the dribble must be thoroughly exploited against today's defenses of all types. Other than the overall presence of Michael Jordan, it was Jordan's and Scottie Pippin's ability to break down defenses off the dribble and utilize a positive option from that penetration that made the Chicago Bulls so hard to defend in their NBA title years. Subsequent players like Jason Kidd, Chris Paul, LeBron James, Steve Nash, Steph Curry and Kyrie Irving have elaborated on those skills.

Other than shooting ability itself, the dribble is the most dangerous offensive weapon in the game today. Ball skills are much better than in previous generations due to a combination of the examples from the past like Marques Haynes, Bob Cousy, Pistol Pete Maravich and modern day training. The teaching of ball skills has grown with the immense growth of the popularity of the sport, due in part to constant television coverage, and even more to the dedication of coaches who work with kids of all ages on skill development.

As with all strengths, however, they can become weaknesses when overused. Over-penetration up against the defense is an recurring problem for most teams. An even bigger problem, however, revolves around the improper movement, or lack of movement oftentimes, of the penetrator's teammates. **Chapter Three** dealt in large part with this proper movement for spacing. In this chapter we will show more detail relative to various uses of the dribble to attack space, create more space and to distort a defense of any kind.

There are six positive functions for the dribble against the zone defenses. The first three actions are fundamental and well recognized. Dribble Rotation and its value as noted in points four and five are far more advanced and lesser understood:

1. **Driving the ball to the goal** for a score, with four teammates moving into positions to complement the attack on the basket, according to our bailout rules.

2. **Punching (penetrating) into a defensive gap** to shoot or to create a shot for a teammate by drawing defenders to the ball, **thereby creating more space for him to operate when receiving a pass.**

3. **Using the drag dribble to improve a passing angle** by bouncing once or twice laterally for a **post entry,** or to shorten the angle and distance for a **perimeter pass,** and especially to key **popping a high post player** out for a catch as an entry into a potential high-low post action.

4. **Dribble Rotating the defense down to stretch or distort the defense.** This is done by dribbling while guarded by a defender out of one zone into an adjacent one toward the sideline or baseline in a non-penetrating angle. The ball handler dribbles the ball one slot over on the perimeter to pull the ball defender to the edge of his area or into the next primary zone area. The intelligent use combined with reading the defense **creates excellent open space options.**

5. **Dribble Rotating the defense up or across the top.** Dribbling **up away** from the baseline, or near sideline, in a non-penetrating angle involves the same process as the Dribble Down, **but offers different space openings.**

6. **Freeze dribbling a defender to make him engage the ball.** This clever action Ken has specialized in serves to have the effect of helping to pull a low wing defender out of his preferred position. It is also a tool used often at the top of the zone to allow better timing for cutters to get into place.

1. Driving to the Goal — Spacing is the key — Know the Bailout Rules on Penetration

We have already dealt with this aspect in the previous Chapter Three, so we will only make short reference here. Most say that there are not as many 1-on-1 driving opportunities against zone defenses as against man-to-man, but there are more than one imagines, if the focus is to attack the basket full and half court and to penetrate into the gaps to create even more open space for a teammate. When these become priorities, the opportunities will develop more frequently. The key is for the perimeter and post players to be educated to the fact that they can find these quick-opening opportunities (spaces) for shots, if they respond properly to the penetration

When facing good ball and player movement, the defense is more likely to shift too slowly to react to a quick 1-on-1 move. Players with the ball handling skill and quickness to make this play need to look to attack the rim when possible, not just to take a bounce or two as in punching, another vital use of the dribble nonetheless. The point is that a player who stays under control can still pull up or pass the ball if he sees the option to the rim close up on him. But if he never thinks, **"Get to the rim,"** he will miss out on such opportunities. They do exist against the zone defense.

Having said that, it is important for a coach to identify which players have the skill to attack with the dribble and to let that be known to the team. The concept here is that it is important to make it clear to players that, for the most part; shooters look to shoot, drivers look to drive or penetrate, and others look largely to pass and cut. The players must know themselves and one another. Along this line, it is important to explain that nothing is forever in this world and they can elevate their game with hard work.

Do not overlook the value of the free throw when attacking zones. The problem with teams that forego the aggressive look for the drive is that they often find it difficult to get to the foul line. Without adequate free throws, a team must score a lot of field goals to win games. However one does it, a coach should inculcate the driving game into all of his offenses, while avoiding overuse.

Note: As driving to the goal is important, the movement off the penetration is equally important in order to keep proper spacing and vision. Spacing is the Key — Know the Bailout Rules on Penetration.

2. Dribble Punching the Ball into Defensive Gaps: See the space — Attack it — Create more Space

It is not necessary to have the speed or athleticism to attack the rim to be able to use the dribble to penetrate the zone. Even the player with that ability will be able to see that he cannot get to the rim every time, but may be able to identify a gap that develops in the defense as the ball is moved that is big enough for him to penetrate a bounce or two for a shot or to draw a second defender, thus opening up space for a teammate to catch and shoot or to make a further play. This is where the ability to read and to execute when to punch the ball into the defense comes into play. It is a critical tool to develop in order to have success against the zones. Oftentimes a team can pass the ball to one side to shift the defense and then swing it to the weak side and find that a lazy defender has failed to recover from help side to ball side and an opportunistic player will be able to attack the gap right away. Many younger players will not be able to see this "gap" or opening or to complete the move successfully, even if they do identify it. The fact is that a higher percentage of college and high school players may be able to acquire this ability through drilling, because many possess better ball handling skills than in years past. It is not easy, but it is worth teaching and drilling in order to discover which players will ultimately be able to do it.

All of the Bailout Movements on penetration in Chapter Three not only apply to driving to the rim, but also apply directly to driving gaps. Four teammates must move to create open space for passes from the dribbler. Once again the dribbler must have his eyes up to read the defenders and to deliver the pass as the defender moves towards the ball before he gets smothered. The movement rules that his teammates follow are the same as those covered in driving the ball to the basket. This total team involvement is necessary to keep the integrity of spacing and to give the ball handler the best chance of finding good options.

As he attacks the defender nearest him and drives the gap to involve another defender, **his first dribble must beat the first man and his direction must be a threatening toward the basket,** or there is no reason to draw help. What each player should understand is that if they **present themselves as a passing option every time there is penetration, they become a part of the play,** whether their number has been called or not.

Diagram 1 illustrates wing man 3 seeing that there is a gap in the

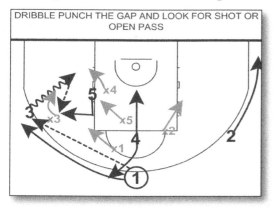

Diagram 1

1-2-2 zone toward the baseline defender. Player 5 must react to this penetration by moving **directly to the area that is at an angle** that is a couple steps up the lane and one or two steps out towards the sideline away from his defender with hands and feet ready to catch and shoot. If the baseline defender on Player 5 does not challenge the attack, 3 can get a shot. If X4, Player 5's defender, does react to 3's penetration, there is a good chance 5 will be open for a little 12-14 foot shot on the drop-off pass.

To keep proper spacing, not only does Player 5 need to open up to 3's drive, but the first player behind the ball, Player 1 here, must follow up 3's drive to give the possibility of a reverse pass if the first two options are not available. As discussed earlier, it is important in all offenses for the top man to follow up any baseline drive; it allows for the swing pass and keeps the geometry intact — triangle with spacing. Just to complete the scene in the team offense, note that Players 2 and 4 also react to the baseline drive of 3. Player 4 may see that X5 has moved over to help on 5, which opens up a cut to the goal for him. If that does not happen, he will loop to the weak side block for rebounding, or will pop to the top if Player 3 reverses the ball to 1. The weak side wing, Player 2, cuts to the opposite baseline to provide the "baseline drive, baseline drift" action.

In Diagram 2 the defense is playing a 1-2-2 or it could be a 1-3-1. In either case, wing man 3 fakes a baseline drive and makes a middle penetration into the gap between his man and the defender on top facing offensive Player 1. If no defender reacts, Player 3 may be able to shoot or possibly get to the basket himself.

Again, there are four responses to the action that are necessary to keep the spacing and geometry intact and to provide Player 3 with the best options. His teammates react to provide him with four options by following the bailout movement rules. Player 4 may have a seal off for a high pass or can spread out to the short corner like 5 does to open up the middle. Note that if Player 3 passes the ball to 2, he would quickly follow his pass with a cut to the corner below 2. In that position

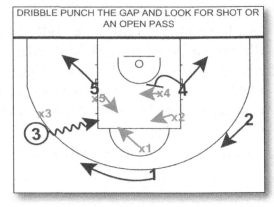

Diagram 2

he will be able to curl up behind 2, if he should decide to attack on the dribble with a second penetration. Player 1 is the safety who could also make a second penetration or swing the ball.

In Diagram 3, Player 1 attacks a gap in the high elbow area between X3 and X1. Player 2 loops toward and behind 1 to provide a safety outlet. Players 3 and 4 create open passing lanes lifting off the baseline. Player 5 may seal up for a high pass, if his man stays home, or he may pop to the baseline to spread the court if his man helps late on the ball.

If the two low post areas are filled on top penetration, as in Diagram 4, the posts read their defenders and usually pop to the baseline for catch and shoot opportunities, or they may slip to the rim, if their man helped early. Most of our offenses tend not to have posts covering both blocks, preferring high/low attacks, but this can happen with single/double sets and there are arguably some very good double low post set plays.

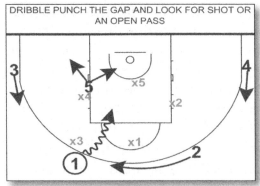

Diagram 3

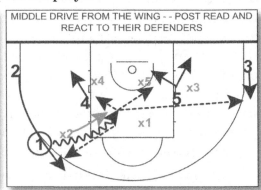

Diagram 4

In the event this occurs a ball side wing would fill behind the penetration for a safety outlet. A weak side wing would preferably move up as shown in Diagram 4, but could possibly find an easy opening by drifting to the corner, if he were on the wing when the play started. He must read the defense and get to an open spot, but coming toward the ball is generally better and safer than drifting away.

Second and third penetrations as options

Obviously, drivers must be able to finish at the rim, if help does not arrive to stop their penetration. However, sophisticated defenses have made getting to the rim much more difficult as the game has evolved. Thus, the increasing ability of players to shoot the 3-point shot has led to the emphasis on driving and kicking to open perimeter shooters. It has become a major emphasis in today's attack, as defenses struggle to stop the layup, and still recover to open 3-point shooters.

Attacking closeouts is as important versus zone defenses as it is against man-to-man. This sets the stage for shot fakes and second and third penetrations. Along that line, a critical concept for the penetrator to understand is **not to stop and stand after passing.** The passer must clear the area immediately upon passing, so that the receiver has the opportunity to have **space to drive** should he attack his closeout defender on the dribble.

The corner angle 3-pointer has become a staple in modern professional basketball since it is the shortest 3-point shot. Defenses are eager to "run the ball" off the 3-point line, especially in the corner. There is a trend in the NBA that has drifted down to college and lower level ball to have what is called **"fly-bys,"** when a player has a look at an open 3-pointer, eschewing the more fundamental act of **closing out — not a good choice in our opinion for many reasons.** In that defensive ploy the defender jumps to threaten the shot or even make an unlikely block and attempts to "fly" on past the shooter with his momentum, with little regard for any contact that could occur. That can work right into the offensive player's hands when he keeps his composure. In fact in a recent NBA playoff series the ESPN commentators were keeping track of the number of these occurrences and noting how often the defender fouled the 3-point shooter. In the end the **fly-bys** don't bother the good shooters and puts the defender out of the rebound game against the bad shooters, especially on the shots taken on the sideline and corner. It is a nice way to meet fans, however.

The passer's general rule of thumb is to **"curl into the area behind the perimeter receiver"** after passing to him. This can result in an open jump shot for the passer on a throw back pass. Obviously, the other perimeter players must be aware of this rule and adjust their movement accordingly.

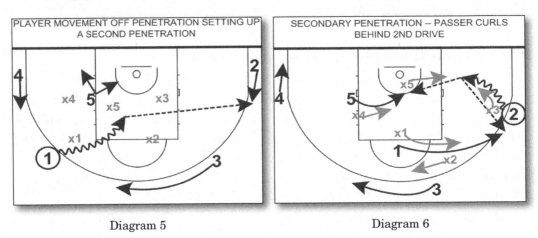

| PLAYER MOVEMENT OFF PENETRATION SETTING UP A SECOND PENETRATION | SECONDARY PENETRATION -- PASSER CURLS BEHIND 2ND DRIVE |

Diagram 5   Diagram 6

In Diagram 5, Player 1 penetrates middle from the wing and passes to 2 lifting out of the corner. Player 2 attacks X3's closeout for a secondary penetration.

In Diagram 6, passer 1 quickly curls behind 2's drive. Post 5 goes to the front of the rim and Player 4 makes the baseline drift on the weak side. Player 3 spaces to the high weak side diagonal angle from the ball.

Note: if Player 2 had caught higher and penetrated middle, 1 would have filled to the corner and Player 3 would move toward the penetration at the top, as opposed to drifting away. Weak side 4 would have presented himself as a down diagonal pass option, reading X4's position.

Creating an opportunity for the drift away move — when there is no apparent gap

In Diagram 7, ball handler 1 performs a clever move to break down the defense and free up a shooter, even though there is not an obvious gap in the defense. Against a 1-3-1 (though it could be any defense), Player 1 dribbles right at the inside shoulder of wing man 2's defender, X2. At the same time, Player 2 cuts away toward the corner to keep proper spacing. If X2's man reacts at all to Player 1's penetration, 1 can loop a soft pass to 2 for a nice rhythm-up jumper. If there is no easy option available, high post Player 4 has responded to the dribble by rotating to the ball handler

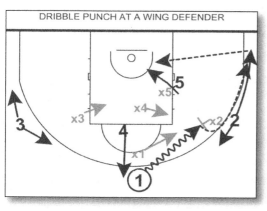

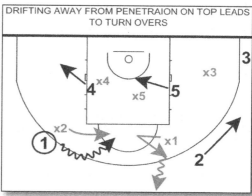

Diagram 7   Diagram 8

for spacing and to provide a reverse escape route. Player 3 reads X3 to provide the weak side option. This simple little technique can often free up a good scorer, Player 2 in this case, for a quick shot or for a pass to 5 who seals his man. This move creates a gap, or space, when there is none.

A caveat in drifting away from the penetrator

Diagram 8 illustrates the increased danger of drifting away from the penetrator that is coming toward a player in the **top area** of the offense. Player 1 punches in the gap between X2 and X1 and Player 2 does what is natural, which is what about 80% of players will do and swear it is the best thing to do - even in the NBA. While the play can be completed often, it is not the best play to make. The reasons are that if the pass is too flat, X1 can get it and it leads to a layup at the other end. If it is too soft or long, X3 may be able to intercept.

On the other hand, if Player 2 moves toward and above the ball, he will be wide open for a catch and a second penetration, if X1 helps stop Player 1. If X1 stays with Player 2 because he is a strong threat, Player 1 can punch in for the shot, or hit 3 coming up out of the corner or find one of the post men for a pass. **In the end the cut also serves for better defensive balance, always a good thing since transition defense is the basis for any effective defensive possession.**

In summary, dribble punching the gaps is an essential tool in attacking virtually any type of defense. It may not be as effective against totally sagging, compact zones, but those defenses are pretty much dead due to the 3-point shot and today's shooters. As is the case with all elements of zone attack, good spacing, ball and player movement with discipline are the foundations upon which offensive success is built. The wise coach will develop and utilize drills to enhance this skill.

We have noted some in our discussions of drills at the end of the book and in the Youth Basketball chapter.

3. Using the Dribble to Improve a Passing Angle

We dealt briefly with this aspect under the discussion of **geometry in basketball,** while noting the importance of breaking the straight three-in-a-row line between the feeder and the low post man in order to facilitate getting the ball inside. In addition to the pass inside, there is sometimes a need for the ball handler on the wing to dribble a bounce or two quickly toward the top when fill-cutters are late in responding to a vacant top area. This exercise by the ball hander can shorten the length of the reverse pass and change a dangerous passing angle to a safer one for the offense, reducing turnovers and speeding up the flow of ball movement. (Diagram 9)

Diagram 10 shows the dribble pull to key a high post entry into the high/low action.

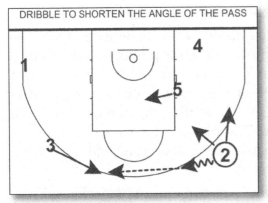

Diagram 9

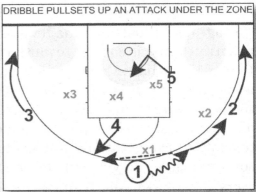

Diagram 10

DRIBBLE ROTATING THE DEFENSE

Zone defenders are generally guided by rules that predetermine the area of the court each man is to defend. Even with sophisticated match-up rules today, players still have a position where they start, if there is a player in the area relative to which defender challenges the ball handler first. There are many zone rules to instruct defensive players how to deal with cutters, overloads, screens, rovers and the gamut of situations offenses throw at them. **But the offense that forces the most adjustments stands an opportunity to force more errors, and the intelligent use of the dribble is key to that.**

The **Dribble Rotate** calls for a specific defensive rule. Dribble-rotating laterally is a **totally different use of the dribble than the aggressive drive to the goal or the forceful punching into gaps** for penetration or the dribble pull to pop a post. The man who dribble rotates does not intend to penetrate. His job is to drag a defender away from his starting spot in the defense or to cause him to hand him off to a teammate who comes to make the adjustment with him. The dual purpose is to distort the formation and to flatten the defense. Mistakes often occur when adjustments are made, and poor ones lead to easy shots. Clever use of dribble rotations with corresponding cuts to open space can be difficult for zone defenses to handle.

4. Dribble Rotating the Defense Down

Point Dribble Rotating against the 2-3 zone. Against a 2-3 zone, the dribble entry to the wing **will force a guard to defend the ball on the entry side nearly 100% of the time.** On ball reversal there will be a hole in the weak side corner, since the weak side low defender will normally have to defend the first pass to the wing on reversal. <u>This forces the low wing out on the weak side, as we say</u>.

In Diagram 11, Player 1 dribble rotates to pull X2 to his extreme posi-

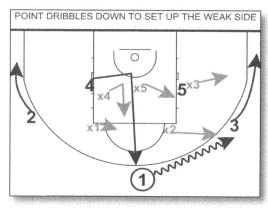
POINT DRIBBLES DOWN TO SET UP THE WEAK SIDE

Diagram 11

tion, pushing 3 to the corner and setting up low post triangle with 5. Player 4 can flash to the rim and inside fill cut to the high post area. Since the play is from a double low post set, Player 2 could fill cut to replace 1 and 4 could flare out to a wide area on the weak side, if he has an outside game. From a 1-3-1 formation Player 4 would pop up for the swing pass automatically. They could work the low post triangle, if open, first of all.

Otherwise, Player 1 pass fakes at 3 signaling him to rove the baseline. It is important that Player 3 cuts quickly to the weak side, as he wants to be in the weak side corner when 2 catches at the wing on the reversal. Player 4 catches high and should have had vision of the middle of the court, which will tell him if he has a shot at 5 down low, his first look, and also if 2 is open on the weak side for the quick relay pass. **This pulls X4 up from the baseline to cover Player 2, which could be**

a mismatch and will expose the corner where 3 will have to be defended by X4 on a rotation or by X5, who would have to leave 5 in the low post to be defended by X3. Of course, an exception would be if X3 had roved along with Player 3 on the baseline cut.

Diagram 12 shows the ball being reversed to two perimeter players, both Players 2 and 3, for possible plays along with 5 possibly cutting across into the low post, especially if X5 runs out to cover the corner. Player 2 should have surveyed the floor and will know immediately whether he has a shot or punch, and whether 3 is open below him for a shot. Another option for attack can be made if the defense is able to rotate X4 down to Player 3 and that is that 4 can dive to the rim upon passing to 2 in an X-cut, in which case Player 5 would read

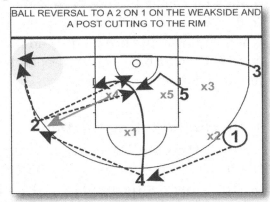

Diagram 12

that and flash into the lane after 4, and then break on up to the high post, if he doesn't get the catch.

Note: it is possible that Player 4 may have to use a **Freeze Dribble** bounce toward X1 to assist the timing of 3 cutting along the baseline, if he reads that he may be late. **See point 6 in this section** relative to that action.

Point Dribble Rotating against the Odd-front zones. Diagram 13 shows a 1-3-1 zone but it will be generally the same against a **3-2 or 1-2-2,** only with players in a different stating place. Player 1 engages X1 and pulls him away from his home spot at the top of the **1-3-1** to a wing. Player 4 pops up into the vacated zone. To keep the integrity of spacing, Player 2 slides toward the corner when 1 dribble rotates toward him. If the wing defender disregards Player 2 and stays to challenge 1, obviously 2 will be wide open, so he will nor-

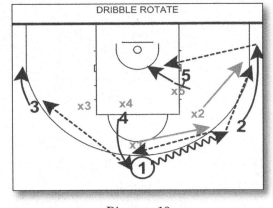

Diagram 13

mally go with him, as opposed to kicking X1 back and forcing X5 to leave the basket area. However, some defenses will have a small man low that will leave and drop the high post down to defend 5. In any case, regardless of the positioning of players, all point defenses must now rotate into a 2-3 formation. Check it out. The zone defense is now stretched and must adjust. The middle man can come up to cover Player 4 and that tends to open up the lane for 5's seal off in a mano-a-mano against his low post defender.

The numbers will vary depending on how the defense wants to move in the 1-2-1 or in a 3-2 or 1-2-2 but we are now looking at a 2-3 to attack. Rotating the ball around to the weak side and running Player 3 along the base line will force a big man, usually X4, to come out to cover 2 on the wing. He will then either be released to get to Player 3 or to make another adjustment to cover him.

Never underestimate the value of forcing an opponent to lift a bigger man off of the baseline to cover outside. It increases the opportunity for mismatches, more open space and mistakes to be made by the defense in adjusting. **Dribble rotating in combination with good passing and timing of cuts is an easier and quicker way to cause these situations than passing and cutting alone.**

Diagram 14 shows the same move against a 1-2-2 or 3-2 with X2 rotating with Player 2 to the corner. Assuming X4 had matched up inside with X5 against offensive posts 4 and 5, X4 is now pulled to the top and X3 has to drop to the baseline to defend Player 3. X5 is on his own down low with X2 and X3 to help.

A Second Dribble Rotation is an option. In Diagram 15, Player 1 has swung the ball to Player 4 who **repeats the move** by dribble pulling right at 1. This creates a chain reaction by forcing Player 2 to rove the baseline and 1 to fill the corner. The defense has to decide whether to continue to rotate and put X1 and X2 on the baseline as in Diagram 16 (next page).

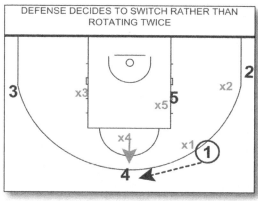

Diagram 14   Diagram 15

This is not a good option for the defense, so the other option is to reverse rotate and kick back by having X2 wave X1 back up as he takes Player 1 in the corner. X1 then waves X4 back. **If that happens, Player 2 may be open immediately in the short corner,** so he needs to look to see the adjustment when he gets into the lane on his way to the opposite wing as shown in Diagram 15.

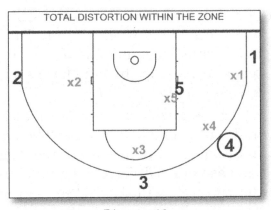

Diagram 16

To clarify, as one looks at Diagram 16, it is easy to see the dilemma the defense has if they continue to rotate with the offense, they end up with players totally out of position in a virtual man-to-man. Post player X4, who began defending in the high post is now out on the wing and X1, who started on the top, is on the baseline where the bigger people usually play.

If the defense hands off initially instead of rotating. If they slide the players off to the defender in the next zone instead of rotating, they must execute the move well or leave an opening for the offense. In Diagram 17 on the **first Dribble Rotate,** X1 goes to the edge of his coverage area and releases Player 1 to X2 and quickly gets back to cover 4 popping to the top. This leaves Player 2 open in the corner, so the defense must decide if X2 will chase to him or if X5 will rotate to cover him. Again, in a 1-3-1 that may be a smaller man to cover the corner, but it will be a back man in both the 1-2-2 and 3-2. Either one does tend to expose the low post to one extent or another and that is good for the offense. **Still, the real trouble for the defense looms on the weak side after the swing of the ball.**

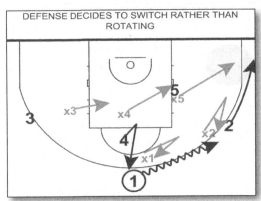

Diagram 17

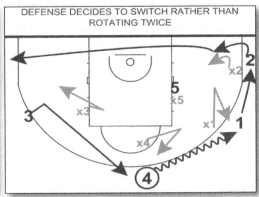

Diagram 18

In Diagram 18 the defender rotated on the first dribble pull, but on the second dribble rotate or pull X2, or whoever is covering Player 2, must decide whether to stay man-to-man with him as he roves the baseline. Otherwise, he may opt to shift off with X3, the weak side defender, and kick back to the corner. X5 cannot leave Player 5 to help.

In any event, if Player 2 doesn't get an easy catch between his corner and the goal when X2 releases him, he will **cut up to the open wing on the weak side when he sees Player 3 has rotated** to the top. **Player 1 will rove** the baseline when 4 passes back to 3 at the top. This will put extreme pressure on the defender on the weak side, X3, to cover the wing and corner, just as before. The point is that the defense has to be sharp in whatever adjustments they decide to make.

It is easy to see how the lateral dribble can antagonize a defense. We went into a lot of detail in this instance just to illustrate that fact. We will not worry about the defense so much generally, since this is about offense.

Wing Dribble Down Option—same principles, but a little different result. Diagrams 19 and 20 illustrate a Wing Dribble Down to the baseline against a **1-2-2, but is as effective against the other 1-front defenses and is difficult even for the match-ups as well.**

Diagram 19 illustrates a key action that is for **post player 4 to pop out** to the wing in an inside fill replacement cut, especially if he is a good outside shooter. If not, Player 1 would make that cut but it is a stronger move with 4. X1 has to cover Player 4 and X2 is pushed on the baseline since X5 is not likely to leave 5 to cover the corner if he doesn't have to. They are now into a 2-3 formation.

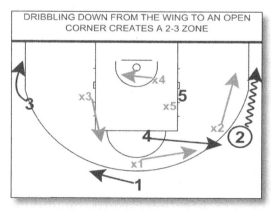

| DRIBBLING DOWN FROM THE WING TO AN OPEN CORNER CREATES A 2-3 ZONE | INSIDE FILL CUT AND BALL REVERSAL CAUSES WEAKSIDE PROBLEMS |

Diagram 19   Diagram 20

Player X3 must lift to the top to defend Player 1, where he may have trouble defending him one-on-one. On the reversal pass by Player 2 to 4 and on to 1 in Diagram 20 (on page 85), Player 2 will run the baseline and 3 will come up to the wing out of the corner and X3 will want to slide to defend him. But if Player 1 engages X3 with a Freeze Dribble move right at him and then passes to 3 on the wing, X3 will be late to get to 3. X4 may be able to help X3 by coming up off the baseline, but that will make it hard for him to cover Player 2 who roved the baseline to the corner below 3. The defense now has to decide how to cover Player 2 in the corner on his cut — to bump X4 down or pull X5 out of the post, unless X2 had been designated to go man-to-man with 2 on his cut. Of course, 5 will be looking to seal off X5 as the ball moves. **Defensive mistakes can be made and that is on just one swing of the ball.**

Diagram 21 illustrates the same action vs. the 1-3-1 set. Assume that Player 1 has just passed to 2 and 2 has pulled X2 down to the corner. Also, Player 4 has fill cut to the wing, leaving 1 on top.

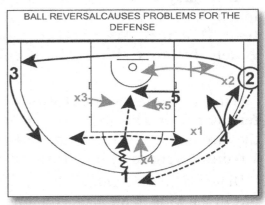

BALL REVERSALCAUSES PROBLEMS FOR THE DEFENSE

Diagram 21

Players 2 and 4 look at Player 5 in the low post on the strong side triangle, but if there is no play, the ball is reversed from 2 to 4 and then to 1 at the top. Player 2 runs the baseline to the opposite corner.

High post X4 in a 1-3-1 has to match up with Player 1, who may be able to take him 1-on-1 as in Diagram 21.

If Player 1 does not attack X4, he can pass on to 3 at the wing and X3 will be defending one against two with Players 3 and 2 on the wing and corner. Again, decisions must be made — bump X3 down, or pull X5 to the corner, unless they decide to let X2 rove the base man-to-man with Player 2. **Even that simple last option exposes the back side to a skip-pass to 4 from 3 because there will be no defense behind X5 who must defend 5 in the low post.**

5. Dribble Rotating the Defense Up

Diagrams 22 and 23 have classic examples of the **Dribble-up** move out of the corner as was shown in Chapter 3. While it may appear to be redundant to mention dribble rotating in a direction toward the middle of the court instead of to the sideline or baseline, the reverse direction

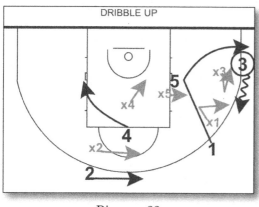

Diagram 22

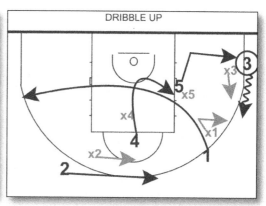

Diagram 23

dribble rotation **causes problems for different defensive players** than does the dribble down.

These diagrams show the **Dribble-up move.** Remember that a **lateral dribble move** in any direction demands corresponding moves to fill the spot vacated by the dribbler, providing immediate pass options in various directions.

In Diagram 22 either the coach from a timeout or dead ball, or Player 1 has called for a "cutback" move on the fly. Player 3 uses a **Dribble-up move** instead of penetrating as he normally does. Player 1 takes a couple steps, as if he is going to cut on through as usual, but then cuts back to the open corner.

Player X3 will have followed Player 3 on the Dribble-up, exposing the space in the corner where 1 may have a shot. If X5 pulls out to cover Player 1, this leaves 5 open in the post. If X4 covers Player 5, the weak side is totally open on the skip pass to 4 at the rim.

In Diagram 23 when Player 5 sees that 3 either cannot penetrate or simply decides to use the Dribble-up move, 5 can move on out further than the short corner to pull X5 further out and open the middle, or else 5 will have a nice open look at the basket for a shot. If he has 3-point range, he can go out past the 3-line for that matter. If Player 5 can pull X5 away from the basket, **4 may be able to dive right into the open block as a great cut or post up option. Either way, player 1 has made a cut to the weak side wing at the diagonal angle from the ball and 5 can skip-pass to him for an easy look.**

Diagrams 24 and 25 show another way that the Dribble-up out of the corner may be used. Player 4 is in the short corner and 5 is in a key position high on the ball side elbow. As soon as Player 2 initiates the Dribble-up, 5 starts to muscle his way down the lane while 1 and 3

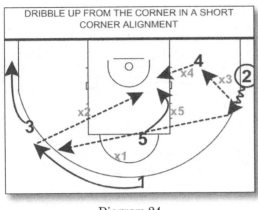

Diagram 24

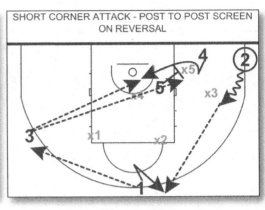

Diagram 25

drift from the ball to keep good spacing. Players 2 and 5 will reach the same level at a point when 5 is about 12 feet from the goal. Player 2 now must read the position of X5; if X5 is on the high side of 5, he may be able to pass to 4 for a shot or a feed to 5 for a layup. If X5 is below Player 5 between him and the goal, 2 may be able to make the direct pass to 5 himself, or he may skip pass the ball to 1 or 3 for a shot or late pass down to Player 5 cutting across to the left block. (Diagram 24)

Diagram 25 shows a counter-move to the play in Diagrams 22 and 23 that may require a special call, such as "hold" or "54", etc. to key it from a time out or dead ball. But is an interesting action for a low post attack. If nothing materializes to allow Player 2 to feed 5 or 4 — a play he would make even on this call when open, he can swing the ball to 1 and on to 3 while Players 5 and 4 engage in screening action for each other as 5 pins X5 and cuts back to the ball opposite the area 4 cuts in order to get a **paint catch against the zone — always a bonus.**

Dribble-across from the top. This operates on the same principles as the Dribble-down and Dribble-up in that it requires the player on the perimeter in front of the ball to slide down a slot for spacing and for a player behind to fill in the spot vacated by the dribbler that can be filled from the perimeter or from the high post.

In **Diagrams 26-27, the offense is facing a 2-3 and will force it into a point defense** with the dribble pull move. In the first diagram Player 2 dribbles laterally toward 1, pushing him into 3's slot and pushing 3 to the corner where **he will hold until the ball is reversed normally, but can cut right away** occasionally for variation on this play.

Here he holds as Player 2 passes the ball to 1 on the wing and on down to 3 in the corner. Post 5 vacates the high post as the ball is caught by Player 3 in an effort to get a low post catch from 3 in the corner, or possibly from 2.

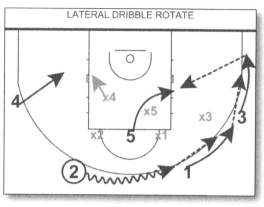

Diagram 26

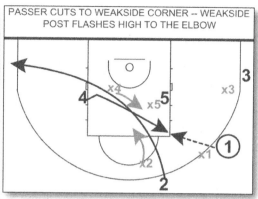

Diagram 27

As Post 5 starts his cut, Player 4 moves down toward the baseline to set up his cut into the slot in the lane that opens up after 5's cut. Player 4 will cut hard into that slot and go as far as a step or two outside the lane to catch from 1 or 3, if he can't catch it earlier. (Diagrams 26-27)

Still in Diagram 27, Player 2 times his cut to the weak side (to the corner if it is open, and to the wing if 3 had cut there earlier), to go just as he sees 4 make his first step toward the ball after 5's cut — important timing. When Player 4 makes the catch he turns to the basket immediately and may have his own move, but mainly he is looking to see if he has a short drop to 5 or if 2 is open in the weak side corner. **As one can tell, unless X2 goes man-to-man with 2, there is no way he will not be open.**

In Diagram 28, **Player 1 could not make the pass to 4** in the mid-

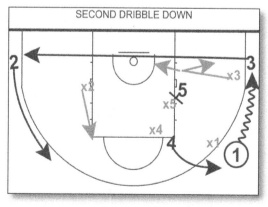

Diagram 28

dle, or simply decided to mix the play up, and runs a second dribble move to force 3 to cut baseline, which forces 2 to cut quickly out of the corner up to the weak side high wing diagonal area. At the same time Player 4 pops out on the fill cut to the wing.

Player 1 may possibly have a drop pass to 5 or could have a short pass to 3 at the goal, where 3 looks back to the ball in the event X3 does not go man-to-man with him, as noted before.

Diagram 29 shows the normal move, which is for Player 1 to pass to 4 who must free himself — should be easy since X1 will have to go at least a couple steps with the ball, even if X3 stays in the corner, and X4 is not likely to want to come all the way out to the high weak side wing to deny 4, totally opposite from where he began in the zone.

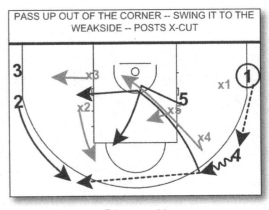

Diagram 29

On the completion of the swing pass, **Player 4 dives in the X-cut** through the paint looking of a catch there or on the block and 5 finishes off the X-cut by coming off 4's tail into the paint and on up to the high post, if he doesn't get a catch before.

Player 2 has many options on the wing — make a move, pass to 3 in the corner or to 4 or 5 on the cuts, or to skip-pass to the diagonal weak side where 1 will be ready. **It is easy to see how the zone can get stretched on this and forced into some man-to-man coverage in many cases.**

6. Use of the Freeze Dribble —
a tool to create favorable match-ups and timing

The Freeze Dribble. In Diagram 30 Player 1 initiates the play with a **Dribble Down move** to the wing, pushing 2 to the corner where he passes to ball to 2 and cuts to the basket for a give and go possibly and then out to the weak side wing.

As Player 1 vacates to the wing, Player 5 flies out of the weak side low post to replace 1, though he could have lined up in the high post to start and popped out as well.

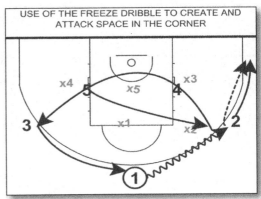

Diagram 30

In Diagram 31, Player 2 reverses the ball to 5 and cuts to rove the baseline. Meanwhile Player 3 had cut to the swing spot at the top to replace 1 on his dribble move and receives the pass from 5.

At this point, Player 3 has to judge if X4 is going to come up to defend 1

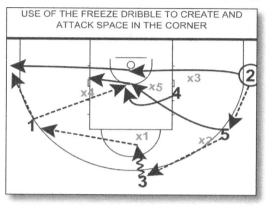

USE OF THE FREEZE DRIBBLE TO CREATE AND ATTACK SPACE IN THE CORNER

Diagram 31

on the wing, which is the hope. He is also watching Playing 2 on his cut across the baseline. Ideally, if he has time, Player 3 would like to take a Freeze Dribble at X1 to make sure X4 has to come up and cover 1 on the wing, thus exposing the corner. If he should happen to read that X4 is flying off the baseline to get to Player 1 on the wing, which is unlikely, he can forego the Freeze Dribble.

He will pass to Player 1 on the wing, who can pass to 2 just as he is set in the corner, or 1 can feed 5 in the paint or on the block as he X-cuts from the wing, after passing to 3 at the top. Player 4 will finish the X-cut right into the lane after 5 clears, looking for a catch and will move up into the high post, if he does not get the ball.

The timing of the cuts of both Players 2 and 5 can be facilitated by 3 and his decision to use the Freeze Dribble or not. At times it is not needed at the top, but it is a good to be able to use it in order to avoid the ball getting to the wing so early that the defense can adjust to the cutters before they are in position to catch and make a move against a defense that is still in transition from strong side to weak side.

Another very useful tactic is to freeze a perimeter man at the edge of

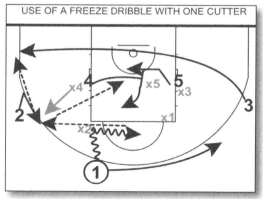

USE OF A FREEZE DRIBBLE WITH ONE CUTTER

Diagram 32

his coverage area when it creates a hole in the defense elsewhere. A good example occurs vs. a 2-3 zone when the team is in some form of cutting game, as in Diagram 32, where Player 1 dribbles at X2 and brings him to the split line. When Player 1 starts this action, 3 cuts through to the corner below 2, rubbing off of the traffic created by 5 and 4 in the post area where

4 picks for 5. When Player 3 gets under the basket, 1 passes to 2 and flares away to the high elbow/wing area. **X2 is now on the split line and cannot go and bump X4 down on the cutter 3.** Player 4 screens across for 5 on the pass from 1 to 2. This is particularly effective against teams that pull X5 to cover the corner.

Player 4 rolls back to see the ball after his screen. Player 2 has options of hitting 4 and 5, as well as 3. Player 4 is the weak side rebounder for any shot by 3, and he rotates to the top if there is no quick shot by 3 or 2. (Diagram 32)

Diagram 33 shows another entry option that would be for Player 1 simply to pass the ball to 3 at the high elbow to get X2 out on him to start the action. Player 3 would return the pass, but the defense will have shifted, allowing 1 to Freeze Dribble at X1.

If there were no good scoring options by the time Player 3 is in the corner on the first rotation of the ball in either case, 3 reverses the ball to 2 and roves the baseline as in Diagram 34 or Player 2 could

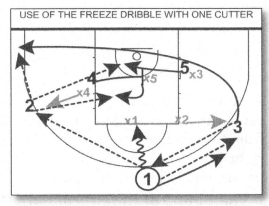

Diagram 33

pass to 3 and run the corner pass Automatic to create movement and 4 would fill cut to the wing.

Diagram 34 does show Player 2 reversing the ball to 4 at the top with 3 on a second baseline run. Player 3 would also cut the baseline if 2 just fakes a pass to him and reverses the ball to the top.

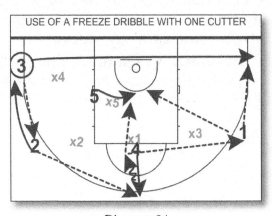

Diagram 34

Possible second Freeze Dribble. In this case with the pass coming quickly to Player 4 on the point, he probably needs to Freeze X1 to make sure X3 has to stay up on 1 and to give 3 a little extra time to get to the corner. Player 4 should also look down at 5 in the low post as he ducks in. If nothing is there in the post, he will pass to Player 1 to force X3 to guard the ball.

Again, Player 1 has 5 and 3 as passing target options on the strong side triangle and will have 2 in the down diagonal pass angle for a skip-pass. X3 is in a bind to cover the wing and corner, unless X4 roves man-to-man with Player 3, but that opens up the weak side corner for a skip pass to 2.

—————— **CHAPTER 5** ——————

SIMPLE SETS UTILIZING THE BASIC ELEMENTS OF ZONE OFFENSE

A Zone Set Using Basics and Automatics — the 13 Series

Obviously this set can be called by any name, but let's call it the "**13**" **series** for now, which is a rather simple zone offense attack that uses many of the techniques previously described. In our diagrams, the player marked **"P"** is one who can alter the look by lining up virtually anywhere on the left side, or if it fits him better (maybe a lefty), coach could invert and put him on the right side. **How P mixes up his positioning and reads the middle slot and times his cuts** are key. He must be a **good passer** and able to make shots from 18 feet or so.

Player **"O"** must be a good outside shooter so that the defense will extend out to cover him when he makes **a high wing catch,** a move that stretches the distance it takes to rotate from the wing to the corner in the event the defense decides to defend him with a low wing player from the baseline, which is not usually the case in a 2-3 and certainly not in a 3-2 or 1-2-2. We want the front defender to defend him in any case, since we are planning to attack the middle first, if possible through player P and then the weak side and even later as the ball and players read and move.

Player **O** should always be able to get open for the first pass, because it doesn't matter if he catches it out of his shooting range. And if a player tries to deny him, he has the entire wing and corner to seal him off and catch. The first pass is just to start the play and to force the defense to make the first move.

Player **"S"** needs to be a good corner shooter. Player 1 obviously is the ball handler and Player 5 is a post man and can be a scoring threat or not, as long as he is a rebounder who can defend his position adequately. Naturally, it is better if he can score down low.

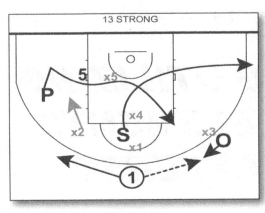

Diagram 1

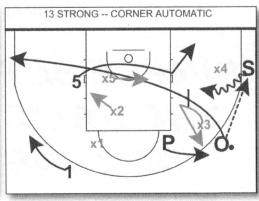

Diagram 2

Diagram 1 shows the basic starting positions, but **P**, the key passer **can start on the wing, in the corner, on a stack with Player 5 or anywhere in between.** He makes a strong cut into the paint to look for a catch in the slot or cuts on up above the foul line. Player **S** starts anywhere at the foul line area but does not leave to cut to a corner (strong side corner here) until the pass is in the air to O. Player O will use his body to free up for a catch. We prefer he catch it in a high position at the edge of or even past his 3-point range. If he gets the ball in the general area shown, S makes a quick cut through the paint to the corner, looking first for an easy catch but the normal play will take him to the corner.

Diagram 1 shows "13 Strong." The Corner pass options. Player O could have attacked with the dribble but it would have had to be a perfect opening. We are just starting the motion with this pass and S will not cut until O catches the ball, and can hold up if O drives. The first look is the middle on the cut by S. Then, if P is open in the paint or on the elbow he will get the ball and work the high/low action already described — look for his own, look under and look opposite to Player 1 drifting to weak side and to the strong corner to S.

In Diagram 2, **Player P** is not open inside, so **O** passes to **S** in the corner and cuts through on the **automatic corner pass cut.** He "drags" a little slowly on his first two steps to see if he is open in the slot for a give and go, and then finishes his cut quickly to the weak side corner while 5 cuts across to post. Player S can shoot the open shot, feed Player 5 or penetrate either baseline or into the middle, preferably. Post man 5 read's S's penetration and if S goes middle, 5 cuts to the short corner. If S goes baseline, Player 5 loops to the front of the rim, moving opposite the penetration angle as per the **Bailout guidelines.**

Player P pops out off of the elbow to the wing on an **inside fill cut** to create a passing lane from **S**. Point man 1 creates a **diagonal passing**

lane on the weak side for **S** and **O** should be in the corner or near it.

Diagram 3 shows the Swing Pass Options. Player **O** reads that there is no easy play to the post or corner. To keep the ball/player movement and to shift the defense, he pass fakes to **S** to key his baseline rover cut and passes to **P** on the **inside**

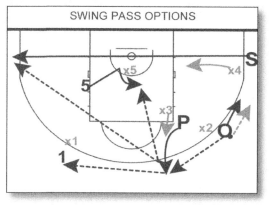

SWING PASS OPTIONS

Diagram 3

fill cut to the top. Then **O fades toward the open corner at least two steps after passing — a key move.** Player **S** roves the baseline and post 5 seals his defender or crosses under to free up in the post as **S** cuts through the paint. This crossing action can be confusing to the defense and allow Player 5 to make a read to get open. Plus the defense has to decide how they will cover the Rover cut. If X3 goes with **S** just part way or all the way, Player **O** will have the corner open for a pass from **P in those first 2-3 steps** with only small X2 on him.

Player **P** will read the coverage and may have own move or a pass down low for Player 5 on the duck-in. If there is nothing immediately open, he will reverse pass to Player 1 who may have a shot, a penetration or have **S** open in the corner. **Key point** here is that if X1 and X2 defended Player 1 and **O** at the start, the weak side will offer open opportunities. The low wing defender will have to be up to defend either the high post or the high wing, depending on how they played **P initially.**

Player **P** could opt to run a dribble handoff to 1, or pass to him and follow with a ball screen for a pick and roll. There are a lot of options here on the first two passes of the ball with all this movement, but we would rather save his options for pick and roll or handoffs until after the ball is swung back to the third side, the original side of entry.

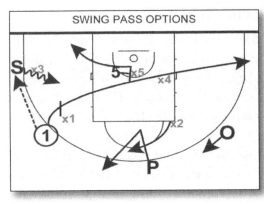

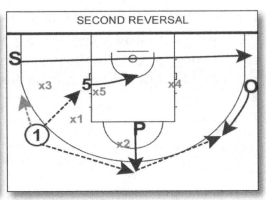

Diagram 4   Diagram 5

In Diagram 4, Player **P** has passed on to point man 1 and gone back into the high post area temporarily. Player 1 may penetrate or have **S** open in the corner, or could hit 5 sealing in the post. Player 1 passes to **S** in the corner and S may shoot quickly; if not, Player 1 will cut through on the **corner pass** auto. Player **S** can pass inside or penetrate right or left and pop 5 out. Player **P** will fill cut for an outlet pass; so the offense will continue to look for open options by following the principles the team will have learned.

Player 1 has other options when he gets the ball than to **pass to the corner** and cut as shown. He has a possible **feed low** to Player 5, and **O** is his **diagonal skip-pass** option on the weak side. In addition, he could signal **P** for a **pick and roll** as noted, but the **preferred action is to swing the ball back to attack the third side,** the original side of entry, as in Diagram 5.

Diagram 5 shows that **P** popped for a swing pass, and **O** presented himself for a catch. If point 1 had pass faked to **S** he would be roving the baseline as in the Baseline Rover Auto again, or he could rove on his own.

Player **P** will look for his own drive to the right, a pass to Player 5 in the post or he can swing and do an **X-cut to the block** with 5 replacing him.

Note: In addition, if Player 1 passed the ball back to **P** without the pass fake and **S** decided to stay, it is a good time for **P to set a pick and roll or pop on O.** There are two shooters spaced in front and **O** is a good shooter.

Play "13 Weak" — an alternative to "13 Strong (Diagrams 6-9)

The original formation is the same as in **"13 Strong,"** but on the call of **"Weak"** Player **S** will cut to the weak side corner when **O** catches the ball. Player **P** cuts into the lane for a catch and score or high/low action with Player 5 just as in the original play.

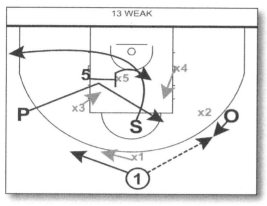

Diagram 6

In Diagram 6, Player 1 fades quickly to the high wing, hoping to draw a low back man, if the ball is swung to him. Player **S** cuts toward the basket and then out to the **weak side corner** this time. Player **P** slashes to the middle just as **S** vacates and if **P does not catch in the lane to make a play, he moves up to the high post area at the top of the circle.** As one can tell by looking at the diagrams, the defense that has been accustomed to having X4 cover **S** when he cuts to the **strong side corner,** now must adjust to designate who will cover the cutter S in the strong side corner, and who will defend **P** on his cut up the middle and still be able to defend Player 1 on the wing.

If the defense covers **O** with X2, then they will have difficulty to defend **P** at the top and Player 1 on the wing and still get to **S** in the corner on a quick swing pass. They could have X4 hustle to cross under and take Player 3 man-to–man, or risk pulling X5 to the corner and expose the low post, but neither is an ideal situation for the defense (Diagram 6).

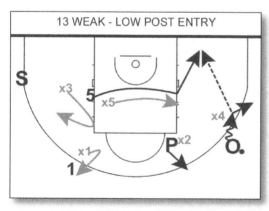

Diagram 7

If the defense decides to cover **O** on the first pass with X4, he will be late getting up to him because he will be expecting to have to defend **S** in the corner. In addition, that still means that X3 will have to cover cutter **P** until he can pass him off to X2 at the top of the circle, while X1 matches to Player 1. And that will make it very hard for anyone to get to S in the corner (Diagram 7).

Diagram 8 (next page) shows the **Swing Pass Options.** A quick option for **O** is to reverse the ball quickly if a low wing defender has moved up to defend Player 1, because the corner will be open for a time normally, as the defense will adjust. Alternatively, **O** may see Player 5 open in the low post. If not, he can pass to Player **P** at the top. Again **P** may dump down to Player 5 in the low post or swing the pass on to 1.

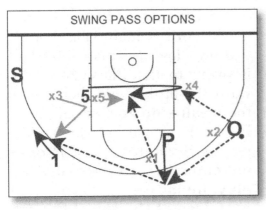

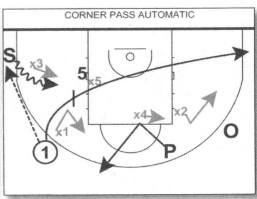

Diagram 8　　　　　　　　　　Diagram 9

In Diagram 9, Player 1 passes to **S** in the corner and cuts as in the **corner pass automatic** move, looking for a return pass or continuing to the weak side corner. Player **S** can feed 5, drive baseline or penetrate middle as **P** pops out to fill cut.

The basic concept of using the Play 13 Weak option is to put a lot of pressure on the defense, causing them to make serious adjustments from 13 Strong. As in the case with the original play action, much depends on how the defense reacts to the distortion these cuts cause to the original zone formation.

The play action continues on just as in **"13 Strong."** There are various options for high/low, pick and roll, pass and cut and punching the ball in a penetration move as gaps appear.

Special call for Cutback option for the Dribble Up play. Just as described in the Dribble Up rotation move shown in Chapter Four, the **Cutback option** can be used anytime the ball is passed into the corner from the wing, but both players need to communicate it ahead of time. This option can be very effective on either the strong side or weak side calls, if not over-used.

In Diagram 10, Player 1 has passed to **S** and starts his cut through, but has communicated he will use the **Cutback** option when **S** dribbles up. As **S** dribbles up into the gap pulling up the corner defender, Player 1 quickly cuts back to the open corner, going in front of posted 5.

Player **P** pops out on the inside fill cut while player **O** puts himself in vision of the ball at the **diagonal angle,** creating an open pass lane to the weak side. Player **S** decides whether to shoot, hit Player 1 in the corner, 5 on the baseline pop, or to swing the ball.

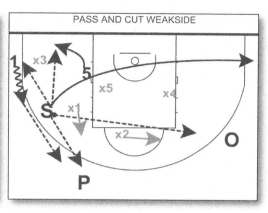

Diagram 10   Diagram 11

If Player 1 gets the ball and has no shot he can penetrate and make a play or swing it on to **P.** After S**'s pass to any player, he cuts through** to the weak side corner. This is a good play to run after a timeout when the basic cuts have already been used. In addition, it can be communicated between just the two men involved, players **1** and **S** any time. It can be used in **Strong 13** as well if Player 5 is a 3-point shooter. (Diagram 11)

The openings will be there, but the offense has to read how the defense adjusts to the various Automatics included in the highlighted explanations of the offense. Of course, the players can punch into gaps any time that those open up due to ball and player movement with spacing.

In quick review one can see how so many of the **Basic Five and the Automatics fit into this set action** that guarantees spacing with ball and player movement, while allowing a lot of freedom to make reads of the defense in the process.

"14" — action from the High 1-4, a versatile and basic weapon

Another simple and easy to learn set for nearly all levels of play that also utilizes many of the Basic Five Elements and Automatics is the **High 1-4.** We have called it **"14"** but others have called it **"X"** or any of many other names. While the details of how to execute the High 1-4 varies with each coach, it has been a popular set for many coaches as one of the weapons in the zone offense arsenal. It is perhaps the most versatile alignment, containing actions that are useful against virtually all types of zones. In addition, it yields itself to advanced options that can be added that create a myriad of possible plays. It puts pressure on zones whether they are lane playing, trapping, matching up or basic standard formations. It can even be used vs. man-to-man, being effective when opponents are using alternating defenses between man and zone, or when a play has been called to attack a zone at a timeout and the opponent comes out with a man-to-man. Run the play call anyway. **There are four simple play actions that can be learned easily: the high post entry, the wing entry, the high pick entry and the point cut.**

High Post Entry — play can start to right or to left with dribble pull and pop the post

In Diagram 12, Player 1 dribbles a bounce or two to pop the opposite post man, Player 4 in this case as has been illustrated. Player 4 must come as high as he has to in order to get open. The pop is important to create space for the pass to the low post, who cuts into the lane in an effort to get open in the paint or on the block.

Ball handler 1 must space away from the post with the ball and be a threat to catch and make a play from the high elbow angle spot. The wing players drop immediately to the corner and have hands and feet set ready to catch and shoot or make a play. As noted in the **high/low action** in the Basic 5, Player 4 looks for his own move, a pass to his post partner 5, or to pass to the corner opposite from the spot the initial pass was made, Player 3 in this case, and then to the new weak side corner, now that the ball has been passed to what was the weak side post.

Diagram 13 shows the **normal X-move** noted in our post play discussion, whereby Player 4 passes to a weak side player, either 2 or 1, and dives through the paint to the goal, while the weak side post man cuts into the paint and on up to the high post, **looking to make a scoring catch if possible, and to be a ball mover, if not.**

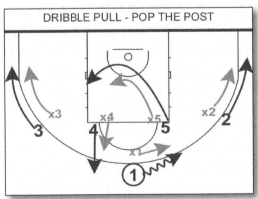

DRIBBLE PULL - POP THE POST	HIGH POST OPTIONS - POSTS X-CUT ON REVERSAL

Diagram 12   Diagram 13

Wing Entry — can be made to either wing

Normally the ball handler will drag the ball to the right or left for the opportunity to enter the **pass to the opposite post or to the nearest wing player.** It is important that he keep his dribble until he decides what to do, so that he has the option of running a pick and roll or to use any of a number of other options that would be unavailable once he kills his dribble.

In Diagram 14 we have a wing entry to the right side. Player 1 drifts away after the pass and the weak side post man 4 cuts into the paint looking for a catch there and gets to the block, if he does not get the ball. Strong side post 5 pops up to fill at the top.

Of course, Player 2 is free to go one-on-one, but if he passes low to 4, he will drift to an open spot in front of the ball for a potential kick out for a shot or to pass back for a re-post or make a swing pass to 5.

If Player 4 gets the ball in the post, Player 5 will read the situation. His options are to dive to the rim looking for the **low/high option but must hesitate,** if Player 4 starts an immediate scoring move. In the latter case he must stay momentarily and ultimately work his way down to the weak side rebound area while reading what his defender does that may give him an opening for a cut or lob.

Player 4 has the option to score immediately, if he can feel his defense, or to pass to Player 5 on the cut, to kick out to the front to 2, or the diagonal to 1 or even to the weak side corner to Player 3.

Diagram 15 shows the swing option with Player 2 passing to 5 at the top where he applies his basic high/low options of making his own move, passing to 4 on a post seal on either block, or to be a ball mover by passing to 1 on the weak side. If he passes to the weak side, his normal move is to utilize the **X-cut action noted in our post play illustrations.**

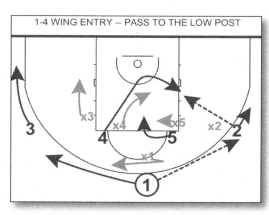

Diagram 14   Diagram 15

While he could run a pick and roll or handoff, the better move is the **X-move** when the ball has just been swung one time.

Note: When a random pick and roll is set on the first swing, it is better for the low post man to run into the pick and roll after the high post has initiated the X-move.

For a change-up, when the ball is passed to the wing, we like for the post players to change their cuts whereby the **strong side post makes the circle cut as the first cut down to the goal** and on to the block instead of the weak side post cutting first. They simply change cuts, which can be done by someone communicating, "change" when players are comfortable with one another, or the back man can just read what the post in front does.

At that point the strong side post can cut down on his own immediately, when the ball is caught on the wing if he has an advantage. Even if the weak side post had already taken a step toward the goal, he can stop and change his cut to go up to the top for the fill cut. The rest of the action is the same as already described in the high/low game.

Of course, the same cuts and options are available by starting the offense on the left side of the court with either the post or wing entry pass.

The Double High Post Pick option — often called "Horns" action

Again, as in all the action out of the **High 1-4,** the action can be run to either the right or the left. In the diagrams we use only the right side for brevity.

In Diagram 16, Player 1 clears his screen, 5 rolls to the rim, and 2 drifts toward the corner, but is ready to come back up against 1's penetration, depending on how his defense plays the action. Post 4 pops to the top for a quick pass back from Player 1 and would like to stay as close to the vertical middle of the court in order to have a good passing angle into 5 on the high/low action. Still, getting a safe pass back from 1 is most important. If Player 4 is covered and has no easy play, he could re-pick, however.

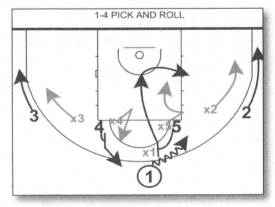

Diagram 16

Player 1 may pass to 5 on the roll and should read X4, as he is the natural "helper" in this situation. If weak side wing X4 does drop too deep to help on the roll, Player 3 must be sure to create a safe pass angle from 1. That angle will normally be on the wing area but may be in the deep corner. As options, Player 1 may pass to 4 for the dump down pass to 5 or to relay the pass to 3 on the weak side. Obviously, Player 2 may be open in the deep corner or may read to cut back up toward the penetration. If Player 1 passes to the corner, he will cut on through to the weak side as in the Corner Pass automatic. If he passes to Player 2 as 2 cuts up out of the corner, he will go ahead and replace 2 in the corner.

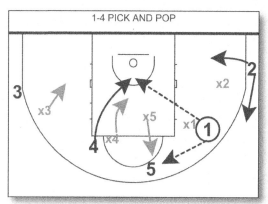

Diagram 17

In Diagram 17 we show the pick and pop option that can be called or just run automatically as the weak side post can read what the picker does and knows he must do the opposite. That is, if the picker rolls, he pops and vice versa.

A helpful note on pops is to <u>pop back</u> a step or so behind the level of the ball to improve the pass angle back to the pop man and to extend the distance to get to him on defense.

Double Post Pick options

The Swing and X-cut Option. Diagram 18 shows the swing option from Player 1 to the high post and on to the weak side player

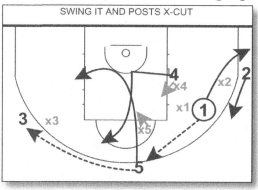

Diagram 18

3. As the diagram shows, either Players 4 or 5 may be in the high post; when the ball is swung, it is better for 4/5 to dive to the goal in the **X-cut** and on to the block. The low post man can catch and work the high/low options or may offer the pick and roll. At any time the high post player can offer a pick and roll or can dribble handoff to either wing.

The Re-pick Option. In Diagram 19 you can see a re-pick action that is a possibility anytime on a read by the player in the high post. In this action Player 5/4 has set the first pick and rolled to the low post. Player 4/5 can re-pick if he doesn't have a good opening himself or if he sees a good opportunity to knock off the defender on Player 1. He can pop or roll. If he pops, Player 4 will post up and if he rolls, 5/4 will roll up behind 4/5's roll.

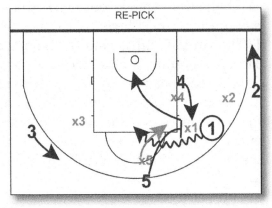

Diagram 19

The Guard Cut Options

The fourth simple move in the **High 1-4** is the Guard Cut action. Without getting too complicated here, Diagrams 20 and 21 show how Player 1 can cut to either corner after the pass to a wing instead of fading opposite the pass. The problem in describing options for openings here is that there are many ways the zone can move to cover this action, depending on whether they are trying to match up or to use standard formation slides. Player 1 can force the defenses to adjust differently depending on what defender covers the first pass. If it is a back man in a 2-3 that covers the wing, he can cut to the strong side corner and force a bump down rotation or for a bigger inside man to have to cover the open corner as in Diagram 20. If a front player covers the wing pass as in a 3-2 or 1-3-1, he can cut to the weak side and force a rotation action of some kind on the weak side when the ball is reversed quickly as in Diagram 21. Giving freedom to players to read this situation makes it more difficult for defenses to adjust

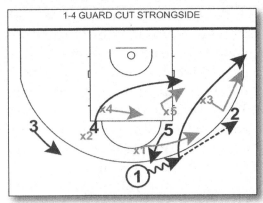

Diagram 20

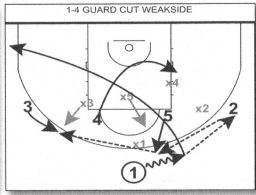

Diagram 21

as readily since the same call can be used at the beginning of the play, but the essence of the play changes when Player 1 is halfway through his cut and makes the decision as to which corner he will fill.

Summary: Play 14, the High 1-4, is a set that can have a place in any coach's arsenal. It is effective against the aggressive, lane-playing or trapping zones as well as the tighter, containing ones. It puts pressure on match-up teams and on teams that alternate defenses after certain actions such as makes and misses on their offense. The reasons for that are that there are good spacing and player movements along with pick and roll options, post ups, cuts to the goal and one-on-one play. It is simple and easy to learn, despite the variety to it.

On the other hand, later in the book we will show some more advanced options that have been used that can be added to the set, if a coach falls in love with it.

THE HIGH -LOW CUTTERS OFFENSE
An Organized Free Lance System Against Any Zone

This offense incorporates all of the basic principles we have noted so far and are adaptable to all zones whether they are containing, laning, or match-up variations. In addition they can be run from virtually any alignment. The perimeter players operate as a three-man team and the posts play as a two-man combo, both guided by the Basic Principles of play and the Automatics. All of the Automatics may come into play as the team is free to exploit the zone with the tools that they understand, based on the reads that they make. Nothing is scripted.

In Diagram 22, Player 1 passes to 3 and sees a defensive guard de-fending out on the ball, so he cuts to the rim and on out to the weak

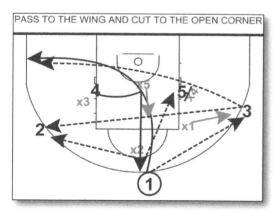

PASS TO THE WING AND CUT TO THE OPEN CORNER

Diagram 22

side corner. Player 4 flashes to the middle and unless he receives a pass, he inside fill cuts high to replace 1, while reading how 5 is being played in the post. Player 3 also reads the defense on 5 and if he cannot feed him success-fully, he reads he can hit 4 who can to dump the ball down to 5 on a quick seal, knowing that X4 is playing on top of him. Alterna-tively, he may skip pass the ball to Player 1 or 2 on the weak side since they may be 2-on-1 vs. X3. If Player 4 gets the ball and cannot pass down low to 5, he reverses the ball to 2 and starts his dive to the rim in an **X-cut** preferably.

In Diagram 23 Player 2 may quickly relay the ball to 1, if he is open for a shot and makes his cut, or he may pass to 4 on his dive to the front of the rim. Post 5 then flashes to the rim as Player 4 vacates the lane and goes on up to the top to fill cut for 1.

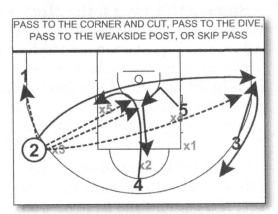

Diagram 23

Player 3 may even be open from Player 2 on the weak side by drifting behind 5's flash, or even by flash cutting into the middle post for a catch and back out, if he doesn't get the ball. If nothing is a clearly viable option at this point, he can hit Player 5 in the high post. Quite naturally, Player 5 will look down low to 4 and to the weak side to 3, if he doesn't have an easy scoring option himself. On the swing of the ball from Player 2 to 5, Player 1 will rove the base as in the Baseline Rover Automatic move. Again, this would **force the zone to rotate as Player 3 would likely now have a low wing out on him,** with a cutter coming to the corner below him. The defense would rotate in a bump move or pull a big man out from the post area.

In Diagram 24, post 5 cuts down the lane after swinging the ball to Player 3 to threaten the basket on the X-cut action. The process can go on, or one of the post men can jump out to set a pick and roll; furthermore, any time a player on the perimeter reads a gap in the shifting defense, he can punch into the opening to make a play.

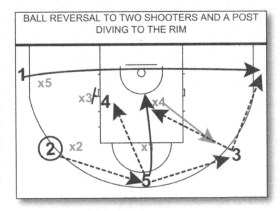

Diagram 24

In Diagram 25, Player 2 passes to 1, thinking he has an open shot or a possible drive, since he is open. Player 2 holds his cut, so as not to jam up on 1. At this time X5 sees that he must pull out to challenge Player 1 and 1 fakes the shot and penetrates baseline. Player 2 drifts back to be a safety on defense since 4 can be a safe outlet for 1 as he moves opposite 1's drive. Player 5 reads the play for a possible basket cut or rebound on 1's drive.

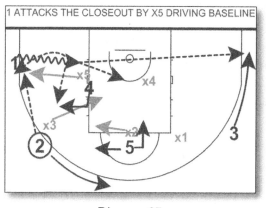

Diagram 25

Player 3 would drift to the weak side corner on the baseline drive/baseline drift move. If Player 2 passes to 1 and he does not have an immediate shot or drive, 2 cuts through on the corner automatic and 1 will look to penetrate into the gap, dribble up or swing the ball to 5 on his pop to fill cut for 2. This creates four good passing outlets for Player 1 on his drive.

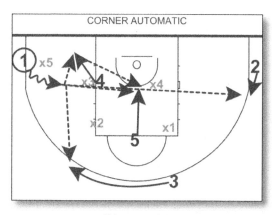

Diagram 26

In Diagram 26, Player 1 dribbles the ball into the gap above X5 after Player 2's cut. Player 4 pops to the short corner. Here is where reading really comes into play in a big way. The normal move is for high post 5 to pop out a step or two on an inside fill cut after Players 2's cut, since 3 is far on the weak side in a good position for a high diagonal pass from 1 on his penetration.

However, when the offense is more comfortable and advanced, they learn to read how X3 down low plays 4's pop to the short corner. If he goes with Player 4, 5 can read to dive to the rim if X4 has not moved into that spot. Or, if X3 does not honor Player 4 on the baseline, 1 can pass to him for a shot or for a low/high action pass to 5 on the dive, if 5 reads that.

In the event that Player 5 does dive to the rim, 3 must cut very hard to get to the safety outlet pass area so that Player 1 can reverse to ball to him to continue the action. Player 2 will move up out of the corner to present himself as an outlet to 1 when 1 penetrates and moves even further up to be able to complete the reverse pass lane from player 3, if 3 gets the ball.

In Diagram 27, if the pass is reversed all the way to the weak side from Player 1 to 3 to 2, it is a great opportunity for **4 to elect to sprint to set a screen for 2 on a good random pick and roll.** There will be two shooters out in front, if Player 2 can penetrate middle, both players 3 and 1. Player 4 can decide to pop for a shot or to feed 5 down low. Or, Player 4 may roll to the goal, in which case 5 would roll up to the elbow area behind 4's cut to the basket.

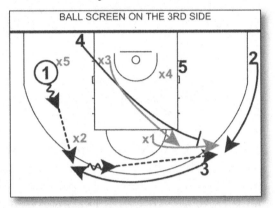

Diagram 27

In Diagram 28, Player 2 uses 4's ball screen looking to penetrate, to hit 4 on the roll or he may hit 5 on the lift behind 4. If Player 4 is denied the ball, he may seal at the front of the rim and 5 has an excellent angle to pass him the ball. As Player 2 penetrates he draws X2, 3 cuts towards the ball and may have a nice rhythm jumper from the top. Player 1 lifts off the baseline and has an excellent opportunity for a catch and shoot or to attack the mismatch with X5 closing out to him. Play would continue if a shot had not been forthcoming, but this

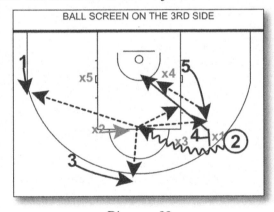

Diagram 28

is the fourth side of the play and seldom do plays go beyond the third side, if the offense is any good at reading defensive mistakes.

The various options just presented demonstrate one offensive possession that show a variety of attack opportunities both inside and out in which the players attack based on the reads they make.

Each half-court possession becomes an opportunity to integrate a combination of many of the principles of attack with all of the potential options that can be used, depending on reads. It is not a continuity play that players must memorize. **Every third or fourth pass should go to a post as a general guideline to keep pressure in the posts and avoid just being a swing the ball around the perimeter, outside only team.**

Dribble punches, rotations, pulls, screening, and cutting all become part of the movement of ball and players. It is very good to run the offense out of transition or to flow into this offense out of a quick-hitting set. This negates the need to pull the ball out and call out "set it up," allowing the offense to stay organized as it attacks throughout the shot clock.

The coach also may choose to use it as a specific action or **"clock ender"** with 8 or 9 seconds on the shot clock, creating ball and player movement with spacing for good shots and defensive balance. While this offense will not necessarily get the ball to the best shooter, it prevents stagnation and forced shots from happening as often, while giving the safety net of rebounding and defensive balance.

Once the players thoroughly understand the principles of playing against the zone and the details of timing and execution that are essential to be successful, they "light up" when they see a zone. Knowing and understanding the Basics, the Automatics and the Bailouts spacing on penetration are important steps toward developing their ability to execute any quick hitters or special situation attacks that the team might run as well.

Their confidence will be high since they have the ability to read and recognize what the defense is doing and spontaneously attack with the tools/actions that fit the situation. This is so vital when up against the toughest of opponents, in the pressure-packed scenarios of league play, and especially in the playoffs and championships.

————— **CHAPTER 6** —————

SCREENING THE ZONE

Screens off the ball

The effectiveness of screens against zones can be nearly equal to that versus man-to-man defense. The major adaptation in screening versus a zone defense is that when screening off the ball, the screen is often set on a player who is not necessarily right on the player for whom the screener is supposed to screen. He will have to seek the person in the zone who will logically try to cover the player that the screener is trying to free. Obviously, the defender being screened will not always be lined up right in front of the screener's teammate as in man-to-man. However, the screener must have the mindset to execute a good screen and should always open up to the ball immediately as the cutter clears the screen. He may be able to slip it for a catch as well.

Another important aspect of screens off the ball is that the screen must be set relative to the potential defender's position to the ball and to the spot the cutter seeks to make the catch. The screener wants to be a hindrance to the direct path that the defender will logically take to recover to the man being freed by the pick.

Screening in on the weak side

In the section on post play, we discussed how posts can **screen in** wing defenders who play inside between them and the ball when the ball is on the wing opposite them. This is illustrated in Diagram 1 (next page) as Player 5 pins in X3. This allows the screener 5 to move on to seal off X5 as well, or to cut up to the top for a catch or just to space the court.

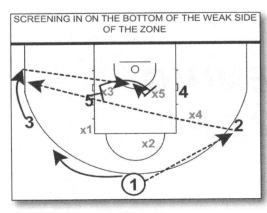

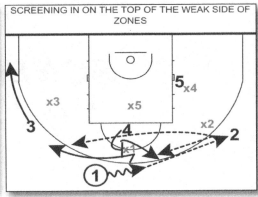

Diagram 1   Diagram 2

Diagram 2 shows post 4 setting a flare screen for the point guard after a pass to the wing. The point guard sets his man up and cuts off the flare to the weak side, just as he would against a man defense. Player 3 on the weak side wing spaces to the corner to occupy X3. Screener 4 pops up off the screen for the 3-point shot possibility, or he may execute any of the basic moves off this action such as to roll or slip cut or re-pick.

Screening in on the ball side

In Diagram 3, Player 1 passes to 3 and cuts to the rim off 5's **"UCLA"** screen. If Player 1 is open he may have a layup. If X5 helps on Player 1's cut, 1 veers to the short corner; 5 rolls to the rim and 3 may hit 5 directly or pass to 1 who hits 5. If X3 helps on either Player 1 or 5, 4 is open in the weak side corner. Player 2 will replace 1's cut at the top.

In Diagram 4, Player 1 dribbles at X3 defending 2, who receives a flare screen from 4. Player 2 sets his man up and cuts off 4's screen. As Player 1 looks at 2, he must see if 5 is open on his dive to the rim. It is also possible that Player 4 could be open cutting to the rim, if X4 jumps out to cover 2.

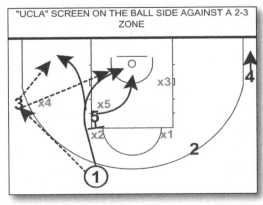

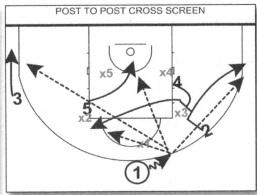

Diagram 3   Diagram 4

However we find that Player 5 has a much better angle for the cut if he can flash cut in front of X5 on his way to the rim. The normal move is for Player 4 to roll back to the weak side elbow, while 3 fades to the weak side corner. Player 1's looks are 2, 5, 4, and 3 in that order as player X2 is put in a tough spot on the weak side to defend 4 and 3.

As in all play actions, the Basic principles and Automatics take over, if there is no shot forthcoming.

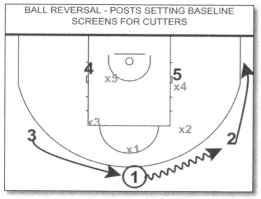

Diagram 5

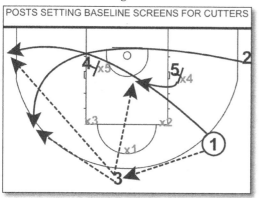

Diagram 6

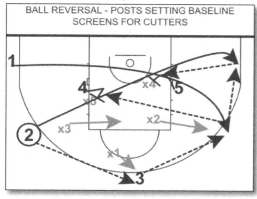

Diagram 7

Baseline screens

In Diagrams 5-7, we show a simple set utilizing baseline screening with strong cuts and ball movement. In Diagram 5, Player 1 dribble rotates 2 to the corner and 3 fill cuts to the point. Before passing to Player 3, 1 pass fakes to 2 to key his cut out to the weak side wing.

In Diagram 6, Players 5 and 4 screen their men in, and 2 speed cuts through off their screens to the high wing area. Player 1 quickly passes the ball to 3 and makes a second speed cut through off of 4 and 5 as well. The posts look for their own opening as 2 and 1 cut off them. It is possible for 1 and 2 to clear 5 and catch for a layup, but normally they get open coming off 4 who seals his man to post up as 1 clears him.

On Player 2's catch from 3 he must see 1 below him as well as 5 flashing into the middle. If Player 2 passes to 1 he may have the shot or a pass into 4 sealing.

Diagram 7 shows that if no shot is there, the ball can be reversed back to 3. Then 1 and 2 repeat their cuts back to the original sides. Note that 1 cuts first this time and then 2. Both 4 and 5 adjust their screens as well as they can and then show to the ball for a possible catch.

Players 4 and 5 can get into a good high/low game to finish off the possession, if no shot yet. (Diagram 7)

Interior screens

Diagram 8 illustrates how post to post cross screens can be effective creating inside-out scoring chances versus a **3-2 zone, or when a defense matches to the post players** in any set, a normal adjustment in most zones. Following is a quick-hitter play action that can be called to work the inside game.

Player 1 passes to 3 who pass fakes to 4 in order to get X5 into a denial stance on 4. Player 1 runs a replacement cut, cutting away and replacing himself. Player 3 passes back to 1; Player 5 sets a cross screen for 4. This creates space for Player 4 to cut to the basket. On the quick pass to Player 2, 4 cuts off 5's screen. If there is a switch, Player 4 clears to the short corner, opening a passing lane to 5 who seals X5. If there is no switch, Player 4 continues his cut to the rim and 5 rolls back to the middle. This is just one sample, but interior screens can be applied effectively in many different sets.

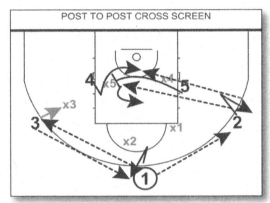

Diagram 8

Screens on the Ball – Pick and Rolls/Pops

Screens on the ball certainly can be effective weapons against the zone. As is the case when going against man-to-man defense, screens on the ball are most effective when set randomly. Defenses can handle ball screens best when the offense comes down the court and uses it as the first move. The more the screen comes out of the flow of the game, and is unscripted, the more effective it usually is. Against good defenses screens on the third side of the offense are definitely the most effective.

A system of multiple pick and rolls is most difficult for the defense to deal with. However, this requires that you have **more than one player** who can handle the ball on a pick and roll. As strong as the move itself can be, not every player has the ball skills and judgment to be the ball man on the play.

Good defenses can usually cover the first pick and roll on a possession fairly well, but they are not ready for the second or third ones as often. In fact the first pick and roll in the multiple system can be a fraud to set up the second one. If possible, your third pick and roll should involve your best ball handler/decision maker, but that can be difficult to set up with random pick and rolls. **Logical suggestion:** be sure to explain, especially to the bigger players, which players are the best ones to offer a random pick and roll for when a play breaks down.

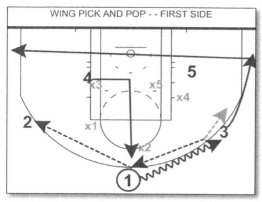
Diagram 9

The most difficult spot for the zone to handle is where a post fires out for a high angle wing pick and roll/pop in the flow of the game on the third side of the court — the second rotation of the ball back to the original side of entry.

Diagrams 9-11 show how simple it is to get to the third side for a wing pick and roll right out of the principles that we have presented.

Diagram 9 shows a dribble entry by Player 1 at 3 pushing him to the baseline. Player 4 flashes into the middle and then on to the point. Player 1 pass fakes to 3 to send him through and passes the ball to 4 who reverses the ball to 2.

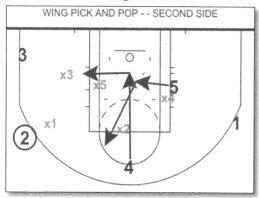
Diagram 10

Diagram 10 shows the ball on the second side and Player 4 X-cutting to the rim on his pass to 2. On the X-cut, Player 5 flashes to the rim as 4 vacates the middle and fill cuts up to the point if he gets no early catch.

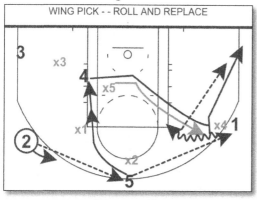
Diagram 11

Diagram 11 shows the third side with the ball being reversed from Player 2 to 5 to 1 on the high wing. Player 4 flashes to the middle on the pass from 2 to 5 and then sprints to set the screen on the wing for 1 as he catches. Player 1 uses the screen by 4 who pops to the corner.

Player 5 should cut hard to the weak side block after passing to 1 to be in a position to rebound if 4 shoots the ball on a pop and to post up on 1's penetrating drive. He must go quickly so as not to jam up the middle, when 1 turns the corner on the dribble.

As Player 1 comes off the screen he may pass directly to 4 on the pop to the corner, hit 5 low or pass ahead to 2 and 3 out in front who may shoot or be able to hit 5 in the post. This action may be used with a "roller" at 4, if he is not a good shooter. In that case, Player 5 can spread to make room, or can cut to the strong side and roll up behind 4 on his cut.

While this will be a called play in most cases to start, we present it to give an example of how to get to a high wing ball screen on the third side of the offense. Once the principles are understood, it is useful in practice to call out the screening situation that you want and on what side of the offense that you want it; then let the players figure out how to do it, being led by the point guard. Players are able to do these types of things when they all are on the same page with the principles of pick and roll offense.

Quickie High Wing Ball Screen. In Diagram 12, Player 5 sets a screen for 1 in the high wing area with two shooters, 3 and 2, spaced in front of the pick on the weak side, the best spots for shooters to get to in the pick and roll game, **and ones they should run to when they see a random pick and roll being offered in the flow of an offense.** Player 5 runs out quickly, and could come up from the weak side low post in an even stronger move to screen for 1, then roll to the basket. Strong side low post 4 lifts to the elbow behind 5's roll.

Diagram 13 shows that as Player 1 clears the screen, he has the pop shooter and two passing options in front of him plus Player 4 posting up. Post 4 reads that 5 is popping and can cross under to post or rebound.

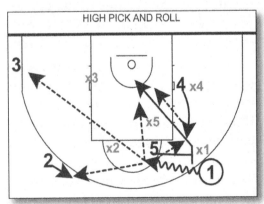

Diagram 12

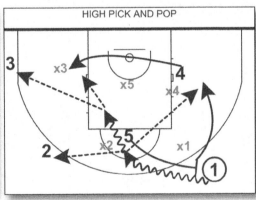

Diagram 13

In Diagram 14 we have the action with only one shooter, Player 2, in front of the dribbler. Player 5 rolls between player 3 and the ball, so 3 lifts up from the baseline behind the roll.

Player 4 on the strong side post **relocates** when he reads that the pick is set on the loaded side. Ball handler 1 again has four passing options,

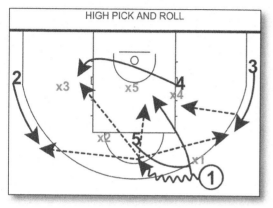

Diagram 14

the roller, the post on the weak side, the shooter out in front and the snap-back, or throw-back, pass to Player 3 on the roll up behind 5. **One of the most difficult options** to cover here is the pass back to Player 3 who has a rhythm-up shot because the defender in his area is most likely going to give help to 5's roll; or he may feed 5 sealing up at the goal. The defender on Player 5 will have to be on the lane side of him to prevent 1's pass to him, so it is easy for 5 to seal the defender off, if the pass reverses quickly on the snap-back. An option is to hold Player 4 on the strong side and let him seal off for a pass from 3. A team needs to employ both options of this play.

Elbow screens can be effective. Especially if the picker lifts to seek the defender, he will give himself more space to roll or pop and

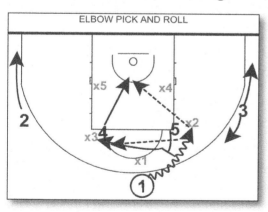

Diagram 15

more room for the ball handler to operate on the drive. We showed this action in the play 14 out of the High 1-4 set earlier in the book.

In Diagram 15, as Player 1 comes off 5's high elbow ball screen, 4 reads what 5 does. If Player 5 pops, 4 dives and if 5 rolls 4 would pop. In this case, if Player 1 cannot turn the corner on X5, then 5 pops to the weak side elbow, or he could decide to turn and re-pick for 1. Player 4 dives to the front of the rim and 2 drifts to the weak side diagonal area, since 5 has the defensive balance for the time being.

Player 3 plays against his man to get open ball side, being sure to keep defender X2 from being in the pass lane. Since Player 3 is up on the wing at the time of this pick, his best move is probably to the corner; if in the corner the best move is to step up. Player 1 reads 4 and looks for his own shot, the pass to Player 5 on the pop, or the pass to one of the wings.

Diagram 16 shows a deceptive move that is a stronger one than the previous standard elbow screen play. Player 2 dribbles to draw X1 and X2 to the left. Player 1 sets up in order to catch near the middle split line guarded by X2. Player 5 steps up and sets the elbow area screen for 1. On 1's first dribble, player 4 flash cuts to the rim and 3 drops to the baseline from the wing, but comes out of the corner, if he starts there. Player 2 fills the weak side corner vacated by 4. Thus, ball handler 1 has every pass option available to him.

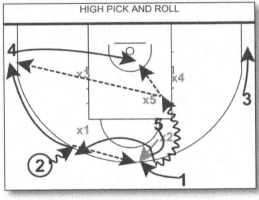

Diagram 16

Double picks can be effective as well. In Diagram 17 Player 1 uses a double high ball screen by 5 and 4. Players 2 and 3 drop to the corners, 5 dives to the rim and 4 pops to the weak side high elbow. Player 1 may have 5 as a clear option, since he might have a deep catch and 4 may also be available on the pop. Again, Players 5 and 4 can alternate cutting and popping by reading or communicating.

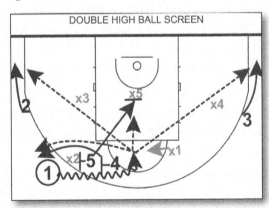

Diagram 17

But What if the Defense Pushes the Wing Pick to the Baseline?

In Diagram 18, Player 5 sets a screen for 1. X1 and X5 turn the play **"down"** as is typical of NBA defenses and the college level has recently seen the advantages of having it as a defensive option. The defender on the ball plays on the high side to prevent the ball from coming over the top of the pick into the middle. **This is ideal defense for the zone because the ball is being turned into the wing and low post players in a standard 2-3 zone and into the two bigs in a 3-2.**

Ideally, Player 5 is a player who can shoot the 17-foot shot and is a capable passer, while 4 needs to be an inside threat. Of course, Players

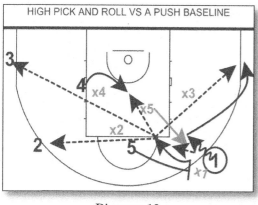

Diagram 18

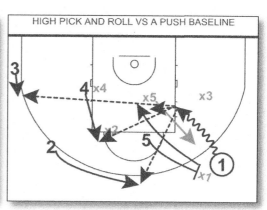

Diagram 19

4 and 5 are interchangeable. Player 1 attacks X5 and 5 opens up quickly on the short roll and looks for a "pocket pass" on the first bounce by 1. The short roll makes it hard for anyone to get to him and he is in a great position to shoot a 17-footer or to pass to Player 4 down low or to swing the ball to a shooter on the weak side. Player 1 flares after his pass.

Diagram 19 shows another attack that can be employed, if the pocket pass option is not available. Player 1 attacks X5 on the dribble and 5 rolls to the basket while post 4 lifts from the weak side to the elbow area. Player 2 fills behind 1 as a safety outlet and 3 lifts in the weak side corner. It will be difficult for Player 5 to be open on the roll, so 1 is alert to read for the open player as he and 5 draw the defense inside. Players 4 and 3 are normally open as threats and Player 2 provides a safety outlet.

The ball handler must be alert **not to take the ball too deep** on this so that he keeps his pass lanes open to the other three players not in the play.

A Pick-and-Roll with a Twist for an Inside Attack.

In Diagram 20, Player 1 dribbles to 3's side and gets X1 to engage him.

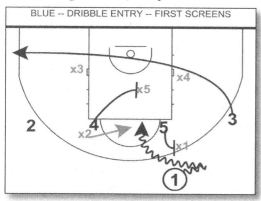

Diagram 20

Player 3 speed cuts to the weak side corner as 1 dribbles to his side and then 5 steps up to set a screen for 1. If X2 stays home, Player 1 has a foul line jump shot, but he will normally give help to the ball.

Point 1 drives downhill to draw X2 as he comes off Player 5's screen. Player 4 cuts toward the rim, just as 1 clears 5's screen and sets a pick on X5 in the middle.

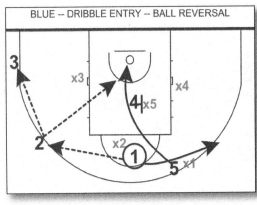

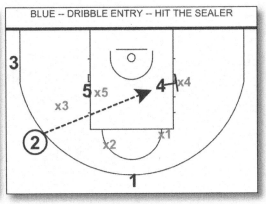

Diagram 21   Diagram 22

In Diagram 21, if Player 1 draws X2, he passes to 2. As Player 1 clears 5's screen, 5 rolls to the basket, cutting off 4's screen. Player 2 may make his own play, relay the ball to 3 or hit 5 on his cut to the basket.

In Diagram 22, Player 4 releases his screen on X5 as 5 clears it and seals X4 facing the ball. As Player 5 cuts he takes X5 out off the passing lane to 4 and there is a direct pass available from 2 to 4.

If on Player 4's cut to screen X5, X5 avoids him, he just cuts straight to seal X4 knowing that 5's cut will take X5 with him leaving him open for an easy pass and shot if he can get a good seal on X4.

Note: To mix up with the play, if the point guard is a good shooter, we can put him in a shooter's position on the weak side, by utilizing a wing to use the first ball screen. So, Player 1 could pass to 3 who must come high enough to draw X1 to guard him. After his pass, Player 1 can fade to the weak wing, pushing 2 down to the corner, or he could cut directly to the corner, if he is a good corner shooter.

While far from being limited to these examples, it should be evidenced here that ball screens are very effective weapons in creating scoring opportunities versus zones. We have not emphasized the opportunities here for quick effective ball handlers to utilize the screens to create penetration opportunities, but clearly, this case exists perhaps even more against zones than versus man to man. Also, zone defenders never seem as "precise" as man-to-man defenders when dealing with screens off the ball. Quick, well-timed execution of screens are difficult for zone defenses.

We both feel strongly that teams that prepare to attack zone defenses and apply the basic elements and principles noted, will have much greater chances of success than those teams that rely only on a few set, scripted plays. The best zone teams are equipped to cover the opponent's set plays in most cases, as are the outstanding man-to-man teams relative to the opponent's actions. Scouting being what it is today in the electronic era gives the advantage to the team that defends better, if the talent is equal or close to it. Conversely, the team that understands how to attack an opponent's defense by making good reads against the schemes that they encounter, and can select counters based on their principles, put themselves in a good position to prevail.

Quite naturally, they need to be able to "knock down shots" that they create. For this reason we also strongly believe in the **inside-out approach of attacking the basket and the inside space to create new space.** This concept gives a team a chance for some **"easy ones"** and free throws that are so necessary to winning, while also setting up the perimeter game.

We acknowledge the necessity for set plays that are difficult for zones to guard, and which may be particularly effective against specific zone alignments and normal zone coverage. In addition, it is important to have sets that are designed to get specific players on your team the ball in positions that they like to operate. Never forget that planning for rebound angles when plotting an attack is of utmost importance.

Thus, we have included many set plays that take advantage of our principles. However, the fact that so much of the world is turning to the 24-second clock makes it is even more important to have the team be adept at reading the defense with some guidelines, or so-called rules, to give some organization to freelance reactions. We contend that it is absolutely vital to be able to **flow seamlessly from set plays into basic principles of ball and player movement with spacing in order to stay organized throughout the shot clock. And planning for even the best plays to have missed shots make it vital to** <u>**plan for the second shot.**</u>

—————————— **CHAPTER 7** ——————————

SOME EASY SET PLAYS VS. THE 2-3 ZONE

The first few chapters covered various principles of zone attack, and laid the foundation for the development of one's own offense by utilizing the **Basics, Automatics and movement on Penetration** that were presented. It is worth repeating that we believe a free flowing motion-style offense is hard to scout and can be used successfully against any zone defensive alignment or system. We believe that zones find that style the most difficult to deal with. Virtually all set offenses can be scouted and the particular zone defense can be adapted to take away the key elements of the offense. Adjustments can be made to the slides of the zones to cover the actions within the set offense. This does not mean that a coach cannot use plays or sets versus zones. Of course, there are many set plays that are tremendously effective zone attacks. We have presented some already and will have a lot more as you read forward. **We do believe, however, that players who understand the fundamental components of zone attack are more effective in executing set plays than those players who just understand the play itself.** With this in mind, the next few chapters will present plays that we believe both challenge the defense and can be "hard to guard" by the particular zone defense in question and provide rebound opportunities.

SOME SETS vs. 2-3 THAT CAN APPLY TO OTHERS AS WELL

Everyone understands that the common alignment of the 2-3 zone places a big man in the middle of the lane protected by his two forwards, one on each side, and the two guards on top. It was originally designed for all players to chase the ball as it moved around the perimeter, but now it is more often played with the guards bumping the forwards down on certain, or on all, wing catches. Basically there are three common ways that the corner may be defended besides everyone chasing the ball:

1. The "bump down" rotation with a front defender sliding to allow the low wing man to cover the corner.
2. The center pulling out with the low wing **X-ing** back to cover inside for the center who had to pull to the corner.
3. Going man-to-man with the cutter.

Beating the Bump Down Rotation. Diagrams 1 and 2 show the bump down rotation that is often used only when the low wing defender is out on the ball and the corner is filled, or becomes filled by a cutter (Diagram 1). That is, the wing defender stays matched on the ball until his partner defender at guard **bumps him down off the ball to the open man in the corner.** (Diagram 2)

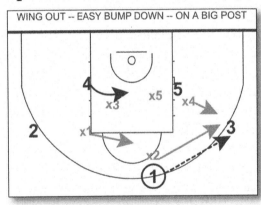

Diagram 1   Diagram 2

For this reason we encourage the **wing on offense** to try to catch high in the high wing extended area when he thinks he will be defended by a low wing, a baseline defender. This lengthens the distance the wing defender has to get to the corner, making it more difficult to get to an open player in time to prevent a shot, whether he is chasing or gets bumped down by X2. However, it is difficult to draw a back man to the wing on the first pass, but that is all right. **It is better to get one out, especially the bigger back wing, on the second side and that is where we really prefer the high wing catch.**

As was noted in Chapter Three on the Dribble Moves and will be mentioned here again, if the low wing is not drawn up on the first side he can nearly be forced to move up on the second side and we prefer to have that advantage on the second side, or even later, when it is read because their rebounding and defense is theoretically weaker in this situation. This is important to know and worth reiteration.

Something that must be avoided is having the point guard dribble over too close to the wing where the ball defender can "chase" the pass to

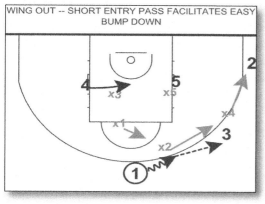

Diagram 3

the wing before the low wing man even has to come up before getting to the man in the corner as shown in Diagram 3. This is when a play has been called for a play like this that gets a shot in the corner or an easy pass down into the post on the first side. Perhaps they need a quick shot, especially by a special player. **Still, unless we are in a short clock situation, we are more concerned in getting the defense to move, so that we can attack on a second or third side when we face a defense that is already set.**

Ball movement alone is not enough. "Reverse the Ball Quickly" or "Rapid Ball Movement" are common themes when dealing with zone offense. However, movement must be in concert with player movement and this is not always the case. **In many instances the ball is swung so fast that it is waiting on the wing for the cutter to arrive on the weak side.** This may allow the defense to call the cutter early and bump down early, and in the best case for the defense, to be waiting for the cutter when he arrives.

Diagram 4 shows Player 2 passing the ball quickly to 1 and cutting

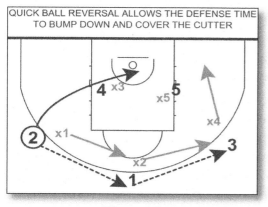

Diagram 4

baseline. Then Player 1 relays the ball to 3 too quickly. In fact, Player 3 has the ball when **2 is still in the lane,** even if 2 cuts hard. This gives X1 or X3 time to call out "cutter," allowing X2 to bump X4 off Player 3 so early that he is waiting for 2 when he arrives. This is a common occurrence even at the higher levels. Normally the quick ball movement outpaces the defense and this can be an obvious

plus. Only this time the ball is moving too quickly for the cutter, thereby working against the offense and giving the defense an advantage.

Using the Freeze Dribble to help timing. Timing of the ball movement is very important to be coordinated with player movement. As explained in Chapter Three, this is the reason that the **"Freeze Dribble"** is important to be for timing when needed for cutting players. It helps to control the proper timing of the ball and player movement, which the defense will find more difficult to cover.

Diagram 5 shows how a clever adjustment by point 1 can make a huge difference in the execution of the play. Player 1 jukes in at X2 to force him to engage and keep X4 up on 3 on the high wing on the second side of the offense. It will be quite unusual for X4 go be able to make the long slide to Player 2.

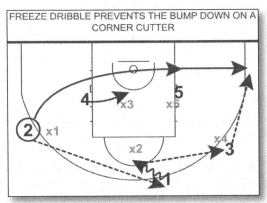

Diagram 5

Literally one of the most important factors in the zone attack that coaches and players need to consider is that if a **guard is out** on the ball on a wing on one side of the floor as in Diagram 5, it is natural that a low wing must come out, if only briefly, when the ball is reversed. In the diagram Player 2 has the ball on the wing with X1 guarding him. He knows that **if its timed properly,** when he cuts to the opposite corner as the ball is reversed, he should have an opportunity to be open, because X4 should have to guard Player 3 on the wing. In fact, Players 4 or 5 could cut to the corner area ahead of X4 when this action is executed well.

As Player 1 catches the pass from 2, he quickly **counter dribbles** generally one bounce **away** from 3. This freezes X2 from being able to pass Player 1 off quickly to X4 and **lengthens the distance** that he will have to run to get to 3 to release X4.

As Player 2 clears the lane, 1 passes to 3 on the counter-flow pass. Player 1 has done a subtle move that has created perfect **timing between the ball and player movement** for a successful play. The main options the defense has are: 1) the bump down rotation, 2) the center pull that exposes the basket, or 3) have X1 or X3 rove man-to-man with the cutter, thus distorting the defense.

The concept of the Freeze Dribble can be used when the ball is reversed from the wing or corner to the opposite side of the court, when timing is an issue, against all types of standard zones. The ball handler at the top must learn to read the situation and how to execute the action.

Beating the Close Out by the Post to a Shooter in the Corner.
As noted above a second method of covering an open corner man in a
low wing out scenario, is to have the low post defender move out to the
shooter in the corner on the pass to him. The wing out defender **"X's
back,** either **short** to front the low post, or **long** where he would take
the weak side low wing position, depending on communication with the
weak side wing defender who must rotate along the baseline to protect
the basket. Not all teams use the X-back, but instead rotate from behind
the center pull and drop a front man, but this usually hurts the rebound
game and makes for a small defensive back line.

Teams who do this well can challenge a shooter in the corner from a
wing out scenario with their length, but they expose the gut of the defense
and help the offense that is focused on having an inside/outside approach.
In addition a big man may be even more vulnerable for the baseline drive,
particularly if he has to come from a higher angle as in Diagram 6 where
X5 is in a ¾ position on Player 5 and may even get held up by 5. Player 2
can show the ball on a shot fake and drive the baseline. Player 5 moves
out to the spot about 2 steps up the lane and 1 step out, ready to catch.
If Player 4 is on the weak side block, he can move to the front of the rim.
If he is further outside, he can move to the baseline on the baseline drift
action. Player 1 will move to the weak side high diagonal angle and 3 will
move to create an open safety pass lane behind 2.

Make it tough on the center, if you want the 3-ball. In Diagram 7
we show a method to make it difficult to use the post to close out to cover
a corner. As Player 1 passes to 3, 5 ducks into the lane. Player 3 feed's
5 if he is open, but pass fakes at him if not, and then passes to 2. **If X5
goes into the paint in covering 5 it is impossible for him to close
out** in time to prevent a shot in the corner.

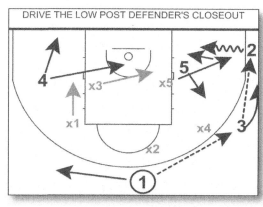

Diagram 6

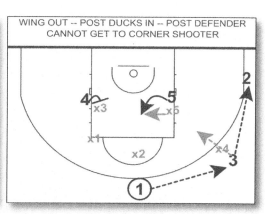

Diagram 7

Beating the Match Up With the Cutter. The final method that is used to cover a cutter to the corner in a low wing out scenario, is to have X1 to stay matched on him or pass him off to X3 to rove with him. This prevents him from getting an open shot in the corner, and it may even be used to deny the catch in the corner.

Diagrams 8 and 9 below illustrate a method to punish the man-to-man adjustment. Here we flash the weak side post man to the middle on the wing catch. For sure X3 cannot leave and give Player 4 a mismatch on X1 (Diagram 9). In an ideal scenario, as from a time out, Player 5 would pull to the short corner to give 4 more room to exploit the mismatch or even to post X3 or X1 at the rim. If, in fact it looks like Player 2 will be denied in the corner by a rover going with him, he can reverse his path and come back off picks by 5 and 4 and 3 can reverse the ball to 1, who will be able to hit 2 coming to his original spot.

In Diagram 9, Player 3 simply passes the ball back to 1 who dumps it down to 4 against X1 or X3 on the flash. It may have to be a lob pass vs. a front, but there is no weak side help. Again, Player 2 could re-trace his cut, if the low post option is not there.

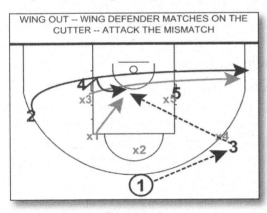

Diagram 8

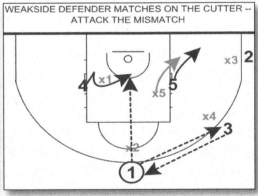

Diagram 9

It is important that coaches get players to understand how to identify and attack these **low wing out** scenarios, as they inevitably present themselves. Understanding these concepts will lead to even more effective execution of the set plays, as well in using their free lance options.

While any play action can be defended, all is not lost if we get no good look in any of these actions. Players can continue moving the ball and making the cuts they have learned in the free lance system instead of looking to the bench for the next move or casting up a bad shot.

Three Simple Plays That Create Options to Attack the Low Wing Out. Here we show three set plays that complement our explanation of how to capitalize on the low wing out in our free lance system with the intelligent use of dribble rotations. We believe players who understand the concept will be able to execute play sets such as these better. Ken has had excellent success with these plays.

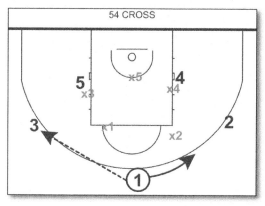

Diagram 10

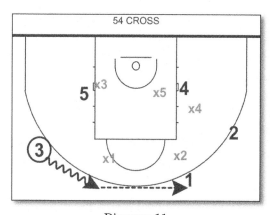

Diagram 11

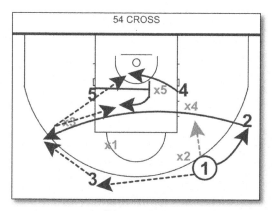

Diagram 12

1. 54 Cross

In Diagram 10, Player 1 passes to 3 and cuts to the weak side high elbow/wing area. In Diagram 11, Player 3 dribbles toward the top and passes back to 1, squaring up the front and putting the defense into a 2-front alignment with the guards up. In Diagram 11 we now have X1 and X2 guarding Players 3 and 1. Player 1 cannot go too deep into the wing area so as to keep space between him and 2 to induce X4 to match to him momentarily. Player 2 may have to move a step or two toward the baseline for spacing as well as to open up the potential pass lane from 1 to 4 in the post.

In Diagram 12, Player 1 pass fakes at 4 as 2 begins his cut to the weak side wing. Post man 4 must really sell trying to get open so that the pass fake to 4 brings X5 over closer to 4, since X4 will go a couple steps with 2 on the cut. Player 2 must cut quickly and 1 then passes to 3 who relays it to 2 on the wing. This brings X3 out to Player 2 on the wing. On the pass from 1 to 3, Player 5 begins his cut to screen X5. On Player 2's catch his first look is for 4 cutting off 5's screen. Player 5 rolls back after setting the screen and may be open for a catch in the paint, or as he moves up into the high post area. Player 1 fades to the weak wing after passing.

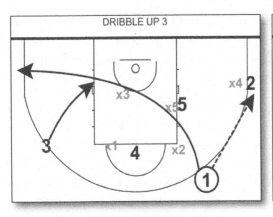
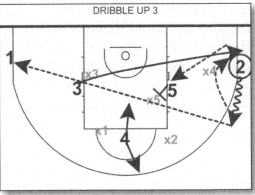

Diagram 13   Diagram 14

2. Dribble Up 3 Play:

In Diagram 13, Player 1 passes to 2 in the corner and cuts to the weak side corner. Player 3 cuts down to the weak side block.

In Diagram 14, Player 2 starts to dribble up the lane, dragging X4 with him while 3 cuts to the open corner below him. Player 2 must be careful not to dribble so high that X2 will bump X4 off so he can get down to 3. Player 3 may have a shot or a pass to 5 sealing X5. He may also have a skip-pass to Player 1 in the weak side corner, if X3 sags deep into the paint. Post 4 reads the defense.

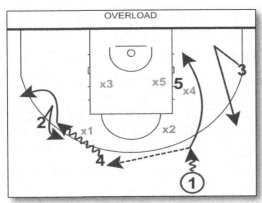

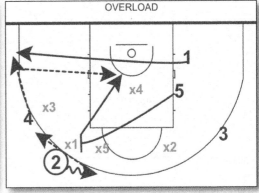

Diagram 15   Diagram 16

3. Misdirection to Overload

This quickie play action features an overload created by a misdirection action that provides a very good opportunity for a team's top shooter. In this case, the shooter is Player 1, but another player can be put into this spot. Diagrams 15 and 16 depict the creation of the overload after the misdirection or counter-flow action.

In Diagram 15, designated shooter 1 passes to 4 and cuts to the weak side block. Player 4 runs a dribble handoff for 2 in the high elbow area and pops back, ready for a catch.

Diagram 16 shows that at the same time Player 4 is dribbling over, post man 5 cuts up quickly to set a pick and roll on X1 that gets the middle cleared. Shooter 1 makes his cut to the corner just after Player 5 gets a couple steps into the lane and gets his hands and feet ready for a catch as the ball is passed to 4 and then on down to him in the corner.

Player 1 may shoot it or pass the ball down into the post to 5 cutting or posting. Player 5 may even slip the pick, because Player 2 is going to snap the pass right back to 4 after one dribble. However, he may see an opportunity to hit Player 5 on his roll for a layup or a short shot. If Player 3 is a capable shooter, he may be open out front the next time the play is run instead of using the misdirection pass back to 4.

1-3-1 Can Offer Simple Options vs. the 2-3

As noted, the containing 2-3 zone is the most popular of zone defenses and the 1-3-1 formation has been the most commonly used starting framework in which to attack the 2-3. It makes an easy starting lineup to initiate the various principles we have promoted: the Basic 5, and the Automatics along with Penetration guidelines. We will illustrate some simple sets that can quickly attack zones that use these factors.

The 1-3-1 alignment is popular for the obvious reason that it lines up easily in the gaps of the 2-3. The point man begins in the gap between the two top defenders, forcing one to commit to him or allow a split into the heart of the defense. The wings are generally in the gaps between the top defenders and the wing defenders, but will come high when they know they can draw a backline, low wing defender. So, the defenders must decide who will cover the ball when a pass is made to the wing , a front player or a wing. We have just discussed how to manipulate the offense when a wing covers up fairly high on the wing, called the low wing out option.

We start with a simple play often called, **"Circle,"** which is easy to learn, but can be effective against more than just the 2-3, when players learn to read the defensive adjustments.

Diagram 17 shows Circle starting in a 1-3-1 alignment. Player 1 passes to 2 and fades to the weak side wing. The high post man, 4 here but it can be 5, dives from the high post to the rim looking for a paint catch and then circles to the weak side block. Post 5 flashes to the rim off of 5's tail and on up to the foul line to clear the 3-second area, then immediately circles on down to the low block. If he does not get a catch by this point, he moves on out to the short corner. Player 3 takes two steps down toward the baseline when 5 steps into the lane and

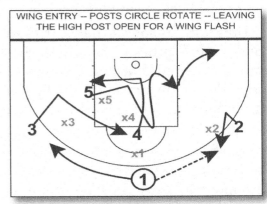

Diagram 17

flashes up into the lane, just as 5 gets to the block. Player 3 would like to get a paint catch where he has his own shot or he will have all the high/low options to work with or the reverse pass to Player 1, who will have drifted down toward the weak side wing after passing to 2 to replace 3. If Player 3 does not have a shot, he looks low at 4's flash and then opposite to 1.

Diagram 18 shows Player 3 in position to create plays at the point. He can quickly dribble handoff to either Player 1 or 2, if he doesn't shoot or pass. It is surprising how often Player 3 gets open because zone teams are set to cover the first cutter and often the second, but not the third.

Diagrams 19 and 20 show a couple other options that Player 3 has other than feeding down low, or running a dribble handoff, or passing to a wing and following it with a pick and pop. For example, if Player 4 has a good match-up to post up, he would stay inside and look for a feed from 1. In that case, Player 3 looks to screen down on 5 and spread on out to the weak side corner. Player 5 might be able to get a paint catch or he

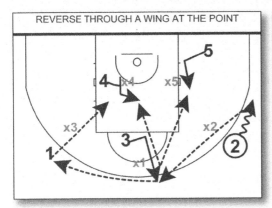

Diagram 18

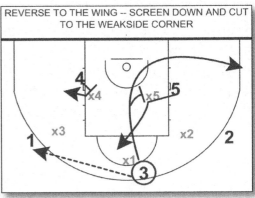

Diagram 19

can run to set a pick and roll on 1. If so, Player 4 would be in a good lift up position behind the roll and the ball handler will have two shooters in front of him, Players 2 and 3 as in Diagram 19.

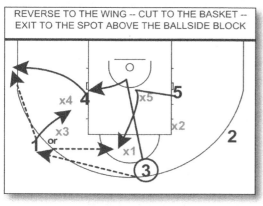

Diagram 20

On the other hand, if Player 4 is a good shooter, he can pull to the corner instead of posting up on 3's catch. If Player 4 pulls, 3 can pass to 1 and dive to the basket and out to the short corner. In that case, weak side post 5 would cut into the paint for a catch and move on up to the high post as a high/low or swing pass man. Then the action can continue with freelance play, following the offensive principles and automatics (Diagram 20).

Diagram 21 shows how the Circle play can be started to the strong side where Player 5 is posted, especially as a change up after the play has been run three or more times to the right side. When the ball is passed to Player 3, he may look inside quickly to 5 to see if he is open because the opponent is expecting 5 to cut up to the top as 1 fades to the weak side wing. Unless he is immediately open, Player 5 starts the Circle action by clearing to the weak side post to open the middle cut up for 4 to attack the paint for a catch.

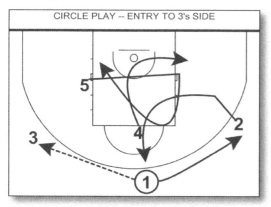

Diagram 21

Player 4 cuts to the basket as soon as he sees 5 start his cut away and circles to the weak side block, if he doesn't get a catch.

Player 5 cuts into the paint and on up to the foul line and loops down to the strong side block. Player 2 sets up his cut by dropping down a couple steps as 5 cuts to the ball side block, and cuts into the paint looking for a catch just as 5 gets to the strong side block. Post 5 can move to the short corner or even to the 3-point line if he is a shooter of that type. The same options to end the play exist if the play is run to this side as when it is run to the right as explained in the Diagram 19 notes. Or, the play can be ended with the free lance system.

The Circle Set provides interesting change of pace movements and spacing, continually making the defense adjust. It provides a balance of inside and outside scoring opportunities and is simple to understand and execute. It is flexible and employable versus most zones as a specialty play, but especially against the 2-3.

For example, from a time out the coach can call for either Player 4 or 5, the <u>better 3-point shooter,</u> to be the <u>second cutter</u> and to cut on out to the strong side corner instead of to the post and short corner. He will be open for a catch on this surprise move. If Player 5 is not a shooter with range, he will start in the high post and 4 will be in the low post.

Michigan State

The next play is from a 1-3-1 set employed at times by Tom Izzo at Michigan State. Player 1 enters the ball to 3 and follows his pass and cuts to the wing. Player 3 takes one or two dribbles down then passes back to 1 (Diagram 22).

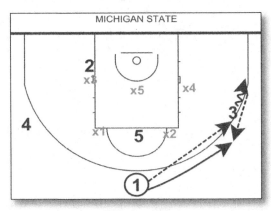

Diagram 22

In Diagram 23, after Player 3 passes to 1, he starts his cut into the lane. Player 5 screens down on X5 in the middle of the zone. As Player 3 gets to the lane, 1 takes two hard dribbles at the top as 3 curls off 5's screen. Player 4 screens down for 2 (shooter) on the weak side at the same time. Player 1's first look is for 3 in the middle. However, if the weak side defenders sag deep into the lane, Player 1 will pass to 2.

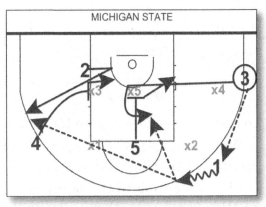

Diagram 23

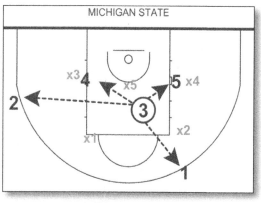

Diagram 24

In Diagram 24, 3 has caught the ball in the middle of the lane. On his catch, 3 may have a shot, but if not, his look is inside to 4 or 5 for a short pass or he can kick the ball out to 2 or 1 who may have easy shots due to the defense having collapsed inside on him.

Double One

Out of a 1-3-1 alignment we have Player 2, our best shooter, starting in the high post. In Diagram 25, Player 1 dribble enters at 3, who runs a shallow cut to the point on the ball side of the split line. Player 2 cuts to the ball side corner.

In Diagram 26, Player 1 can fake pass to 2 to cue him to start his cut, if he is not clear for a shot. He then will pass to Player 3 as 2 cuts hard off the double screen set by 4 and 5 on X3 and X5. Player 3 may need to use a freeze dribble to aid the timing of 2's cut to the weak side corner or wing.

We now have two picks for wing X3 to negotiate to get to the corner area to cover Player 2. As Player 2 gets to the screen, 4 flashes to the middle. If he can flash in front of X5, he may get a paint catch. However, if X5 bumps his cut, he screens X5, often freeing Player 5 for a lob pass and a layup at the rim. If X2 takes this away by dropping low, Player 2 has an open shot (see Diagram 27 on the next page).

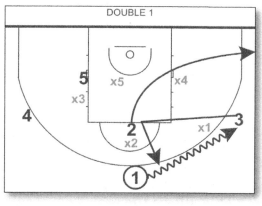

Diagram 25   Diagram 26

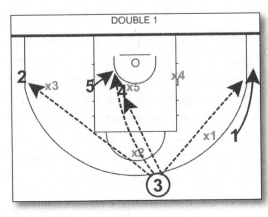

Diagram 27

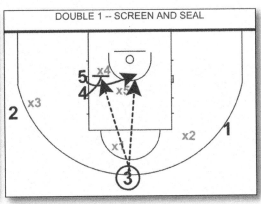

Diagram 28

In Diagram 28, X4 roves the baseline cut with Player 2 and releases him to X3. Therefore, Player 4 screens down on X4, and 5 curl cuts off 4 to the rim. Player 5 may be open for a catch. However, if he is not, Player 4 will be open by sealing X4 and opening up back to the ball for a pass from 3.

Flash and Seal: Quick Hitter From a Low Double Attack

One of the simplest, but most effective plays out of a double low post alignment starts with Players 4 and 5 setting up behind the defense almost at the level of the backboard, as shown in Diagram 29. Player 1 dribbles at X2 and takes him inside the lane line. Player 4 flashes up and into the lane at the high hash mark to clear out the weak side as Player 1 passes to 3, who must be guarded by low wing X4. On the flight of the pass to Player 3, Post 5 flashes

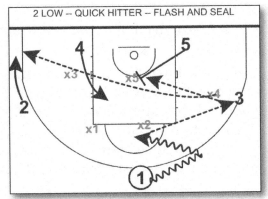

Diagram 29

and seals X5 deep and close to the split line. Player 3 passes to 5 who has an excellent deep scoring opportunity, or he can make a pass to 4 in the paint or a skip pass to 2 since Player 4 will draw X3 inside.

Play Series "2 Low"

Versus a zone defense, particularly a 2-3 zone, the coach on offense gets to decide who guards who by placing offensive players in the areas covered by specific players in the zone. This allows the offense to create mismatches with our initial actions. This is a play set that Ken has had success with at high levels from universities to national teams. The play is called **"2 Low,"** since Players 4 and 5 start low in a low double post formation, just below first hash mark above the block. Most 2-3 zones have a small forward and a big forward playing on the low wings with a bigger man in the middle, so we line up in the slots.

As we approach the attack area, everyone on the court must read, *"how are our posts being played?"* Are the wings of the zone playing on top of our posts, or slightly outside of the posts, so that they can get out on the wing shooters? Or are they playing slightly inside the posts so they are able to deny post flashes into the lane?

We place our strongest post, usually our 5 man, on the lane on the side of their smaller wing, X3, to set up the mismatch action. Our best shooter, Player 3 here, goes to the wing on the same side. Point 1 lines up at the top with the other wing, Player 2, lining up in the seam of the zone opposite our best shooter, as shown in Diagram 30.

In Diagram 30, point 1 has drawn X2 and passed to Player 3 who has to be covered by low wing X4. This time Player 4 is on the strong side block and is being played from behind by X5. Post 5 has a mismatch on small low wing X3 and seals him off for a high pass from 3, who reads the mismatch. Player 4 can help the play by popping off the lane to the short corner area, taking X5 with him.

In Diagram 31 defender X3 plays inside Player 5, or was able to get inside of 5 to ward off the pass in Diagram 30. In that case post 5 screens X3 in to open up the corner pass for Player 2 potentially. Ball handler 3 reads Player 5 screening X3 in and looks to skip-pass to 2, who has drifted behind the screen.

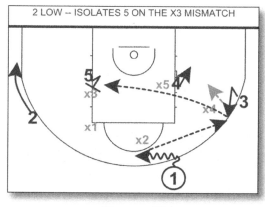

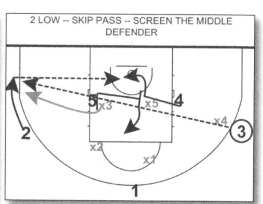

Diagram 30   Diagram 31

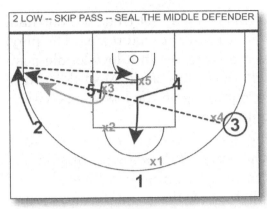

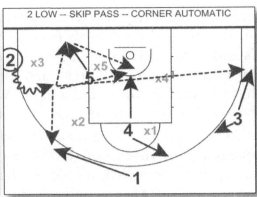

Diagram 32   Diagram 33

As the ball goes over Player 5's head, he releases the screen and quickly seals off X5, screening him into the middle of the zone. The options now are that Player 5 may be quickly open, or post 4 can use 5's screen to cut to the basket as in Diagram 31.

Diagram 32 shows that Player 2 has the option of the open 3-point shot, or attacking the closeout of X3, or hitting 4 on the high cut off 5's screen, or 5 on the roll back after screening for 4. As noted, if Player 5 has a size advantage on X5, 4 flashes to the high post to let 5 have the post as in Diagram 32.

Diagram 33 shows none of these options being open so Player 2 has the options of penetrating like he would, if the strong side wing had passed him the ball and cut, called the Corner Automatic. Or, he could swing the ball up to point 1 who is fill cutting into the open area and rove the baseline as in the Rover Automatic move.

In Diagram 33, Player 2 runs the dribble up move by punching into the seam between X3 and X2. In fact he may have a shot, or he may be able to hit Player 5, who pops to the short corner area. Player 4 Is reading to see if a hole appears near the rim for a scoring cut. However, if there is no obvious cut, he should step out opposite Player 1 where he can shoot if he has 17-18 foot range or become a ball mover to attack the weak side.

Player 2 must also read the weak side defenders, regardless of what 4 does because he may have a weak side pass to 3, who puts himself in position to catch and shoot.

What if the defense is able to have X1 bump the low wing X4 back to the low post? This allows X5 to sit in the middle of the lane and take any passes to Player 5 on the weak side. This takes away our initial play, but it opens up a secondary option. Any time the front defender is able to get to the wing on the initial pass or with a bump

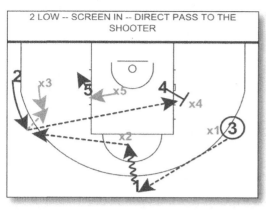

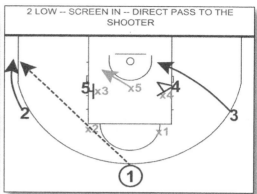

Diagram 34   Diagram 35

down rotation, that is a key for wing 3 immediately to pass back to Player 1.

In Diagram 34, Player 1 can freeze dribble X2 on the split line before passing to 2 lifting out of the corner, which brings low wing X3 up off the baseline. Player 1 passes to 2 and he can feed 5 if he is in great position, or can pass fake to 5 if he is not.

If 5 does not have a great postup, he steps out low on the ballside lane, while 4 seals X4 who was bumped down on him and may be playing outside of him. If so, player 2 passes to 4 on the seal.

Diagram 35 shows a quick hitter read. As the offense enters the scoring area and they read X3 and/or X4 play inside the posts, the posts screen in on them, and Players 2 and 3 drift behind the screens. Player 1 passes to the shooter 2 in Diagram 35. On the airtime of the pass, Player 5 screens in on X3. If Player 2 shoots, 4 wedges in as the weak side rebounder and 3 also attacks the weak side board. Again, a key aspect of a well-planned play is to plan for the rebound, as is the case on this quick-hitter.

Two Low allows us to go at the mismatch between our 5 man and the smallest wing defender as our first mode of attack against a 2-3, using our perimeter player looking **"strong side post," "weak side post," "skip-pass"** coinciding with our Inside-Out attack philosophy.

It is of paramount importance in attacking any zone for the players to recognize when the zone is matched up against the offense. They then should flow right into some cutting action to break the match-up without having to reset. In this latter case, the team identified the situation and called out a signal to alert the team to react as shown.

——————— CHAPTER 8 ———————

SPECIAL ATTACKS FOR THE 3-2 OR 1-2-2 ZONES

The 3-2 zone has grown in popularity since the 3-point shot has become such an important part of offense. With three active perimeter players and two big mobile post players the 3-2 zone can be a formidable defense. Clearly though, the baseline and the middle of the zone, from the rim to the high post area, are exploitable areas, since in most 3-2 zones the posts have to cover from the rim to the corner on each side of the court as well as having to move up into the high post area to cover flash cuts. When a post has to go to the corner to defend a shot, rebounding problems often occur on the weak side. We understand that coaches on both sides of the ball will make adjustments to help both the defense and the offense to make things work for them in counteracting the opposition.

Repeating one of the basic premises, the simple starting point in zone offense is to attack odd front zones with an even front offense and vice versa, we start here by attacking the 1-guard front zones with a 2-guard front formation.

2-1-2 Baseline Attack — Starting Simple

The simplest alignment follows the principle of aligning in the seams of the zone. The two guards on top are aligned in the gaps between the point and wings of the 3-2, looking to attack three offensive players against the two defenders on the bottom of the zone when possible. This makes the defenders have to decide who is responsible for the ball and brings that defender to the edge of his coverage area.

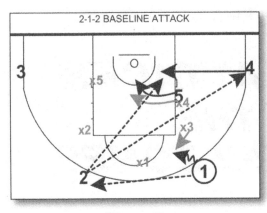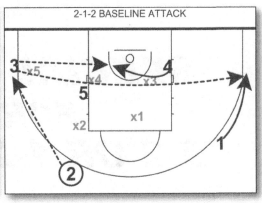

Diagram 1   Diagram 2

In Diagram 1 the original attack formation has the 5 man, the bigger inside player, starting at the level of the middle of the first hash mark above the block, while the wing players play a step or two above the baseline at the 3-point line. Player 1 punches deliberately into the gap of X3 and X1 to draw them and passes to 2. Player 5 flash cuts to the front of the rim and, if open, receives a pass from 2. However if X4 takes the cut away by denying it, 4 reads the play and cuts to the rim along the baseline. This amounts to a cut and replace action between 5 and 4, only it occurs at the rim as opposed to the perimeter. If X3 does not drop to guard him he has a layup. If Player 4 is a good mid-range or, especially, a 3-point shooter, he may possibly hold his position and receive a pass for an outside shot, but that pass has to be strong, since X3 may be alert to steal. If X3 drops to cover Player 4, 1 should be open because he must fade after his pass to 2.

In Diagram 2, if X3 drops to cover Player 4 down low, he may get a postup, and 1 should be open in the weak side 3-point area on a pass from 2. If Player 2 passes down to the baseline to 3, 5 seals his man halfway up the lane in the post. Player 4 must be alert on the pass to 3 that if X3 is in a help position on 5, he can flash into the open middle. If Player 5 cannot catch, 4 has the option to flash under the basket and present himself as a scorer. Actually, Players 5 and 4 can get together on this and 5 can tell 4, "I will seal X4," thereby taking X4 out of the play and creating more space for 4 under the goal.

Diagram 3 shows another option for Player 3, which is to punch the gap between X5 and X2. Player 5 pops to the short corner, and 4 may either seal at the rim or pop baseline as well. Player 1 gets into position to create a passing lane from 3. Player 2 cuts towards the ball to provide a safety outlet for 3.

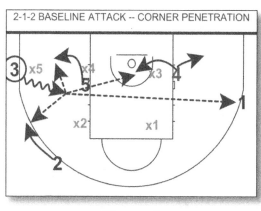

Diagram 3

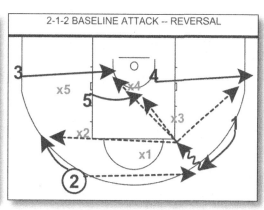

Diagram 4

Diagram 4 shows options if Player 2 does not pass to 3 or into the posts, but swings it back to 1. Player 4 pops hard to his corner spot and 5 flashes to the front of the rim. Player 3 follows with his cut to the space near the rim vacated by 5, just as 4 had done on the first side. Player 1 looks at 5, 3, 4, and 2 for the skip pass, who faded after passing. The 2-1-2 attack focuses on three baseline players attacking the two low defenders utilizing the principle of cut and replace. Against a straight 3-2, it provides multiple interior options in keeping with the inside/out mentality.

2-1-2 Baseline Runner — Simple Continuity Option

Diagrams 5 and 6 show another approach with the 2-1-2 alignment featuring an attack with screens and a baseline runner. When the ball goes guard-to-guard, the baseline man from the ball side runs off baseline screens on or in the lanes, set by his two post partners, 5 and 4.

In Diagram 5, Player 1 passes to 2 while 5 and 4 set baseline screens for 3, who cuts off 5's screen and is 2's first look. Player 5 rolls back to

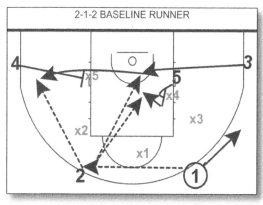

Diagram 5

the middle after his screen. Player 4 pins X5 in and 3 continues his cut to the corner. If Player 2 passes down to him, he may shoot or hit 4 sealing X5. Player 5 reads from the weak side and may flash to the middle high, but more likely since 4 is playing high in lane, 5 may be open flashing under the rim below X5 like Player 4 in the **2-1-2 Baseline Play** last shown.

In Diagram 6, Player 3 may reverse pass to 2 or even make a skip pass to 1 and then repeat the same baseline cut off of picks by 4 and 5. If nothing materializes after the second swing, the free lance principles and Automatics should provide good options and there is always the opportunity for random pick and rolls set on the wing, preferably set after a quick run by the weak side low post player. Naturally, at a youth level, the offense could be repeat-

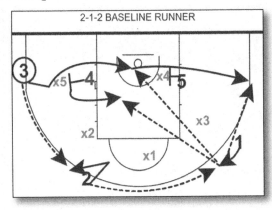

Diagram 6

ed until a shot is forthcoming, and **there are always opportunities to penetrate** when the defense commits an error.

2-1-2 Baseline Screener — Quickie Play

In Diagram 7 we start 2-1-2 as we did in Diagram 1, with the bigs along the baseline and the guards up top. Player 1 passes to 3 in the corner and 5 gets to the ball side block.

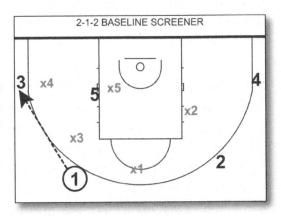

Diagram 7

In Diagram 8, Player 3 skip pass-es the ball to 2 at the high diagonal angle or passes to 1, who quickly re-lays it to 2. As the ball is released, or slightly before, Player 5 steps out and flex screens for 3, who cuts to the basket off 5's screen. Player 4 pulls to the corner.

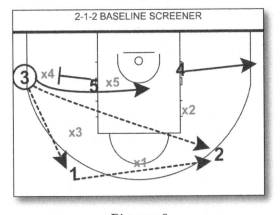

Diagram 8

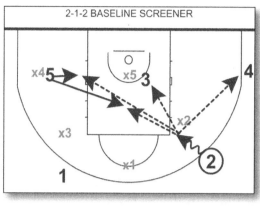

Diagram 9

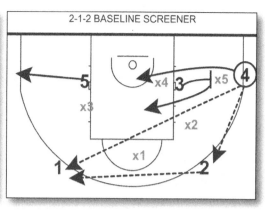

Diagram 10

In Diagram 9, Player 2 penetrates a dribble or two in order to draw X2. If X5 switches to Player 3 on the cut, 5 seals X4 and may be open for a direct pass from 2, or he may be open on his roll back to the middle. Player 3 may also be open on his cut and 4 may be open to catch in the corner, if X5 can't get there and X2 does not respond in time. It is possible that Player 2 could freeze dribble to draw X2 away from the corner to help open up 4.

In Diagram 10 Player 2 has passed it down to 4 in the corner, whether X5 or X2 is covering to distort the defense. As Player 4 swings the ball back to 2, the play continues with 3 stepping out to back screen 4. As Player 4 cuts, 3 seals and rolls back to the middle. Player 2 may even get X5 to move out on 4 enough to set him up for 3's pick with just a pass fake. If so, he has him set up for the back screen from Player 3 without a pass, allowing 2 to reverse the ball directly to 1 — a quicker move. The continuity may continue or the freelance options can apply.

Flare Screen — An Option on Baseline Screener

It is wise not to overlook the value of the flare screen against the zones. This is an excellent way to create space for a good 3-point shooter who may not be able to get his own shot. Even if he can, **this tactic can open up space,** when combined with a ball handler who is skillful enough to juke with a believable dribble pull in one direction to draw the defense off of a prime 3-point area, and then deliver a quick pass in the opposite direction behind the flare pick.

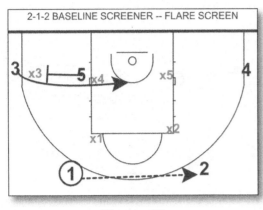
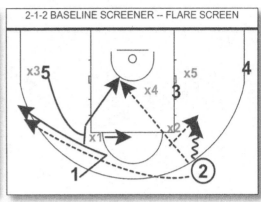

Diagram 11   Diagram 12

In Diagram 11, Player 5 sets the back screen on the baseline for X3, as he would normally do on the play.

Only as Diagram 12 shows, after his back screen, he immediately sprints up and sets a flare screen for Player 1. Player 2 dribbles into the X2/X1 gap at an angle to draw X1 enough to let 5 get a screen set. Player 1 helps by jabbing toward the penetration a step to set up X1 and then uses 5's pick. Depending on his read, Player 1 may curl off the flare, pop back or cut deep in the wing area. In addition Player 5 may slip to the rim, if X3 helps early on 1's cut, or he may dive later.

It is possible for the players to re-set and run the same action from the right side this time with Player 3 setting picks for 4 and then 2. When playing with a shot clock it may be necessary to go to freelance Automatics.

There are many effective attacks that do not adhere to the principle of attacking odd-man front defenses with even front attacks. We will present some simple but effective ones next.

Hi/Low — Looking to Play Inside-Out

Out of a 1-3-1 set, in Diagram 13, Player 1 dribble pulls and pops 4 for an entry and spaces away from X1, now being effectively in a 2-guard front to attack. Player 5 ducks in on X5 at the front of the rim as 2 and 3 drop to the baseline. Player 4's first look is for 5 ducking in and then for 2 or 3 in the corners.

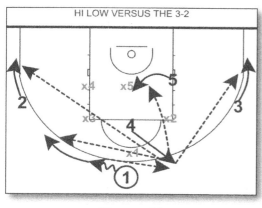

Diagram 13

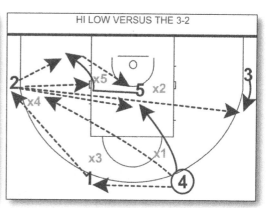

Diagram 14

In Diagram 14, Player 4 passes to 2 in the corner, either via 1 or directly. Player 5 cuts ball side since he was not open on the duck-in. Player 2 may pass directly to him on the seal, or when he cuts to the short corner. Player 4 times his cut to the rim. As Player 5 drags X5 out of the middle, providing 4 with a lane to the rim, 4 makes the cut. This is a set play so we are not in the Automatics that would call for the **X-cut** until after the freelance options begin. However, if the opening is there, we allow players to break the play and use whatever principles they have learned, as the Automatics are guidelines as opposed to hard-set rules. The teammates will adjust accordingly. Player 2 or 5 may hit 4 on his dive. Player 3 lift's to the diagonal angle from the weak side corner and may be open on a skip-pass from 2.

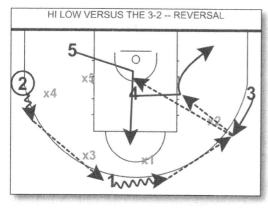

Diagram 15

In Diagram 15, Player 2 dribbles up from the corner and reverses the ball to 1, who swings it to 3. Player 4 fills the ball side block and seals his man on the pass to 3. Player 3 may pass to 4, or to 5 who flashes into the middle of the lane as 4 vacates. Then Player 5 fills to the high post, if he is not open on his flash. Basic high/low action can finish it.

In Diagram 16, Player 3 may pass to 4 in the short corner whereby 5 would dive to the front of the rim looking for a pass from 4. Of course, Player 4 may pass to 2 cutting into the middle, just as 3 could have if 2 had read the opening earlier, or to the high diagonal to 1. He can always outlet back to Player 3 in front of him.

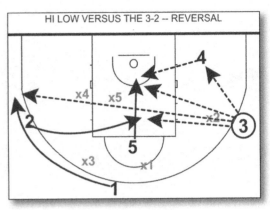

Diagram 16

High Stack into High Low — Pressuring the Posts

Perhaps one of the simplest plays versus a 3-2 zone is a simple ball screen out of a high stack, into High Low action. Starting with 4 and 5 stacked at the nail, and 2 and 3 as wings, 4 steps out and screens 1.

In Diagram 17, Player 1 comes off the screen, 5 dives down the split line to the rim and 4 pops away from the ball outside the 3-point line. Wing man 2 drop's to the corner, while Player 3 reads the defender on the wing and moves to create a pass lane from the ball. Point man 1 may have a pull-up jump shot, a feed to Player 5 on the dive, 4 on the pop or either of the wings. If nothing comes quickly, the Automatics and Penetration opportunities will keep the offense moving.

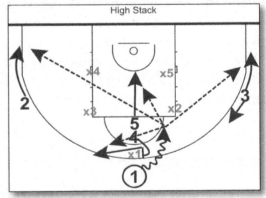

Diagram 17

Attacking the 3-2 Out of the 1-4 Alignment — Always a Good Default Alignment to Possess

We have already presented the **basic 1-4 attack in Chapter 5,** but to be a little more specific when going against the 3-2, we include it briefly here. We do believe the high 1-4 to be adaptable to virtually every defensive formation in the hands of an inventive coach. The 1-4 is particularly effective since it is one alignment that gives four possible initial entries from the point. Of course, the offense can flow right into the principles/ automatics from the entries.

In Diagram 18, Player 1 passes to 4, usually after bouncing once or twice opposite 4, who will step up off the lane to catch. Automatically, 4 pivots and faces the basket seeing both corners, looking for his own move and then for 5 diving to the front of the rim, which draws either X4 or X5 to stop the layup. The wings drop to the baseline and 1 goes opposite his pass. If no easy play materializes, 4 can pass to 1 and dive in an X-cut, or follow for a pick and roll, or he could execute a dribble handoff to 2 or 1.

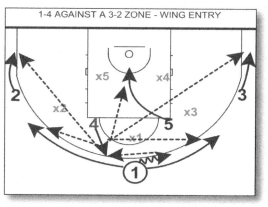

Diagram 18

Double Runner — Operating Out of a Double Low Post

In Diagram 19, Player 1 dribble-rotates 2 to the corner and 3 fill cuts to the point for 1. Post man 4 flashes into the high middle, creating two passing triangles into Player 5, basically front and back. Player 1 may pass to 2 in the corner for a pass to 5, or to 4 in the middle for a shot or a dump down to 5.

In Diagram 20, Player 1 may wave 2 through, or call out "through," and then reverse the ball to 3 and cut through himself. If Player 1 had passed to 2 and there were no play, 2 would reverse to 1 on this set play and cut through, followed by 1's cut to the weak side corner on his reversal pass to 3.

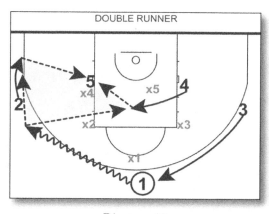

Diagram 19

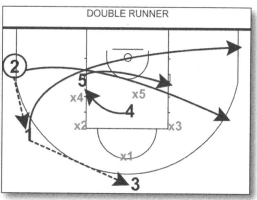

Diagram 20

In Diagram 21, on the catch by Player 3, 5 cuts across the lane to his spot above the block and 4 clears to the weak side block. The ball is reversed from Player 1 to 3 and on to 2 and we have a re-set now on the second side. We are back to having the two triangles created for passing to Player 5. The same options are open as the continuity goes on and the offense can call out to go to free lance autos at any time.

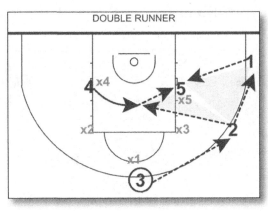

Diagram 21

5 X — Quickie Play from a Timeout

A simple quick-hitter play that creates a good inside scoring opportunity is one we can call 5X, but can have any name.

In Diagram 22, Player 1 passes to 3, then jab cuts and replaces himself. He receives a return pass as Player 3 speed cuts through to the corner after his pass to 1. This cut forces X5 to cover him, as he is a respected shooter.

Player 1 quickly reverses the ball to 2, who may have 3 open for a shot or may have 5 in the post. If X5 has to cover Player 3 in the corner, players 5 and 4 can attack smaller X4 and X3 inside. Another option is shown whereby, if he is not open in the post Player 5 can cross-screen for 4 and then open back up to the ball in the middle of the paint. If there is no play, the ball can be rotated and the same action repeated on the weak side or the offense can go to the Basic 5 and Automatics.

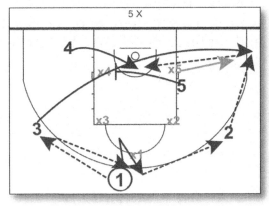

Diagram 22

Double Stack — Always a Challenge to Match the Alignment

Here is a quickie play out of a Double Stack that is useful versus the 3-2 zone at any level of play, especially after a timeout. It is also confusing for other formations and match-ups as a quick set play.

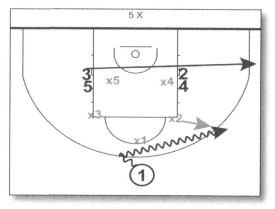

Diagram 23

In Diagram 23, Player 1 can drag the ball to his left, then reverse and come back to the right to entice X2 to guard him high on the wing. As Player 2 reaches this spot 3 cuts to the ball side corner.

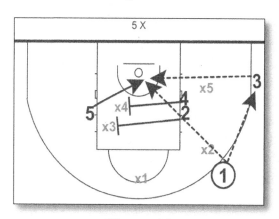

Diagram 24

When Player 3 clears the stack of 4 and 2 (Diagram 24), they screen across on X4 and X3. Player 5 uses the screens to cut to the rim, looking for a high pass at advanced levels, but is on his way to the strong side block.

On the play, Player 1 reads X5 who will come to the corner with our best shooter, Player 3, if 1 draws X2. If Player 1 is successful, 5 will be open at the basket. If X5 stays in to protect the basket area, Player 3 may be open for the corner shot. Players 2 and 4 will split, with 4 normally cutting up to the top and 2 spreading to the weak side wing for a reversal, if there are no good options on the initial play. Player 3 can rove the baseline on the reversal in the Automatic Baseline Rover option.

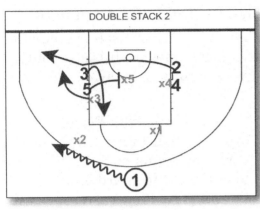 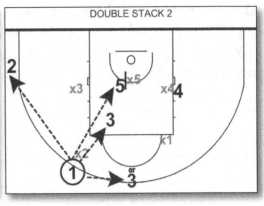

Diagram 25   Diagram 26

Double Stack Two

Diagram 25 shows another quick action as Player 1 dribble-enters to the wing on 3 and 5's side. Player 2 cuts off the double screen set by 3 and 5. As Player 2 gets to the screen, 5 screens in and seals X5 as deep as possible, giving 3 space for his cut, so 3 cuts up between 5 and his defender and loops into the middle of the lane.

Diagram 26 shows Player 1's passing options: 2 in the corner, 5 on his deep seal, or 3 in the middle. If Player 3 is not open early, he continues on up to the top to the swing spot. On Player 3's catch at the top he can drag dribble over to the weak side where 4 will seal in on X4 and 2 will reverse and rove the baseline back to the corner. Player 5 will cut up to the high post and the regular high/low post action can follow to produce a shot, along with the Basic Principles the team will know.

Create and Attack the Mismatch — Always a Good Strategy

As is stated so often, in man-to-man the opposing coach decides who will guard our players. However, **versus the zone the coach decides who will guard his players** based on how he aligns them versus the zone. **Just as we created and attacked a mismatch in the 2-3 zone with Player 2 low,** we can do a similar thing versus a 3-2 zone with this quickie move. Diagrams 27 and 28 illustrate how we isolate our 5 man versus the opponent's 2 man (their smaller wing).

In Diagram 27, Players 5 and 2 line up on X2's side. Point 1 passes the ball to Player 3 and cuts to the corner below 3. Wing man 2 fill cuts to the point, replacing Player 1. Player 4 cuts through to the short corner on the ball side, just after 1 clears the lane. The normal coverage would have X4 take Player 1 in the corner, X5 take 4 in the short corner, and **X2 would have to drop down to cover 5.**

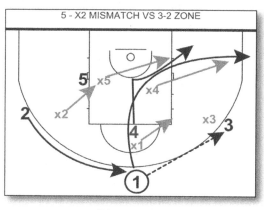

Diagram 27

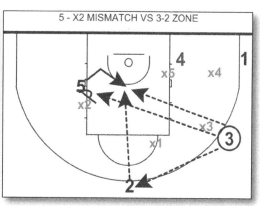

Diagram 28

In Diagram 28, post man 5 moves up a step or two and seals X2, who had to rotate down. If he is unable to seal him, he ducks in to the front of the rim. Player 3 may be able to pass directly to 5, or he may pass it back to 2 who can dump it down to 5, if 2 gets inside on 5.

While the 3-2 zone has obvious strengths, especially vs. the strong perimeter teams, it can be exploited both inside and outside with proper organization combined with good spacing, passing, and movement.

---------------- **CHAPTER 9** ----------------

SPECIAL ATTACKS FOR THE 1-3-1 ZONE

The 1-3-1 zone can make typical ball movement difficult in comparison to the previous zones we have looked at. If they have a big post man and long athletic wing men, they can present problems, regardless of the level of play. The standard containing 1-3-1 defense has its obvious holes along the baseline, and one would think that simple ball movement should be able to free up corner shooters. This chapter will set forth several play actions that can be used as simple offensive sets or as quick-hitter plays from a time out. Understand that all of our sets and quick-hitters are actions that can be used to stand alone as a part of a coach's war chest, but are best used to attack a particular formation to get an easy shot. But we know all plays look good on the board, but none will work every time. If that were the case, we would have discovered that play by now and we all would be using it. What we have are **entries into an offense that probes the weakness,** but our main thesis is that when these entries fail to produce the desired shot, that the team will have the knowledge of the principles we have established in the opening chapters to be able to continue to attack a broken up defense with proper reading and reacting to what the defense allows after it has been put in motion.

As we have noted in the opening chapters as well as in our assessments in attacking the 2-3 and the 3-2 or 1-2-2, we believe our principles and many of the set attacks and entries we present can be adjusted to be effective against more than one zone defense formation. For example, as you read over **Chapters 7 and 8 we stated that the 1-4 set and the 2-1-2 sets can adjust to be effective vs. the 1-3-1 and match-ups.** Toward the end of this chapter we will present some additional 1-4 play actions that are more specific to the 1-3-1 defense. At the start here we will note some simple 2-1-2 entries that can be successful against the 1-3-1, but can be included along with those previously written.

Having said that we will proceed here with some simple special actions vs. the 1-3-1, while confessing that not all 1-3-1's will have the same lineups and slides. Some will be tight and containing, others extended into the lanes and will involve trapping in key spots or situations. This is all part of the coaching challenge.

2-1-2 Versus the 1-3-1 — Simple Starting Point

As mentioned, the **2-1-2 Baseline Runner and the Baseline Screener in Chapter 8** can be used to attack the 1-3-1 zone as well. In this chapter we will go with some 2-1-2 entries that are more specific to the 1-3-1. A standard approach is to attack the odd front with two players and align two other players along the baseline while placing one player in the mid post area in a 2-1-2 starting formation. The attack is very similar to that which we used versus the 3-2 zone that also features a one-front defensive alignment.

Diagram 1 shows the basic first movements. We feel that we can use this alignment to attack the basket along the baseline for some high percentage interior shots. We can do this by using Player 5, our mid- post player, to engage X5, the middle man in the zone. At the same time, our weak side baseline player (3 in the diagram), attacks the basket when the ball is reversed between the two top players, 1 and 2. The ball side wing player, X3, is responsible for covering the block area below him when the ball is reversed to the weak side and we try to put pressure on him.

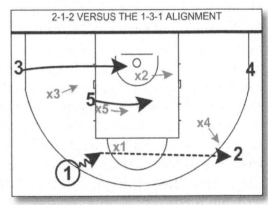

Diagram 1

Our mid-post player 5 engages X5, the middle man in the zone, by flashing to the ball side on all ball reversals. If Player 5 is open for a good catch, he must get the ball. But, our primary look in this action is for the weak side corner man, Player 3, attacking the rim before the wing defender X3 can drop. The other option is for Player 3 to seal X3 on his back as the ball is passed, a part of attacking under the zone.

If Player 3 cuts to the rim, 2 looks to hit him with a diagonal pass if he is clearly open. This pass must be practiced, however, as it requires judgment, skill and timing!

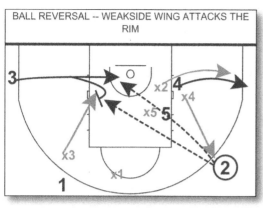

Diagram 2

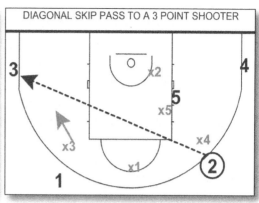

Diagram 3

Diagram 2 shows simple possibilities. Note that we have now distorted the 1-3-1 to become a 2-3 with X1 and X4 up and X3, X5 and X2 on the baseline. All zones become 2-3 when the corner is threatened as noted earlier.

If Player 3 is a good 3-point shooter we may hold him in the weak side corner on the pass to 2 if X3 still has a very long drop to get to him, but that depends on the skill level of the players involved. Skip passes are not for everyone.

Player 2 must be skilled enough to throw the quick diagonal pass to 3 for the 3-point shot as is shown in Diagram 3. This action is extremely difficult to cover for a straight 1-3-1 zone, since it also means that this long, poor closeout angle puts Player 3 in a great driving situation as well.

In Diagram 4, Player 2 does not throw the diagonal pass to 3, but passes to 4 below him. This is an excellent option if Player 4 is a good 3-point shooter. If Player 4 in the corner is not open for a shot, he has the option of passing quickly to 5 who has sealed X5 on the pass to 4. On the weak side Player 3 reads 5, who needs to seal X5 well above the block at the first hash mark. X5 may be occupied enough defending Player 5 that 3 can cut under to the basket since it stretches X3's coverage, who will at best be behind him, and he quite often is open. Player 4 may also hit 1 on the weak side diagonal spot. In addition, he can run a dribble up move or simply reverse the ball to Player 2 and rove the baseline off of 5 and 3.

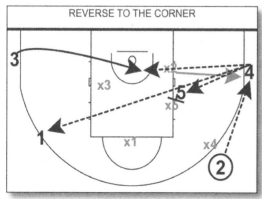

Diagram 4

Diagram 5 shows the many options Player 1 has upon receiving a skip pass from 4. He may shoot it, pass to Player 3 popping to the corner, drive it at the closeout, look for 5 busting back across the lane, and 4 attacking the basket or sealing X4 on his defensive drop. Of course X4's drop usually leaves Player 2 open as well.

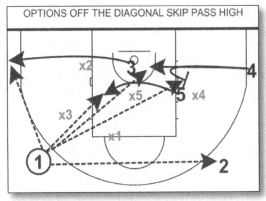

Diagram 5

Quick High/Low action to attack a smaller baseline runner. The fact that the next aspect of the 2-1-2 attack is the last action covered, certainly does not diminish the importance of the high post entry shown in Diagram 6. As we have maintained, **the high post is a most effective point of attack** in any zone offense.

Diagram 6 shows that Player 1 attracts X1 and dribble pulls him to the wing near X3, hopefully drawing X3 to some degree, and passes to 2 to draw X4. Post 5 flashes to the high post and catches from Player 2. As Player 4 ducks in on X2, (usually a smaller type player), 2 and 1 fade away from the high post.

As Player 5 turns and faces the basket he may have a shot, or he can make the high low feed to 4 sealing low. If Player 4 seals up

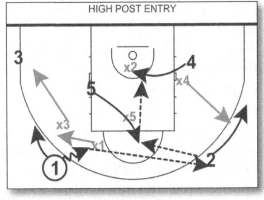

Diagram 6

and thereby take's X2 out of the play, it can also provide 5 with a good driving opportunity, especially if X5 is slow afoot.

In combination with the other actions in the 2-1-2 attack, the high/low game is a particularly lethal weapon. Player 5 has the pick and roll as well as the dribble handoff options to either 1 or 2 at his disposal.

Strong Tight — A Pinch Post Option
that Puts the Defense in a Virtual Man-to-Man

Another attack that may also be run out of a 3-2 or a 2-1-2 alignment has two different actions to start. One action is labeled **"Strong Tight"** and the second action is called **"Strong Wide"** and are illustrated in Diagrams 6 and 7. In fact, this is a standard man-to-man action that is basic to the Triangle Offense. As we noted early on, this is one of the standard offenses that combined ball and player movement with spacing, so it is no surprise it translates to the zone game as well. In addition, it contains another element that is consistent with many zone defense antidotes, an overload. We showed previously how the standard UCLA rub cut could be used against the zones as well. Certainly these offenses are also effective against the match-ups for obvious reasons.

In Diagram 7, Player 1 passes to 3 and cuts to the ball side corner. Player 2 cuts to the point and 4 flashes up to the weak side elbow. If we have high percentage scoring opportunities on the first side, Player 3 may pass to 5 or to 1 for a shot, or for a drop pass to 5. In most cases these options will not be there, so Player 3 will pass to 2 at the point.

Diagram 8 shows that on Player 2's catch, Player 4 may set an elbow screen for him to use on a pass and cut or it could be mixed occasionally with a quick pick and roll. It is amazing how often Player 2 can get a handoff and take a hard drive to the basket, if X5 is concerned with 5. If Player 2 does not receive the ball, he continues to space to the corner.

Again, an occasional option once the play has been run a few times is to let 4 pass to 2 in the corner and dive to the goal for a give and go. If he doesn't get it, he can run through to the weak side post and 3 can run the cut that is set up in the original set that is shown in Diagram 9 and 5 can cut to the mid-post for a possible catch or high low action.

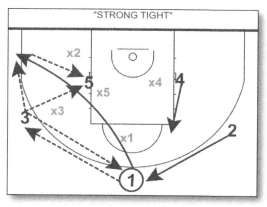
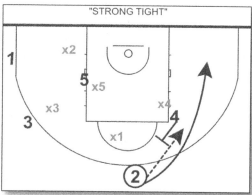

Diagram 7   Diagram 8

ATTACKING THE ZONE DEFENSES

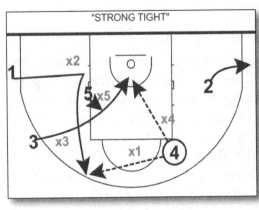
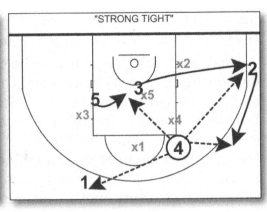

| Diagram 9 | Diagram 10 |

Diagram 9 shows the completion of the basic play with Player 2 spaced at the corner. Player 4 squares up to the goal to face his defender, as 3 makes a wing Shuffle cut off of 5's pick to the front of the rim. Player 1 cuts hard to the lane and then up the lane off 5 to the high elbow area. Player 4 may hit 3 on his cut to the rim or 1 on his cut to the high elbow. Post 5 may be open late on his flash in the mid-post.

Diagram 10 shows a good inside option. If X5 helps on Player 3's cut, 5 will be open on his step to the ball. If X5 stays home on Player 5, 5 ducks in on him and may still be open for the pass from 4. If Player 4 passes to 1 or 2, he cuts to the basket and 5 will read 4's cut and stay spaced. From here the Basic Principles and Automatics take over.

Strong Wide — A Counter to Attack Low on the Weak Side

In Diagram 11, 1 passes to 3 and cuts to the ball side corner and 4 flashes up to the high post. Again, if there is a high percentage scoring opportunity here, 3 may pass to 5, or he may pass to 1 who relays to 5. However, if none of these is easily achieved, 3 reverses the ball to 4.

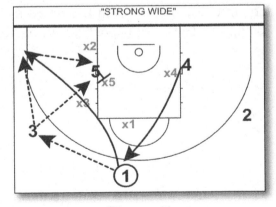

Diagram 11

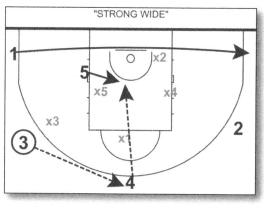

Diagram 12

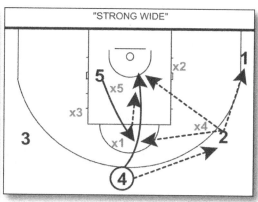

Diagram 13

Diagram 12 shows a possible pass down to Player 5, who may be able to get an easy one, if he can lock and seal X5 when the ball is swung from 3 to 4 on 4's flash cut. Player 3 would read that X5 is in a high position on 5 and snap the ball quickly to 4 in that case as 1 roves the baseline. Good post players have a signal to let the wing know when he feels he has an advantage.

In Diagram 13, Player 4 swing passes the ball on to 2 and dives to the basket on his pass. Player 5 X-cuts high and may catch for the shot or for a quick dump down to 4. In review, Player 2 may hit 4 on the dive, 5 on the flash high, or 1 in the corner. If we have not achieved a good scoring chance we finish with the Principles and Automatics.

1-4 Versus 1-3-1 — A Good Default Offense

The most versatile alignment with the most available entries is the 1-4. It makes it very difficult for the defenders in the middle line of three to prevent entries to the line of four in the 1-4. The wing defenders must decide if they are going to try to sit on the posts at the elbows and give free entries to our wings. Bringing the bottom man, X2, up with X5 to defend the posts is unworkable. Passing to the post guarded by their middle man and having our other post dive to the rim, with their smaller man on him, would be a big advantage. They can match big-to-big and small-to-small, but are no longer in a 1-3-1. There are other adjustments possible, but the 1-4 does cause problems for the 1-3-1. So, to begin let's look at the easiest entries and follow our principles in Diagram 14 (next page). The High/low Automatic yields many good options against a straight 1-3-1.

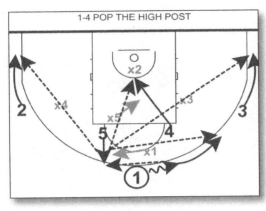
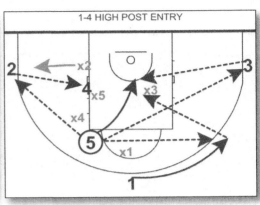

Diagram 14   Diagram 15

Player 1 will drag the ball opposite 5 who pops up to catch and looks to get a quick 4 on X2 mismatch at the front of the rim. Player 5 will have options to pass to the corners as the wings drop or can pass back to 1 who drifts away from him (Diagram 14).

In Diagram 15, if Player 5 cannot pass to 4 in front of the basket, 4 continues his cut to the spot above the block and can pull to the short corner as well. Player 5 may pass it to 2 in the ball side corner. Player 2 may have a shot or a quick relay pass to 4 sealing X5. If Player 5 passes to 1 or 3, he can cut to the rim and exit to the ball side post and short corner, while 4 flashes in to the rim in the X-cut behind him, then into the high post. The play can be finished by running a high/low game with the Basics and Automatics.

Guard Cut Option — Strong Side Attack for a Quick Inside Attack

In Diagram 16, Player 1 passes to 2 and cuts to the ball side corner since the big wing is up. Player 4 dives and sets a brush screen on X5. As Player 4 rubs X5, 5 cuts hard to the basket off the screen. Player 4 continues his cut and seals X3, then looks back to see if he can get a paint catch. If X3 gets in front of Player 4, then 4 locks him in to give 3 an open 3-point shot on a pass from 2.

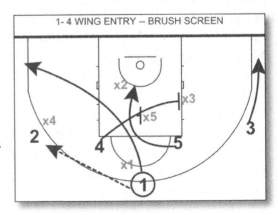

Diagram 16

In Diagram 17, Player 2 may find 1 open on the cut, but normally his first option is for 5 cutting to the rim and then to 1 in the corner be-

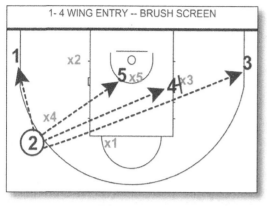

Diagram 17

low him, who may have a shot or a better feed angle to 5. His next look is for Player 4 sealing X3, or for 3 drifting to the weak side corner. A major point to be observed is for Player 4 to come to a quick stop so as not to pick up a blocking foul as 5 cuts. In addition, Player 4 must seal and vacate to the top so as not to draw a 3-second call. Player 2 must be quick and decisive on his passes. If none of these is open, Player 4 can fill cut to the top for a swing pass or high/low action. He could even set a pick and roll for Player 2. It is easy to get into the basic freelance principles either way.

Throughout the book we have emphasized that when a guard dribbles to the wing, the point zones become a 2-3. Virtually anything that you ran against a 2-3 becomes a menu from which to select actions. The Basics and Automatics are based largely on this fact.

Dribble entry to rotate the defense for a low post threat. In Diagram 18 we illustrate the Dribble Rotate entry with Player 5 quickly diving to the rim. This immediately creates double triangles to exploit getting the ball inside to Player 5. We have Player 3 in the corner and 4 popping to the high post as possible passers to 5, depending on how X5 plays him.

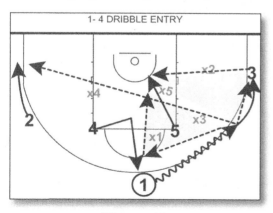

Diagram 18

The other option, which often comes available, is the diagonal skip pass to Player 2 for the 3-point shot and/or excellent penetration possibilities for him against a closeout or fly-by, particularly. If none of these options is available, Player 1 can just go to the Automatics to finish the play with the corner pass auto or the swing pass auto for the baseline rover, high/low action, etc.

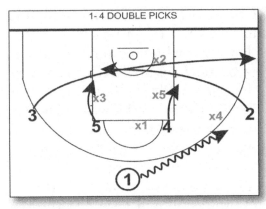

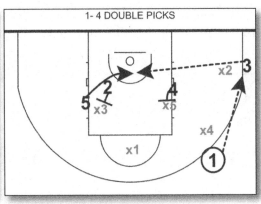

Diagram 19   Diagram 20

Double Picks — A Quick-hitter Special for an Inside Shot

Diagram 19 shows another play off a dribble entry that is a quick-hitter action, suitable for timeouts or specials. Player 1 dribble enters, pushing 2 to cut to the rim. Player 3 cuts to the ball side corner, while 4 and 5 slide down the lane.

In Diagram 20, Player 1 passes to 3 as 2 sets an up pick on X3 and 4 seals X5 on the lane. Player 5 cuts under the basket and 3 passes to him for a score. If nothing works on this quickie option, Player 3 can reverse to 1 and 2 will pop up to the top while 3 will rove the base and 4/5 can get into a high/low game as it flows into the free lance operation. The posts could execute an interior screen and pop the picker up to the high post before initiating the high/low game for that matter. This is the freedom they should have to contest the defense.

Double Stack — Another Inside Game Approach with a Quick-hitter

In Diagram 21, Player 2, who is our best shooter, forms a stack with our best big man, Player 5, on X3's side of the lane. Players 3 and 4 start in a stack on the other block. Player 1 dribbles away from 2 and 5 to engage X4. Meanwhile, Player 3 pops to the corner pulling X2 while 4 seals off X5. Point 1 pass fakes at Player 3, unless he has an easy open look, because the meat of the play is to go at X3 with 5 in the post.

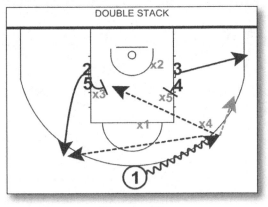

Diagram 21

For that to happen, X5 needs to be concerned with Player 4 in the post so 1 and 3 have to look like they are on the attack with 4. Player 2 cuts off 5 to the high elbow area, while 5 seals X3 on the inside for a direct pass from 1. If X3 slips inside, Player 1 can lob over the top to an open side. If neither option from Player 1 is open quickly, 1 passes to 2 at the elbow. Player 2 should have a good angle to dump the ball down to 5 in the post. This all has to happen quickly with some deception to keep X5 from jamming the middle.

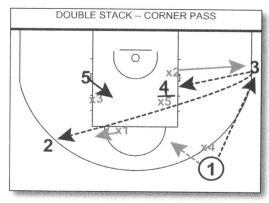

Diagram 22

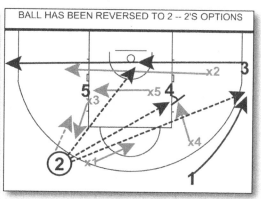

Diagram 23

If the weak side post game does not produce a good look, Player 1 can always look back to 3 in the corner, and try to post 4 (Diagram 22).

In Diagram 23, Player 1 completed the pass to 2. If Player 2 does not have a shot, he pass fakes at 5 posting on the lane. Player 3 cuts to the basket under the zone and on to the corner, if he does not catch. Player 4 releases his seal of X4 on the pass to 2 and looks to seal X4 on the inside of the lane. Player 1 drifts towards the corner. Player 2's first look after his pass fake inside is at 3 on his cut or in the corner. His second look is at Player 4 on his seal, and his third look is at 1 fading behind 4.

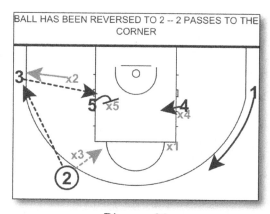

Diagram 24

Diagram 24 shows that if none of these options is available, he may pass fake at Player 4 stepping to the ball and then pass to 3 who has cut to the corner below him. Player 3 may have a shot or a post feed to 5 sealing on X5. Player 1 cuts back to his original spot. From here the play can be finished with Player 3 reversing on the baseline cut off of 5 and 4 to apply the Basic Principles and Autos.

High/Low Stack — Inside and Outside Options

The High/low Stack also puts players in an alignment that can create excellent scoring opportunities both inside and outside. In Diagram 25, Players 3 and 4 are in a high stack at the left elbow and 2 and 5 are in a low stack just above the right block. Player 1 dribbles away from the high stack to engage X4. A key part of the play is for Player 1 to pass fake to 4, who takes a step out to the top, as Player 2 cuts across and screens X3. Player 3 cuts hard to the ball side corner, coming off of screens by 2 and 5. If Player 3 is open immediately, there may be a play for him and/or 5 on the seal on X5.

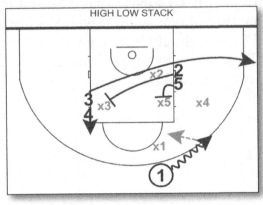

Diagram 25

In Diagram 26, Player 1 passes to 3 in the corner if he is clear, as 4 cuts over or under 2's screen, looking for a paint catch or lob from 3.

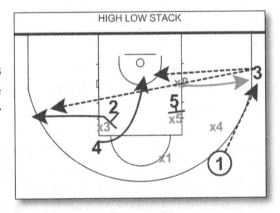

Diagram 26

Diagram 27 shows another option with the focus on the weak side instead of the strong side corner, as in the first look at this play. To involve either Player 4 or 2 primarily this time, 1 pass fakes at 3 on his cut and passes directly to 4 on his cut in the paint or to Player 2 on his pop to the 3-point line. Player 5 will pop to top to get into high/low if there is no shot.

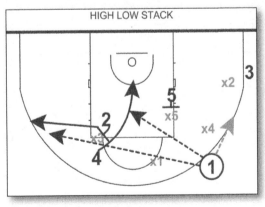

Diagram 27

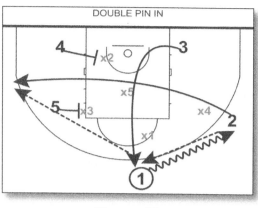

Diagram 28

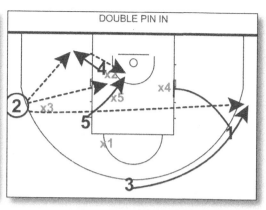

Diagram 29

Double Pin In Play — 3-point Options with Possible Inside Play

Screening/pinning in on the weak side of the zone can be an effective means to obtain a 3-point shot, followed by some excellent options to score inside. Diagram 28 shows Player 1 dribble entering toward 2, who will drop down and then cut off of 3's tail, who is fill cutting for 1, when he is halfway through the paint. Player 2 continues to the 3-point line. Quickly, Player 1 passes to 3 and on this pass, 5 pins in on X3 and 4 pins in on X2 to free up 2 for a pass from 3.

In Diagram 29, as Player 2 catches, 5 dives to the rim on X5 and 4 pops to the short corner. Player 2 may pass directly to 5, or he may pass to 4 for a short jump shot or for a relay pass to 5.

At the same time, on the opposite side, Player 1 pins in on X4 and 3 fades behind the screen. Player 2 has the option to skip- pass to 3 for the 3-point shot.

Note: If Player 5 is fronted by X5 on his cut to the rim, as in Diagram 30, Player 1 must read it and flash up into the lane area for a direct pass from 2 and a quick dump down to Player 5.

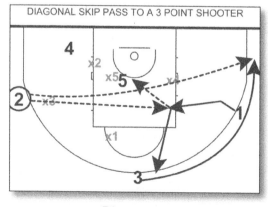

Diagram 30

If that is not open due to X4 shutting it down, Player 1 may be able to pass to 3, who cuts to the weak side behind 1's cut for the skip-pass. Player 1 will pop to the top for a swing, if there is no easy play and action can resume.

─────── **CHAPTER 10** ───────

ATTACKING THE MATCH-UP ZONE DEFENSES

The Match-up Zone has evolved into a defense best described as a zone with man-to-man principles, or a man-to-man with zone principles. The fact is that many of today's zone defenses begin with defenders matched up with whatever alignment the offense presents to them. This takes away any decision of who takes the ball on the first pass, since the match-up begins by challenging the ball handler and matching up around that. The defense makes the normal shifts required by their particular defense rules to cover cutters, screens, etc. There is no single match-up zone defense. Each coach determines what the basic rules will be to govern the team and individual techniques in the defense, and will be flexible to make adjustments as challenges are presented by different opponents.

A coach who has an advanced understanding of the match-up can take a scouting report and structure the game plan to be able to cover the prime moves of the opponent, if their zone offense is based on a few set actions, which is the case for most teams. Match-up rules may determine that the team will stay with some cutters and not others. They may switch on cutters and screens, or go in and out of staying with cutters. Coaches develop their own particular match-ups by studying others and combining that with their own ideas to formulate their special rules that cover cutting and screening actions.

One objective with match-ups is to create hesitation or confusion, as the opponent sometimes questions, "Is it man or is it zone?" There is normally as much man-to-man coverage as possible while still playing a zone primarily. Therefore, coaches often go to their man-to-man offense, if it has good spacing, including ball and player movement with screening. The man offense is well known by your team and may well be very effective against the match-up. On the other hand, it is easier to scout and make the adjustment plans easier on the part of the opposing team, who knows your offense as well.

Because match-ups can be particularly effective against pattern type offenses, be they man-to-man or zone, our purpose in presenting the Basics Five and Autos is to present principles that will enable teams to create their own free-lance, motion-type offense that can be employed to produce continuity of ball and player movement subsequent to a broken set play action instead of having to re-set the offense, or one that can stand alone similar to one of our offenses, the **High Low Cutters on Chapter Seven.** The concept has proven to be very effective against both standard and match-up zones in our experience.

In the following pages we present various special sets, both series actions and quick-hitters, which have been effective against various match-up styles, as well as the standard zone defenses in most cases.

1-4 Pass and Cut

The alignment that arguably provides the most difficulty for match-ups is the 1-4. Many match-up teams take the easy way of matching up, which is to match this align-

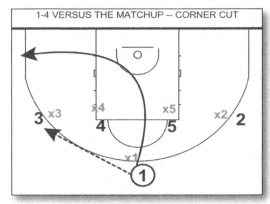

Diagram 1

ment by covering the posts with their posts and the wings with their wings. Others have a more sophisticated way; regardless, the first problem that occurs for the defense is how they cover a wing entry when the passer cuts deep inside through the lane, as shown in Diagram 1, and cuts out to either corner. Do they pull X4 to the corner, or go man-to-man with the deep cutter in the standard match-up? A shallow cut to the ball side corner provides the easiest opportunity for a bump down by the cutter's man to the wing, but the inside cut prevents a bump down, since there is no one to cover Player 1's cut to the goal without exposing an easy high/low game for the offense. Again, there are rules team set for this, but this cut forces the team to have knowledge of the difference in the nature of the initial cut.

In Diagram 2, X1 stayed matched with Player 1 on his cut to the ball side corner. Of course this already distorts the defensive alignment by putting a small on the baseline, but it is one option that teams use on the first deep cut. It does tend to disguise the fact that the team is going to zone up on the possession.

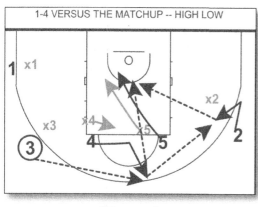

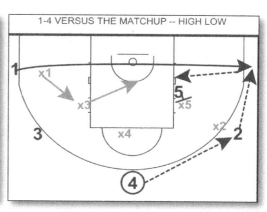

Diagram 2   Diagram 3

Player 5 dives to the rim, if 1 is not open and 4 pops out to a good passing angle inside, on an inside fill cut for 1. Wing man 3 could pass to the corner and cut, but here he quickly passes to Player 4 and 1 begins to move toward the weak side corner, but times his cut to be sure not to jam the post area for 4 and 5.

Player 4 may have a move or a dump down to 5, otherwise he swings sharply to 2 who V-cuts toward the ball for a shot or a good passing angle to 5. Player 2 hits 5 on a deep seal at the rim. This must be a very quick series of passes in order not to draw a 3-second call on Player 5. If Player 5 is unable to catch, he empties above the ball side block and 1 finishes his cut to the baseline corner.

In Diagram 3, Player 1 has roved the baseline after the high-low options were explored. The defense has to decide how to cover this baseline cut as well, either to pass Player 1 off from X1 to X3, or to use another option. This is not a book on defense, so all options will not be noted, though here X3 has chased Player 1 to the corner to keep X5 inside. In the diagram, Player 2 passes to 1 in the corner for a shot or for a possible post feed to 5.

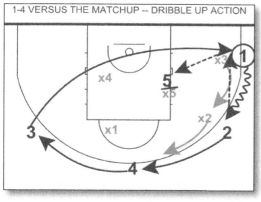

Diagram 4

This is a **set play action** vs. the match-up, otherwise the team could go to the free lance options and Player 2 could cut through in the corner pass automatic. But in this set action, if Player 1 has no shot or easy post play, he **dribble-rotates up** in Diagram 4. His dribble up from the baseline, is a key for Player 3 to speed cut to the ball side corner below 1.

The whole exercise is intended to force decisions on the part of the defense. Because Player 2 had not cut through, the dribble up **causes a chain reaction for spacing** whereby 2 and 4 each slide over to maintain 15-18 foot spacing between each of them. Player 1 pushes 2 to the point and 4 to the weak side wing, ready to attack the board if 3 shoots. A rebound plan is always essential.

Player 3 may be open for a shot or for a post feed to 5 sealing. At this point another option available is to call for the **Dribble Rotate up "cutback"** move shown in **Chapter Four,** a difficult move to match.

UCLA Cut from the 1-4 Set

Another difficult action to guard out of the 1-4 begins in Diagram 5. Ball handler 1 dribbles to set him-

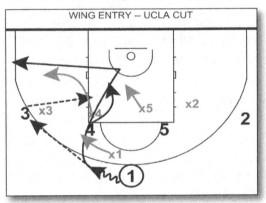

self up above Player 4 then passes to 3 and runs a UCLA cut to the rim off of 4. If X4 switches onto Player 1, then 1 cuts down and out to the corner and 4 dives the rim where he should have position on X5 who will have to move over to defend him, since X1 cannot drop down on 4 with any hope for success. After this cut Player 5 pops and the offense is in a high-low attack.

Diagram 5

In Diagram 6, X1 has followed Player 1 and Player 4 pops out off of

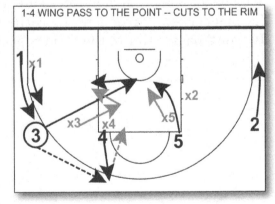

1's cut. Wing man 3 passes to 4 and cuts to the front of the rim. If Player 4 cannot hit 3 on his cut, he pass fakes to him to ensure that X3 is on top of him and 1 lifts out of the corner, behind 3's cut. We have the defenders shown with X3 going with the cutter, but in reality he may have gone just two steps and passed Player 3 off to X5 on his drop, in which case 3 can still post to occupy X5, possibly open-

Diagram 6

ing up a cut for 5 behind them for a high pass over X2. Either way, the defense must adjust to stay matched.

In Diagram 7, Player 4 can fake pass to the weak side to 5 or 2 to try to get the defender on 3 to be inside the lane, but snap passes back to 1. Player 1 passes to 3 sealing at the rim, or on the block. If Player 1 cannot hit 3, post men 5 and 4 set a staggered screen for Player 2 who takes his man down a step or two toward the base and then quickly cuts off the staggered picks. Player 1 dribbles towards the point and hits 2 coming off the picks, if he is open. Either Player 5 or 4 may have a slip cut option.

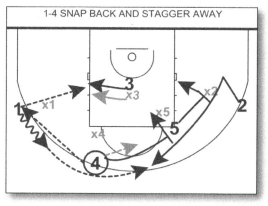

Diagram 7

In Diagram 8, Player 2 comes as high as he must to get a catch, while 4 and 5 form a double screen on whatever defenders are in the area. Player 3 cuts off the double screen. Player 3 may split between 4 and 5 and use them as a "mouse trap" or "elevator door" screen, or he may cut under the screen. Posts 4 and 5 will form a split action as shown in Diagram 9.

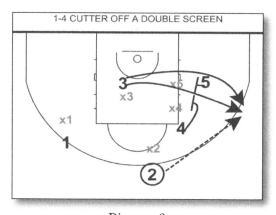

Diagram 8

In Diagram 9, Player 3 catches, but has no shot coming off the double screen. Player 5 sets a flare screen for 4 who pops to the corner for a 3-point shot. Player 3 will look to pass to 4 on the fade or to 5 on a seal. Or, he can reverse the ball to Player 2 and cut hard through to the weak side corner where he would probably draw X5 out to the corner.

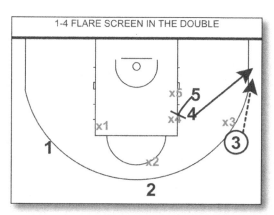

Diagram 9

Player 3 could have curled off the screens set by 4 and 5 to get to the corner earlier and 4 would have still had the flare cut off of 5's pick to the corner from player 2. Of course, Player 3 will be an option for 2 to pass to in the weak side corner in that event. If there are no shots yet, the team would continue with the **Basic 5 and Automatics in a read and react motion offense geared to forcing movement and decision making. Dribble moves, punching into gaps and setting picks will be central elements vs. match-ups.**

1-4 Dribble Rotate Entry

Dribble actions such as the Dribble Entry in this play always cause decisions on the part of the match-up as to when to pass off a dribbler to another defender as explained in **Chapter Four** on the positive aspects of the use of the dribble against the zones.

In Diagram 10, Player 1 dribbles to the wing, pushing 2 to the corner and trying to get to the line of 45 degrees as 5 dives to the rim. Players 1, 2, and 4 read how X5 plays 5. If X5 gets caught on top of Player 5, 1 passes to 2 who feed's 5 on the baseline side as he seals X5. If X5 denies Player 5 high on the ball side, 1 may feed 5 directly. If X5 fronts Player 5, 4 pops quickly to the point to catch from 1 and dump down to 5, or there could be a possible lob from 1 to 5, depending on the location of the defense behind 5. Player 3 keeps his dribble.

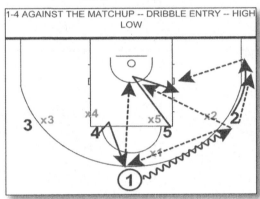

Diagram 10

Diagram 11 shows a **double rotate action** that can be used if there is nothing quickly in the high/ low game. Point 1 wave's 2 through and dribble rotates down one more slot to the corner. The defense must again determine whether to stay with their men or to hand off. Player 2 cuts through to the high wing spot on the weak side and 4 pops out for an inside fill cut for 1 while 3 fill cuts to the point.

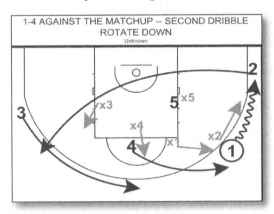

Diagram 11

In Diagram 12, Player 1 passes to 4 and roves the baseline. Player

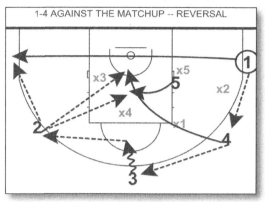

Diagram 12

4 swings it to 3 at the point and busts to the front of the rim as 3 swings the ball to 2. Player 2 may have a shot or a punch move or can possibly pass to 4 on his cut to the basket. Post 5 flashes to the rim as Player 4 exits to the ball side and may have good position for a paint catch from 2, or 2 can pass on down to 1 in the corner at any time.

Note: Remember that Player 3 at the top may want to use a Freeze Dribble move to help the timing of 1 and 4's cuts from strong side to the weak side.

High Post Pop. A simple entry to the 1-4 versus the match-up is the basic high post entry. In Diagram 13, Player 1 bounces away from 4 to automatically pop him up for a possible catch and fades to the wing.

Player 5 stops his cut on the split line and screens X5 to seal off the lane for a take by 4. Player 4 sets up his drive with a fake away, then drives to the rim off 5's screen. Player 4 can score it or draw and kick with 3, 2 or back to 1. Post 5 may roll or pop, but must be sure that he does not draw a 3-second call.

Handback Option that can be keyed or called for a possible 3-point shot. In Diagram 14, Player 1 passes to 4 and gets a hand back. As Player 4 is handing the ball back, 5 flare screens X4. Shooter 4 flare cuts off the screen at the weak side high elbow area and is ready for a catch and shoot 3-pointer. If it closes up, Player 4 may be able to pass to 5 slipping to the goal or to 3 or 2 who may be open for a shot, or else can

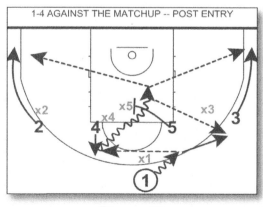

Diagram 13

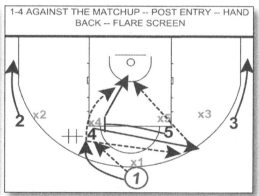

Diagram 14

pass down to 5 in the post. If X5 shows at any time during Player 5's cut to set the screen, Player 5 slips for the rim. Player 1 must be aware of this option. If he were to slip, Player 1 or even 4 may be able to hit him at the front of the rim.

If Player 1 does not pass to 4 after getting the hand back, 5 turns and set's a screen for 1. Player 1 comes off 5's screen looking to make the quick "pocket pass" to 5 or to turn the corner to attack the rim himself and has 4, who must spread wide if he does not get the pass from 1, and 3 in front of him for outlets for shots. In the process Player 2 lifts behind the screen and may be open for a snap back pass for a shot or a dump down pass to Player 5, if 5 can seal X5 in the lane. (Diagram 15)

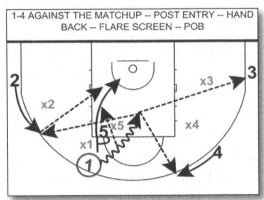

Diagram 15

1-4 Elbow Pick and Roll Quick-hitter option

The 1-4 elbow screen provides an opportunity for a 3-point shot for one big man and a deep catch for the other, with spacing that makes it difficult to bring help to either action. In Diagram 16, Player 1 passes to 2 and spaces away past 5 to the wing. Players 1 and 3 spread on the weak side as 4 sets a screen for 2 just off the elbow, the higher the angle the better as opposed to the foul line extended — giving more space for the defense to cover.

Diagram 17 shows Player 2's options much more clearly. Player 2 comes off the screen looking to penetrate, while 5 dives to the rim and

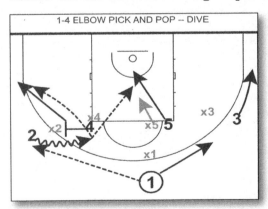

Diagram 16

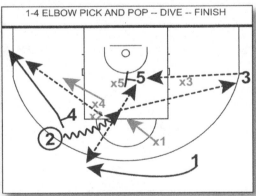

Diagram 17

4 pops diagonally to the 3-point line. Player 2 may be able to pass to 5 inside or 4 for the 3-pointer quickly. If neither is open he has Player 1 on the wing and 3 in the corner. Player 3 has a great angle to feed 5 sealing at the front of the rim. Player 1 is an option for a shot or as an outlet to set up the finish of the possession.

Dribble-rotate entry option

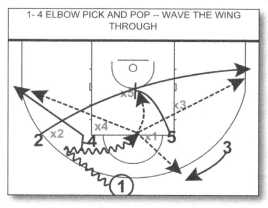

Diagram 18

Diagram 18 shows Player 1 waving 2 through to the weak side corner on the dribble rotate move and cutting back to use the screen set by 4. Again, Player 4 pops diagonally, and 5 dives to the rim as 1 comes off the screen. Player 3 lifts behind 1 to present himself as an option and as a safety outlet. Player 1 may turn the corner and attack the basket, or feed 5 sealing, 4 popping, 3 lifting or 2 in the corner.

If the defense turns the ball to the baseline, Player 4 can slip to the goal and look for a pocket pass or pop back, while 5 will read 4 and do the opposite of whatever he does. Player 2 will be on the baseline drift and 3 will fill to the weak side diagonal area and is a safety for defense.

1-4 Screen the Screener after a Dribble Rotation

In Diagram 19, Player 1 dribble-enters toward 2 who cuts into the lane ahead of 5's cut. When he gets to the basket, he reads the coverage for his next move. Post 5 rolls down the lane off 2's tail and 4 pops to the top.

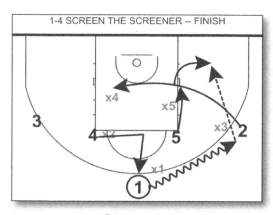

Diagram 19

Player 2 can decide to cut to the weak side corner area if X3 just stayed two or three steps and released him and then moved up to release X1, who has followed Player 1 to the wing. Or, he can pull to the corner, even if X3 did stay through the lane with him. Either way, he may get a good shot on a skip-pass. However, if X3 is following him all the way, he can cut out on the weak side off of 3's down pick. He is basically going to try to take advantage of X3 the best way he knows how.

Player 1 gives 5 a low post look and reads where 3 decides to go as well. He will at least pass fake to Player 5 to freeze the defense, then swing pass to 4, if there is no play to 5 or 3. With the pass in the air to Player 4, 3 must decide the logical person to screen to set up 2. He may screen down on X4 or may pinch the wing on X2, depending on who he thinks will try to cover Player 2.

In Diagram 19 if X3 does not stay with Player 2 into the free throw lane, Player 2 can cut back to the corner..

Diagram 20 shows the more logical defensive formation in which the defender, X2, would rotate to Player 4 at the top and 3 would pick down on X4, or X3 if X3 stayed man-to-man on Player 2. Obviously Player 2 can cut or fade off 3's screen. Alternatively, Player 2 can read to curl cut off of 3 and 3 would pop out to the wing for a catch.

But Wait! There can be more — or not. Look for the rest of the story on Diagram 21. With the ball now in Player 2's hands, **3 continues his cut to screen X5**. Player 5 cuts to the rim off 3's screen. And the set can continue with the **pick the picker** as Player 4 sets the down pick for 3 on X1.

Feeder 2 may pass to Player 5 on the cut, 3 on his cut high, 4 on his roll back after he picks on X5, or can skip pass to 1 as he fades to the weak side diagonal. As we have consistently reminded, the set can be called off at any time in lieu of running the Basic 5 Principles and Automatics, but this is a good semi-continuity set that has some choices of options as opposed to following the dots totally that forces a lot of adjustments for the defense.

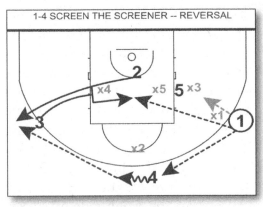

Diagram 20

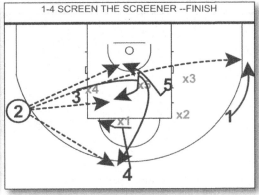

Diagram 21

Dribble Pass and Cut —
DPC Series: Using the Automatics in a Set as in Chapter 4

Following is a good series (Diagrams 22-27) with ball and player movement using the dribble effectively that creates match-up problems throughout. It becomes a question then of which team can execute better.

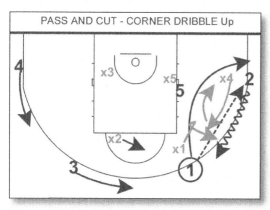

Diagram 22

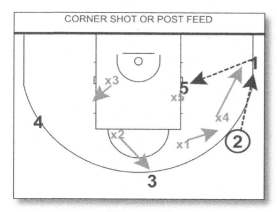

Diagram 23

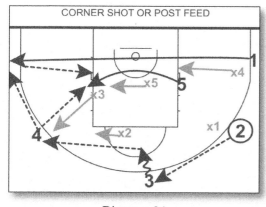

Diagram 24

Diagram 22 shows it starts by getting a small matched up with a big in the corner. Player 1 passes in the corner to 2, drawing a back defender X4 here. Player 2 uses the dribble up move as 1 loops inside to replace 2 in the corner. It is a simple play that may create a quick corner shot for Player 1 or an attack off of the dribble, if X5 pulls out to cover, or if X4 tries to pass off Player 2 to X1.

Diagram 23 illustrates the situation when X4 is late to recover. Player 1 may still be able to penetrate before X4 can get to him or to feed 5 down low on a seal off. It is simple to see how this dribble up action provides decisions for the match-up zone. The **Dribble Rotate Up** here is similar to the **"cutback"** option presented in Chapter 4 that explains this excellent exercise against the match ups.

Diagram 24 shows what happens if the ball is swung to Player 3 at the top. Player 1 cuts baseline on the Baseline Rover option when the ball is reversed from the wing, an automatic if 2 pass fakes to key his cut first. Player 4 rotates up to the wing toward the ball.

Player 5 flashes across the lane

toward the ball. There is a chance that Player 3 may have to freeze drible at X2 to ensure that we get the timing right for Player 1 to get to the weak side corner for the 2-on-1 attack on X3, along with post 5 cutting.

In Diagram 25, Player 4 passes to 1 and cuts through as in a **corner pass automatic** and looks to seal on the inside of X4, if possible. Player 1 quickly dribbles into the gap for his own move, or to make a play. Post 5 pops automatically to the short corner, perhaps for a short jumper, or makes a full cutback move to the corner, if he is a 3-point shooter.

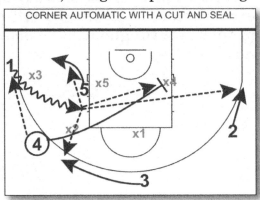

Diagram 25

On the punch, Player 1 has a lot of options other than to 5. Player 4 seeks to seal X4 on the inside and weak wing 2 creates an open pass lane at the high diagonal angle. At the top, Player 3 makes his cut toward the penetration for a safety outlet and defensive balance.

Diagram 26 shows yet another option on the play. If Player 4 does not pass down to 1 in the corner, he then looks to 2 flashing hard into the middle gap. If Player 2 catches, he may have an open shot or a quick dump down to 5, sealing his man on the pass to 2. Note that Player 3 fades to the weak side when 2 gets the pass and is therefore a back-door option for 2.

Player 4 could have simply reversed the ball to 3 at the top for high/low action and upon that pass, 1 would have the option of running the baseline in the Baseline Rover automatic. If the pass went from 4 to 3 at the top, player 2 would have to pull back out to the weak wing. (Diagram 27)

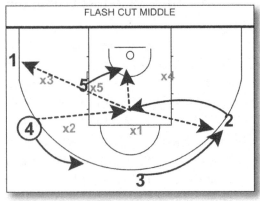

Diagram 26

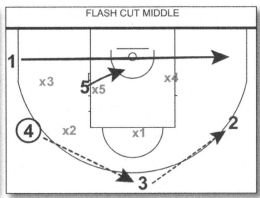

Diagram 27

Elbows — A Quick hitter Play vs. Matchups

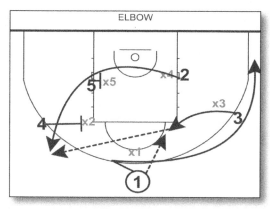

Diagram 28

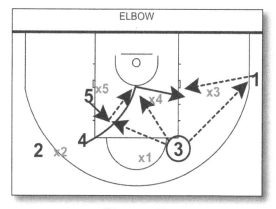

Diagram 29

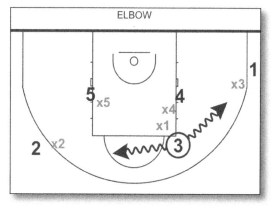

Diagram 30

In Diagram 28, Player 1 passes to 3 who puts his body on X3 and flash-posts to the elbow for a catch. Player 1 then cuts outside of 3 to the corner. Just after Player 3 started his cut, 5 and 4 pinch screen in on X2 and X5 and 2 cuts off of their screens.

Player 3 passes to 2, if he is open for a shot, but 4 and 5 both are options to slip, as the players they pinch in will likely try to get up on top of them to be able to help on 2's cut and pick him up, depending on whether 2 comes up to the high wing or fades to the corner.

In Diagram 29, as Player 2 comes off 4's screen, 4 dives to the rim and 5 flashes into the lane behind him. Player 3 may pass to 4 or directly to 5, if 4 is fronted on his cut. Post 5 may have a shot or can make a play. If 4 is not open on the cut he exits above the ball side block. At that point 3 may then pass to 1 in the corner, who may have a move to make, or can pass to 4 sealing on the lane.

If nobody is open, as shown in Diagram 30, Player 3 may dribble at 2 or 1 and run a dribble hand-off for either one, a man-to-man offensive option that is equally effective at any time as an alternative free lance move, when there is no easy scoring move to be made otherwise.

Note: For those who want to invest in the play as more than a quick hitter, Diagram 31 shows how Player 3 may dribble at 1 in a misdirection drag dribble and spin back to hit 2 on his fill cut to the top as a swing man. Player 1 roves the baseline when 3 starts his dribble move at him and looks to cut off of 4 and 5 for a shot. Player 2 can pass to 1 for either a shot or a feed to 5 sealing on his screen, or to 4 flashing to the middle for a shot or pass.

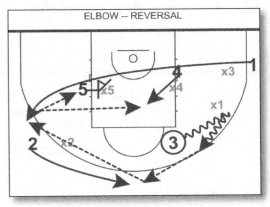

Diagram 31

—————— **CHAPTER 11** ——————

ZONE ATTACKS
OF
RICK MAJERUS

Our dear friend Rick possessed what was considered by many to have been one of the world's great basketball minds. He was relentless in his pursuit of knowledge about all facets of the game. One of the things that made Rick one of the best was his ability to "take it to the court" as he would say. He was a master teacher who could communicate his information succinctly and in a manner easily absorbed by players. His attention to detail was meticulous, always focused on the elements most critical to execute the specific exercise of the moment. Coaches are judged by what they get out of their athletes, and while some could not survive in the extremely demanding environment that he created, there is no question that his athletes played to their potential. Rick shared his knowledge willingly, but to our knowledge there is little on record of his works dealing with attacking zone defenses. It is with a great deal of pride that we devote this chapter to Rick as we describe some of his basic zone sets and special plays.

RICK'S FAVORITE PLAY SERIES
HE NAMED YANKEE AND REBEL

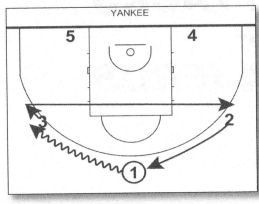

Diagram 1

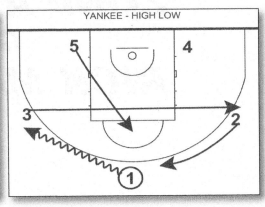

Diagram 2

Yankee Series

The movement in Diagram 1 is **"The Yankee Action."** Rick loved the dribble entry versus zones because it distorted the zone without having to make a pass, thus protecting from turnovers and tending to keep the ball in the best passer's hands, plus it flattened down the defense. It developed in various combinations, but the flat cut across and slightly under the foul line from one wing to the opposite with the weak side wing filling the point are common actions of **Yankee.** He then involved the posts as cutters, pickers, sealers and rebounders with their actions fitting into the various combinations of the perimeter players' movements. For instance, the action may start with his posts in a 2-low format, but could easily flow into a high/low action as in Diagram 2.

Diagram 1 shows Player 1 dribbling at the 3 on the wing in the Yankee action with 2 filling at the top for 1 and 3 clearing across the lane to the weak side wing. Diagram 2 illustrates the high/low action as post man 5 flashes into the high post, getting "ahead of the ball" so that he is facing the basket at the nail when he gets the catch from Player 1.

Diagram 3 shows Player 1 dropping to the corner after his pass to 5. When Player 5 flashes up early, **2 shortens his fill cut to the point,** leaving 5 more open space at the top for his catch as in an inside fill cut. Both Players 2 and 3 then quickly cut to the wing and the corner on the weak side as potential targets. Player 4 quickly ducks in to the low post at the split line as 5 pivots wide to the right to improve his passing angle into 4, who seals his man on the split line in front of the goal, if possible. This

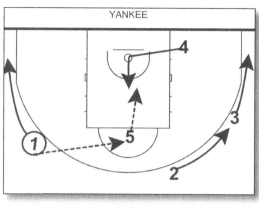

Diagram 3

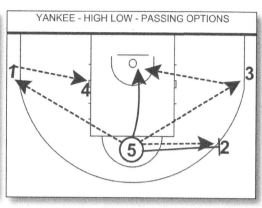

Diagram 4

is Player 5's first option. Player 4 must be counting in his mind and must clear to the weak side lane line above the block to avoid the 3-second call.

Post 5 may then pass to either corner or pass to Player 3 and cut to the rim or pass to 1 as 4 seeks to seal his man. Or, Player 5 may also pass to 2 and set a ball screen for him (Diagram 4).

This is but one example of the posts integrating their action with the perimeter players. By the end of the season Rick could call upon an incredible number of combinations of moves in Yankee (and Rebel, which we will show next). Over the course of the season he would have a few moves that he thought would be effective against the next opponent and would concentrate on those in the practices before that game.

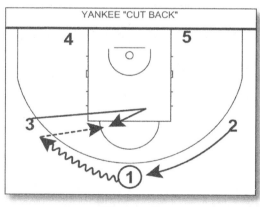

Diagram 5

The three perimeter players over time learn other actions that can be effective in Yankee, by simply making a call in which the cutter might **"Duck Back"** for a catch as in Diagram 5, or to **"flop"** his cut into the ball side corner such as in Diagram 6 (next page). On the **duck back,** Player 3 looks to make a play on his catch, and post 4 and 5 will open up to each short corner to give him space and be ready to catch.

In Diagram 6, the cutter "flops," i.e. changes, his cut to the ball side corner, which cues the posts to react to the cut. Post 5 attacks his man with a seal as the ball is coming to his side and his partner 4 on the other side looks to come high for a possible high/low action. Player 1 may pass to Player 2 in the corner for a shot or a quick relay to 5 on his seal, or

1 may also pass to 4 flashing into the lane for the high/low action, or skip pass to 3, who is fading to be on a diagonal angle from the other wing when he has the ball. This diagonal spacing was one of Rick's favorite and most effective principles: **when one wing catches the opposite wing must drift to be diagonally opposite the other wing.** This skip pass may be effective against any zone.

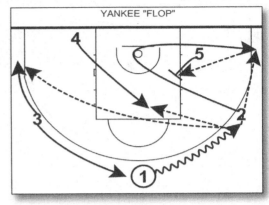

Diagram 6

As shown, the posts have their set moves that they bring to the play that are **coordinated** with the perimeter player's movements. They may run an **"Interior,"** which is a cross screen by the ball side post for anyone in the weak side post position — usually his post partner as in Diagram 7.

In Diagram 7, point man 1 has already dribbled at Player 3, who ran the flat Yankee cut to the weak side. Player 2 has made the fill cut to the point. Point 1 passes to 2, who relays it to 3, while 5 screens across for 4 on an **Interior** pick. Post 4 uses the screen, so Player 3 reads the defensive reaction and may hit 4 on the cut, or 5 sealing or rolling back on his screen. He may also skip pass to Player 1 on his diagonal movement on the weak side. Rick mainly ran **Interiors** for his best shooters to come off the low cross screen.

Sometimes the posts or the ball handler may call **"Hold,"** and the low post would attack/seal his man in the middle of the lane (Diagram 8). Again, Player 1 has dribbled at 3 who ran the flat cut across to the wing position. Player 2 ran a fill cut to the top and 1 passed to him and he relayed it to 3.

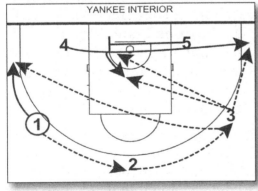

Diagram 7

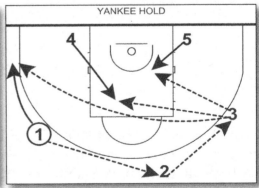

Diagram 8

Wing 3 looks for Player 5 sealing deep, then looks for 4, who would be flashing into the middle for a possible high/low feed to 5. Finally, Player 3 may hit 1 on the weak side diagonal position (Diagram 7).

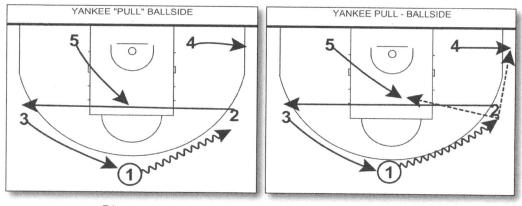

Diagram 9   Diagram 10

Another of Rick's favorites, **Yankee Pull** (Diagram 9), involves the ball side post pulling to the corner to pull out a big defender, as the perimeter players execute their Yankee action. Point 1 dribbles at Player 2 to **drag the top of the zone below the free throw line,** an important concept in Rick's philosophy of attack. Wing 2 sprints across the lane below the free throw line and wing 3 fill cuts to the point in regular Yankee action, as Player 4 pulls to the corner and 5 flashes into the high post. Diagram 10 shows Player 1 passing to 4 or to 5 in the middle; 2 and 3 drift down as 5 gets the ball. Pulls were restricted to posts that could shoot the 12- to 15-foot shot minimally. Rick was never shy about identifying the roles.

Diagrams 11 and 12 show **Yankee Pull-Reversal** that Rick might call when **the ball was not moving well.** Players 1-2-3 run the Yankee cuts and then swing the ball to the attack side. Diagram 12 shows Player 1 reversing the ball to 2 and on to 3 with his various passing options, or he could have a penetration, of course.

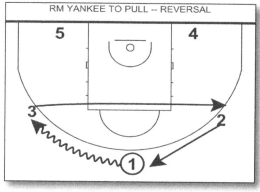

Diagram 11

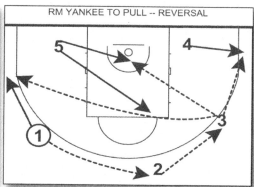

Diagram 12

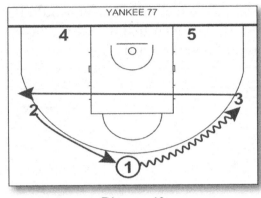
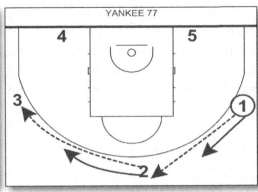

Diagram 13   Diagram 14

Diagrams 13 and 14 show the start of a Yankee **lob option called Yankee 77.** Players 1-2-3 run the Yankee entry in Diagram 13 and then 1 passes back to 2 on the point and slides up to the high elbow spot. Player 2 relays the reversal pass to 3 and cuts to the ball side high elbow spot. Posts 4 and 5 line up below the basket.

Diagram 15 shows Player 3 quickly passing the ball back to 2 as post man 4 cuts up to the high post for a catch. At the same time post 5 sprints and sets a back screen just off the lane for Player 3. Player 2 pass fakes at 4 coming into the high post, and then quickly passes the ball to 1, who looks to make the lob pass to 3 cutting off 5's screen. If the play is not there, Player 3 cuts on to the corner and high/low action can continue.

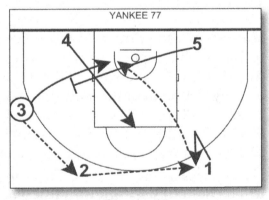

Diagram 15

The movement options available to the perimeter players are numerous. Rick was the master at using perimeter actions in combination with his supply of post actions to build a play to attack any zone defense.

The "IN" and "OUT" Calls

The "In" call. He could start the offense with a pass and an **"in"** cut

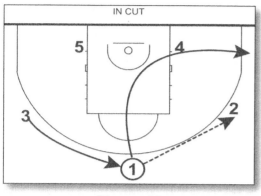

Diagram 16

shown in Diagram 16 and then have post action to follow such as **high/low or interior, etc.** Obviously, the "in" call refers to a 1-2-3 player making an inside cut down the middle and going to the strong side corner. Rick's calls apart from the series often tended to help a player remember what the play action entailed as opposed to requiring players to remember just numbers and parts of the body such as "thumb" or "chest" or some geographical location to delineate the move.

An "In Cut" variation. Diagram 17 shows how an **"In"** call can be

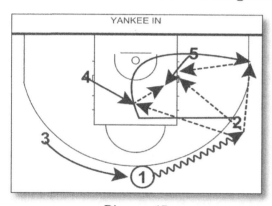

Diagram 17

altered from Player 1 making the cut to a **wing making the inside cut.** Player 1 dribbles at 2, who fakes the flat cut and cuts to the ball side corner. Player 3 fill cuts to the point while 5 posts hard above the ball side block. Player 4 flashes into the lane on his way to the nail at the high post. Point 1 may pass to Player 2 in the corner for the shot or to feed 5 sealing. He may also pass to Player 4 flashing into the lane where 4 may have a shot or a dump-down pass to 5.

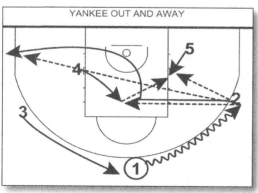

Diagram 18

In Diagram 18 we see the **"out cut."** Point 1 dribbles at Player 2, who fakes a flat cut, but breaks it off and cuts to the **weak side corner** instead of to the strong side as in the **"in"** play. Player 3 fill cuts to the point as 5 posts hard on the ball side block. Player 4 screens in on the weak side for 2 and 4 then flashes into the lane on his way to the high post, if he gets no paint catch. Point 1's options are to hit Player 5 posting on the ball side block, or hit 2 with a skip pass as 4 screens in for him. He can also hit Player 4 flashing into the lane, where 4 may have a shot or a dump-down pass to 5, or swing to 3 at the top or to 2 on the weak side.

Rebel Series

The other favorite play series of Rick's was called **Rebel,** a play with numerous options based on Rick's post sequences, or movements, in concert with the different perimeter actions. For instance in the play **Rebel** shown in Diagram 19, point 1 makes a dribble entry at Player 2 who cuts to the ball side block. Wing 3 fill cuts for Player 1 and 4 cuts up diagonally to fill for 3 at the weak side wing.

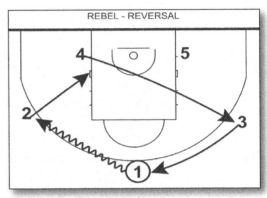

Diagram 19

In Diagram 20, Player 1 passes the ball to 3 who relays it to 4. On the pass to Player 4, 1 drifts to the corner and 5 sets an **Interior** (cross screen low) for 2. As Player 2 comes off the pick, 5 seals on the defender and shows back to the ball. The options for Player 4 are to hit 2 early or late, send it low to 5 in the block or pass to 1 cutting to the **weak side diagonal angle,** since that defender is usually occupied helping the screening action by 5. Player 1 may have a shot or be able to slip the ball low to 5 as well.

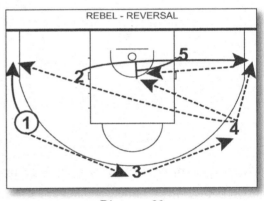

Diagram 20

Diagrams 21 and 22 show the **Rebel Flop option**. In Diagram 21, Player 1 dribbles at 2, pushing him down to the block, while he drags the top defender below the free throw line. Player 3 fill cuts for 1 to the point and 4 fill cuts up diagonally to the high wing area to replace 3. Player 2 takes a step toward 5, but then **"flops"** his cut back to the strong side corner, as 5 cuts for a paint catch or a spot above the block.

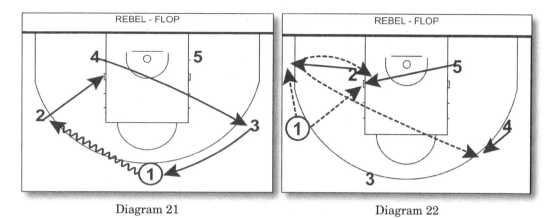

Diagram 21   Diagram 22

In Diagram 22, Player 1 may pass to 2 in the corner, who may be open for a shot, or may pass directly inside to 5 on his seal. Player 2 may also pass to 4 stepping up to the weak side high elbow area, or he can reverse the ball to go to other options or free lance the next cuts.

Rebel Pull: Pull action comes on the second side. See Diagrams 23 and 24. Again, Player 1 dribbles at 2 pulling the top of the zone down as 2 cuts to the ball side block. Player 3 fill cuts to the point for 1 and 4 fill-cuts to the weak side wing for 3 (Diagram 23).

In Diagram 24, Player 1 passes to 3 and fades to the corner. Player 3 relays the ball to 4 on the weak side wing. Player 5 pulls to the short corner and 2 flashes high then dives to the basket on a pass to 5. Player 4 may pass to 5 pulling who may shoot or pass to 2 diving. Post 4 may also pass fake to Player 5 and hit 2 diving. Finally, Player 4 may skip-pass to 1 in the weak side corner.

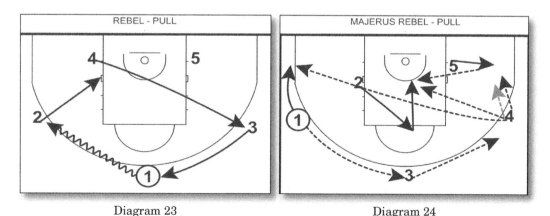

Diagram 23   Diagram 24

Rebel with an "In" to an "Away": This action sets up **Interior** and **Pull** actions on the second side. See Diagrams 25, 26, 27 and 28. In Diagram 25, Player 1 passes to 3 and runs an "In Cut" to the ball side corner. Player 2 fill cuts to the point for 1. (Diagram 25)

In Diagram 26, Player 3 passes to 2 at the top and runs an **"Away"** flat cut, meaning a cut to the weak side. Player 1 comes back to the wing to fill cut for 3, while 2 pass fakes at 3, then reverses the ball back to 1. These apparently meaningless actions cause the defense to adjust a bit to cover the corner and gets the defense moving to set up the **next move.**

Diagram 27 shows Player 1's passing options as 5 sets an **Interior** pick on 4, so 1 can pass to 4 on the low post, to 5 on the step back after his **Interior** pick, or make the skip pass to the diagonal man 3. Of course, he can always swing it back to Player 2 at the top.

Diagram 28 illustrates the **Pull** call to a high/low action, after the first Rebel cuts have been made as in Diagram 26. Wing 2 now at the top pass fakes at 3 like he did in the Interior play and passes back to 1.

Instead of setting the Interior, Player 5 **Pulls** to the short corner and 4 flashes to the middle for a paint catch or goes on up to the high post.

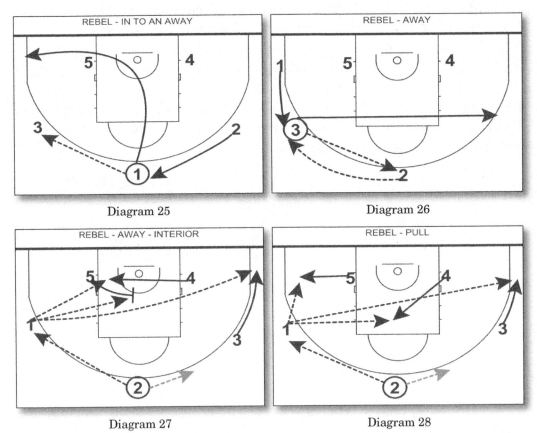

Diagram 25   Diagram 26

Diagram 27   Diagram 28

Player 1 may pass to 5 in the short corner or to 4 on his flash for high/low action, or he may make a skip pass to 3 at the weak side diagonal. Each of these adjustments causes the defense to react a bit differently, yet the offense is working on simple adjustments that are well-rehearsed on their part.

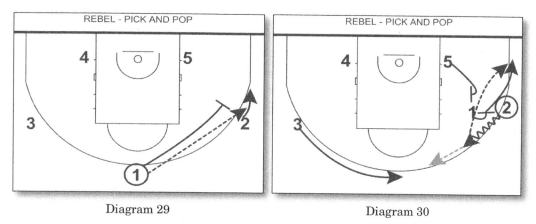

Diagram 29   Diagram 30

"Rebel - Pick and Pop" option. Diagrams 29 and 30 show a play Rick liked for a **last second shot against a zone or man-to-man defense.** Player 1 passes to 2 and then follows his pass and screens for 2 (Diagram 29).

In Diagram 30, Player 2 dribbles high off 1's screen and pass fakes at 3, who is fill cutting to the point setting up the counter-flow (misdirection) action. Post 5 cuts up and sets a screen on Player 1's man on the baseline side, whether there was a switch or not. Player 1 pops to the corner off 5's screen and 2 pivots to hit 1 for the 3-point shot in the corner. Post 5 dives to the goal.

The Yankee and Rebel Series are genius in their simplicity in that they force the zones to make an adjustment at the start of each play, and then the actions that follow the Yankee or Rebel initial entry can be adjusted to become different plays that require the defense to make a decision on adjustments, depending on the play that is called.

Rick also had many other plays that he used at will over the years. We cannot include all by any means, but we want to share some favorites in the following pages, keeping in line with our intent to show a lot of different play calls against zones that coaches may select from according to their personnel or personal likes.

This is a selection of plays only, chosen from many more that we do not have space for in this book. In fact, Rick was such a student of the game that he kept things he picked up from coaches in restaurants and many of these he would keep on napkins or transfer to legal pages.

If he really liked the play or concept, it would be a part of what he would talk about the next time he was doodling with a coach at the next restaurant. But they were in his repertoire, no matter what, and between the two of us, we had a lot of them on paper as well. Had he lived to coach another 10 years, he might have gotten to use most of them. We think you will appreciate this addition.

SOME OF RICK'S FAVORITE ZONE PLAYS

Rick was able to integrate his principles of play into some simple but effective plays to attack zones. The first set of zone attacks, along with Stacks and Rebel are effective against 2-3 or 1-1-3 zones.

1. Double Back from Yankee Series: see Diagram 31

- He always wanted the shot going to Player 2 or 3 on this.
- Run "Yankee" then yell "Double Back."

In Diagram 31, Player 1 dribbles at 3 who runs a Yankee flat cut to the weak side and 2 fill cuts to the point for 1. Then Player 1 skip-passes to 3 to complete the "Yankee" starting action.

In Diagram 32, Player 5 screens in on the bottom defender of the zone while 1 screens in on the top of the zone. Player 2 jukes down a step to set up and cuts from the point to the weak side behind the screens. Player 3 skip-passes to 2. In addition Player 1 can pop, 5 can slip.

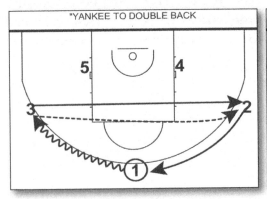

Diagram 31

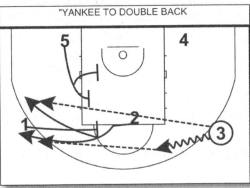

Diagram 32

2. Triple Replacement (Diagram 33)

- Usually can get the skip-pass option.
- Effective versus Match-up or 1-1-3 Match-up.

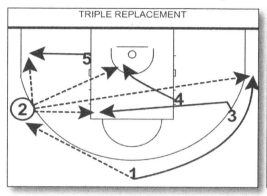 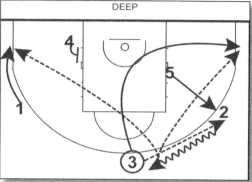

Diagram 33   Diagram 34

1. Player 1 passes to 2 and cuts to the weak side diagonal spot from the ball.

2. Player 3 runs a Jordan Cut, as Rick labeled it

3. Player 2 lateral Dribbles Up a bounce or two (not shown) and pulls 5 on the baseline to the corner.

4. Player 4 dives to the rim.

5. Player 2 may pass to 5, 4, 3 or 1.

3. Deep (Diagram 34)

1. Player 3 passes to 2 and cuts **inside** to the ball side corner — the In cut move.

2. Player 2 dribbles to the point as 5 steps out to replace 2 on the perimeter.

3. Player 4 screens the backside of the zone and 1 drifts behind the screen.

4. Player 2 may pass to 1, 5 (not shown) or 3.

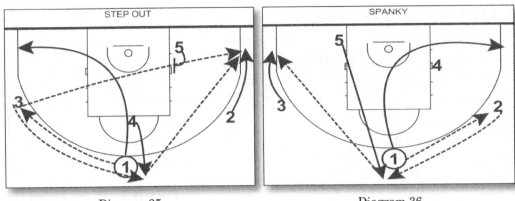

Diagram 35   Diagram 36

4. Step Out (Diagram 35)

1. Player 1 passes to 3 and inside cuts to the ball side corner on an IN, as 4 steps out to replace 1.
2. Player 5 screens in and 2 drifts behind the screen in the corner.
3. Player 3 may skip pass to 2, pass to 4 to relay to 2 or work high/low.

5. Spanky (Diagram 36)

1. Player 1 passes to 2 and in cuts to the ball side corner.
2. Player 5 flashes high to replace 1 and 3 drops to the corner.
3. Player 5 passes to 3 in the open corner, or to 4 posting up or to 1.

Deployment (Alignments): Stack Options

6. Split Stacks (Diagrams 37 and 38)

1. Players 2 and 4 (best shooters) are on the bottom of the stacks. They break out and Player 1 passes to 3 (Diagram 37).
2. Player 2 catches from 3 slightly above the foul line extended, to draw the zone farther out and to extend it (Diagram 38).
3. When Player 2 catches he looks to shot fake, gap dribble right or left, or make a "Quick pass" to Player 4 or 5 (Diagram 38).

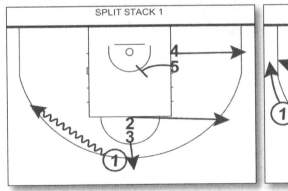

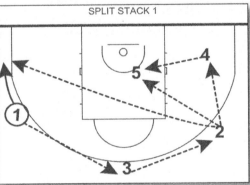

Diagram 37   Diagram 38

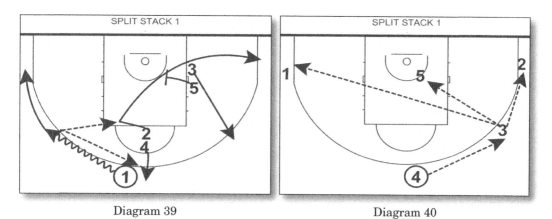

Diagram 39   Diagram 40

"Stacks Big," pop your best big out for a shot (Diagrams 39-40)

In Diagram 39:

1. Player 1 dribbles to the left high elbow area.
2. Player 4 pops to the point as 2 cuts toward 1 then breaks it off to cut off 5's screen to the weak side corner.
3. Player 3 pops to the high wing on the right side.
4. Player 1 passes to 4 and then spaces away.

In Diagram 40:

5. Player 4 passes to 3 who may pass to 2, or 5 sealing in the middle, or he may skip pass to 1.

Stack Interior play (Diagrams 41-42)

1. Player 1 drags his man below the free throw line extended while 4 pops to the point and 3 pops to the weak side wing. Player 2 drops to the strong side block.

In Diagram 42:

1. Player 1 passes to 4 and spaces to a diagonal angle from 3.

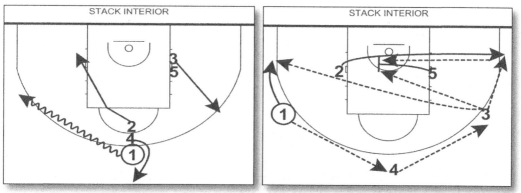

Diagram 41   Diagram 42

2. Player 4 Reverses the ball to 3 and,

3. Player 5 screens the middle of the zone, and 2 cuts to the corner off of 5's screen.

4. Player 3 may pass to 5 sealing, to 2 for a shot or a feed to 5, or he may skip pass to 1.

7. Baseline Runner (Diagrams 43-44)
   Effective against odd front zones: 1-2-2, 3-2, and 1-3-1.

Baseline Runner (Diagram 43)

1. Players 1 and 3 play off each other off the lane line extended. (High Elbows)

2. Player 2 (best shooter) runs off 4 and 5 along the baseline.

3. Players 4 and 5 screen the bottom of the zone and look to step up on their screens for a possible catch, as 2 cuts off of their picks. They are set to rebound.

Baseline Runner – Back Out (Diagram 44)

1. Player 1 drags the ball a freeze bounce toward 3 and is reading 2. If he cuts back off of Player 5's pick before 1 passes to 3, he can pivot and pass to 2, but the normal play is to pass to 3.

2. Player 3 reads 2 to see if he comes all the way off of 4 or if he cuts back off of 5. In that case Player 3 would throw the ball quickly back to 1 who can feed 2 or 5 on the step up.

3. If Player 2 continues on through to the weak side, 3 can pass to 2 on his cut, to 5 sealing or to 4 stepping up off his screen. Or, Player 3 may swing to 1 for weak side action.

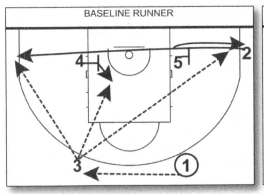

Diagram 43

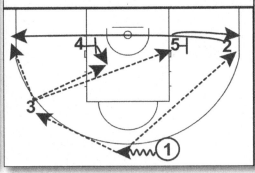

Diagram 44

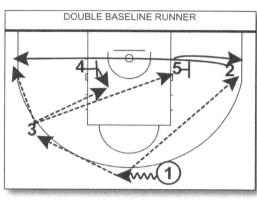

Diagram 45   Diagram 46

Double Baseline Runner (Diagram 45, 46 and 47)

In Diagram 45:

1. Player 1 drags a freeze bounce and passes to 3, or may read to pass to 2 on a duck back.

2. Player 4 screens in and 5 screens out and both seal and step to the ball after they screen and look for the ball.

3. Player 2 cuts off 5, then off 4's screen to the strong side corner.

4. Player 3 may pass to 2, to 5 or to 4. In the diagram, he passes to Player 2 for a possible shot of a feed to 4.

In Diagram 46:

1. Player 2 had no play so he passes back to 3 and cuts back off 4 and 5 who screen again,

2. Player 3 may have to take a couple quick dribbles to improve his angle and shorten his pass to 1.

3. Player 1 may pass to 4 or 5 on step ups or pass to 2 coming off 5 for a 3-point shot.

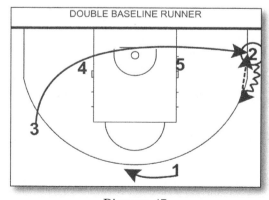

Diagram 47

In Diagram 47:

1. Player 2 had no shot so he dribbles up to keep the bottom defender on him. As he starts, Player 3 sprint cuts to the ball side corner off of 4 and 5.

2. Player 2 passes to 3 in the corner for a shot.

Diagram 48:

   1. The continuity can continue if Player 2 passes back to 1 and 3 sprint cuts back to the wing off 4 and 5, and 2 follows to the corner. Lots of action.

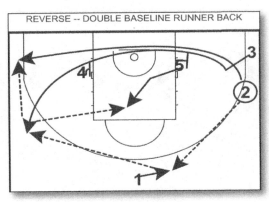

Diagram 48

8. Weber: This action was designed to be used against **Extended and Trapping zones. Spacing is Vital!** (Diagrams 49-54)

In Diagram 49:

   1. Player 1 dribbles down in transition and,

   2. Player 3 makes a hard loop cut to the weak side high elbow area.

   3. Player 5 loops to the ball side block and,

   4. Player 4 fill cuts for 3.

In Diagram 50:

   1. Player 1 passes to 3 who reverses the ball to 2.

   2. Post 5 busts across the lane and Player 4 flashes to the ball side elbow.

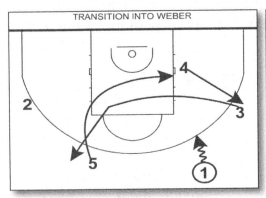

Diagram 49

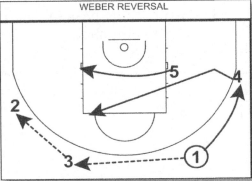

Diagram 50

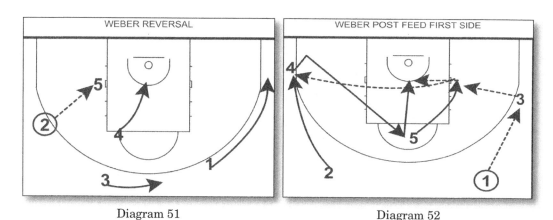

Diagram 51   Diagram 52

In Diagram 51:

1. Player 1 Spaced to a weak side diagonal on the pass to 2.
2. Player 2 passes to 5 in the post, if possible.
3. Player 4 dives to the rim, and 3 spaces to the weak side high elbow area.

In Diagram 52: A different pass option when the ball comes down the court.

1. Player 1 comes down the floor only this time 5 moves into the high post instead of hanging back in the swing spot as he did in Diagram 49.
2. Player 4 runs to the weak side corner, instead to running to the strong side block.
3. Ball handler 1 enters the ball to 3. Player 2 cuts to the weak side diagonal from the ball.
4. Post 5 cuts to the ball side low post.
5. Player 4 makes a hard slash cut into the high post.
6. Player 3 passes the ball to 5, if possible, and 4 dives to the basket.
7. Player 5 may pass to 4 on the dive or skip pass to 2 on the weak side.

If there were no easy options into the post or out of it, the ball would be reversed to Player 4 and they can finish with high/low action until they get the shot they want.

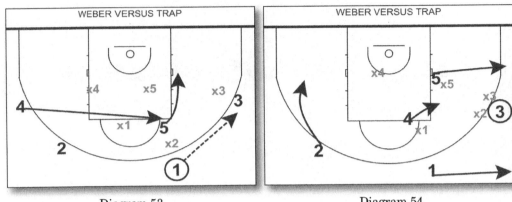

Diagram 53   Diagram 54

In Diagram 53: action vs. wing trap.

1. Player 1 passes to 3 on the ball side wing.
2. Player 5 dives to the ball side block and 4 flashes into the ball side elbow.
3. Player 2 cuts away to a diagonal on the weak side.

In Diagram 54:

1. X2 and X3 trap 3 on the wing.
2. Player 1 cuts to the wide wing above the trap in the "crack-back" position for a safe outlet angle.
3. Player 4 flashes to the middle position while 5 flashes to a wide spot up the court from the trap
4. Player 2 cuts to the weak side diagonal as a potential cross court pass outlet.

—————————— CHAPTER 12 ——————————

NCAA AND EURO ZONE ATTACKS

We want to include contributions that some of the top coaches in the world who are NCAA coaches sent when we asked if they would contribute a play they have used against zones as part of the tribute to Coach Majerus. Obviously, these are isolated plays and are not meant to indicate the overall theory, philosophy or strategy of these great coaches. In addition both of us would like to honor the contributions that international coaches are making to the overall knowledge of the game. Del started coaching FIBA basketball in the 1960s while Ken was still playing. Ken began coaching in the 1970s and we both have witnessed the incredible growth of the sport in the coaches and players worldwide.

At that time, there were just a few pockets where good basketball was being taught and played. Countries like the Soviet Union, Italy, the Slavic countries, Spain and Brazil along with tiny Puerto Rico and Israel were at the forefront early on. There was a great hunger among coaches and players to learn more. As a result, they read all the literature they could find that was coming out of the U.S. in terms of books and magazines such as *Athletic Journal, Scholastic Coach, The Converse Yearbook* and others. In addition many came over to the U.S. to spend some time at the practices of American coaches particularly at the college level.

There were many college and NBA coaches who went to basketball camps and clinics in the various foreign countries to spread the word, particularly to outstanding ones in Italy. American coaches also went to foreign countries to coach in the leagues and even the national teams. Most notably Dan Peterson became a pioneer in that regard in Italy with his clinics, camps and his coaching of the top teams there. Over the years many nations around the world have developed excellent coaches, players and teams. The impact on the NBA has been phenomenal in affecting the style of play, the work ethic necessary to compete and in terms of talent. By the middle of the second decade of this century, over 20 percent of the NBA players each year are men born in nations or territories apart from the continental United States, representing about 40 different countries or entities. As recently as 1975 that would have been deemed to be unthinkable. As recently as 1987, Del's Bucks team beat Russia severely in the first McDonald's International Tournament, leading by as many as 50 points at one time with a pre-season camp lineup. Such has been the growth of basketball worldwide.

First, we will present a few of the plays that coaches sent to us at our request and then add some actions of other top coaches that we have gleaned from seeing their teams play. There may be nuances to these plays that we will not denote, but will include the major aspects. Of those who sent us plays, we will present them in alphabetical order by the coaches' names out of respect to all of these great coaches. Following that we will show some of the strategies of a sampling of world-class FIBA coaches we have coached against.

Steve Alford is the coach of UCLA, who has had a great run in coaching at the University of New Mexico, the University of Iowa, SW Missouri State and Manchester College. His teams have won the conference tournament at each of these stops. His teams have qualified for post-season play in 15 of the last 17 years.

UCLA Stack Play vs. Zone

Diagram 1:

1. The team lines up in a tight high stack at the top and a loose stack with the posts 4 and 5 low.
2. Point 1 drag dribbles to the open wing, keying the pop out move of 3 cutting to the top.
3. Player 2 splits to the weak side wing as 3 comes off of him and 1 swings the ball quickly to 3.

Diagram 2:

1. Player 1 swings the ball to 3 and 2 drops to the corner, hoping to draw the baseline defender off of player 4.
2. At the same time post 5 puts a hard screen on X5 and Player 4 slides to the goal looking for a high pass from 3.
3. If there is no play, Player 3 can drag the dribble down a bit toward the wing and play can continue in a high'/low action as 5 steps up into the high post area.

UCLA Stack Variation

Diagram 3:

1. The team lines up with Player 3 in the high post and this time 2 lines up in the short corner opposite a tight stack on the right side of the basket.
2. Player 1 dribble drags the ball to the open wing.
3. Player 3 pops hard to the top to catch.

Diagram 4:

1. As the ball is passed to Player 3, 5 breaks up to set a pick on X2 and 2 starts on his way under the goal.
2. Player 4 immediately cuts off of 5's cut and sets a pick on X4.
3. If the timing is right Player 3 will be coming off of 5's pick as 2 clears under 4's pick on X4.
4. Player 1 must rotate back for safety and to be at a diagonal pass angle from 3.

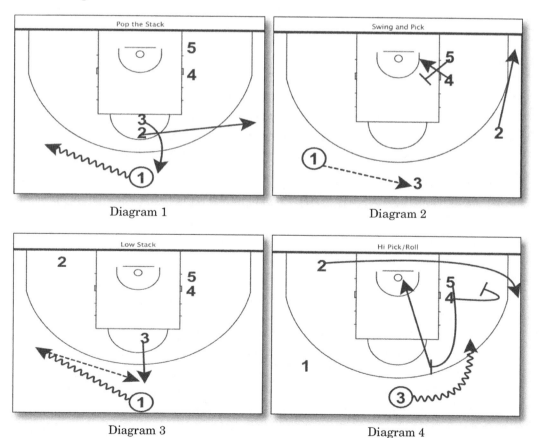

Diagram 1

Diagram 2

Diagram 3

Diagram 4

John Calipari is the Hall of Fame Coach who has won an NCAA Championship at the University of Kentucky and has led all three of his assignments, including also UMass and the University of Memphis, to the Final Four. He has stocked the NBA with multiple high draft picks since 2000. He also led the Dominican Republic National teams to a gold, a bronze and a fourth place finish in international FIBA competition in directing them to their strongest finishes in Dominicana's history.

Here is a simple move that was effective for him with the record-setting 38-win Final Four team he coached at UK in 2014-15. In Diagram 5, the team lines up in a 1-3-1 or in a 1-2-2 that cuts to the 1-3-1 with their best low post player generally in the low post.

Diagram 5:

1. Point man 1 initiates by dribbling at wing 2, who loops over him to the top replacing 1.

2. As Player 1 is dribbling to the wing, 3 cuts hard from the weak wing to the strong side corner.

3. Post 5 seals off his defender as Player 3 cuts past him. If Player 3 is open for a shot, he takes it, but the play is mainly to get the ball to the low post to 5 from 3 or from 1.

Diagram 6:

1. If there is no play, Player 3 or 1 reverses the ball and cuts back to the weak side as 4 drops down to set a pick for 3 to rub off of.

2. Player 1 reverses the ball on to 2, who drags it a bounce or two and can send the ball on to 3 or feed directly to 4 in the low post, or even to 5 breaking up to the high elbow.

3. Ultimately, Player 5 can run at 2 and set a pick and roll, as 1 is spaced out in front, with 4 rolling up behind 5 and 3 coming up from the corner of a snap back pass from 2.

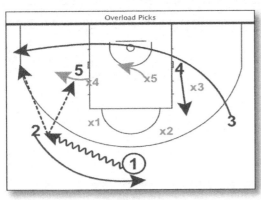

Diagram 5

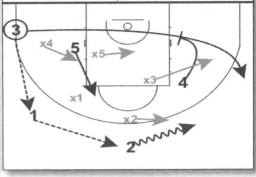

Diagram 6

Variation on the same play.

Diagram 7:

1. Point 1 dribbles at the wing to Player 2 and this time he cuts away to the weak side instead of looping up behind 1.

2. As he gets to the high wing area between the top and the flat wing area at the foul line extended, Player 4 runs at him for a pick and roll.

3. Players 2 and 3 are spaced in front of the pick-and-roll action. If Player 4 is a shooter, he can pop for a 3-pointer or a 17-foot shot. If Player 4 is a shooter, 5 relocates to the weak side for a post up pass from 1 or one of the players spaced in front, or for rebound position in the event 4 shoots.

Diagram 8: option if 4 is <u>not</u> an outside shooter.

1. On the dribble over when Player 2 clears on through, if 5 is not already on the strong side block, he should move across to the strong side post so he can curl up behind 4 on his roll as shown.

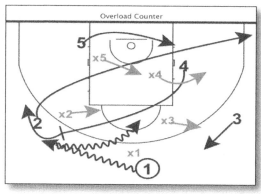

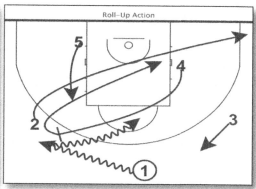

Diagram 7   Diagram 8

Mike Krzyzewski is a Hall of Fame coach at Duke University, who has been the most winning Division I coach of his era, as well as the coach of the USA Olympic Team, having won four national titles in one and four gold medals in the other. Every coach is familiar with his biography as he has crossed the 1,000-win mark and sent so many players to the NBA.

The diagrams following describe a play he calls, **"Wide."** The team lines up in a 1-2-2 vs. a 2-3 set.

Diagram 9: The players line up in the gaps in the 2-3.

1. Point 1 passes to Player 2 and drifts away to a shooting spot in the high wing, pushing 3 to the corner.
2. Post 4 runs from weak side to set the pick and roll for Player 2 with shooters 1 and 3 in front.
3. Player 4 pops for a shot or 2 advances the ball to 1, as 5 flashes to the low post for a triangle attack.
4. Generally you will be able to attack 3-on-2 on the weak side. Both the Duke and USA teams have used this set with great success against the 2-3 and even the 1-2-2 - simple and effective when executed well. (Diagram 10)

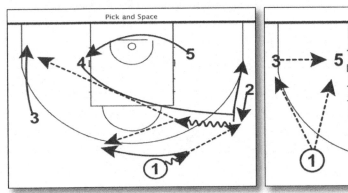

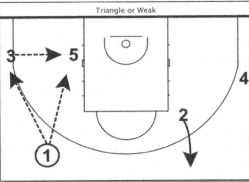

Diagram 9   Diagram 10

Sean Miller is regarded as one of America's elite coaches. At Xavier, Ohio and the University of Arizona, he has coached teams to six Sweet Sixteen and four Elite Eight appearances in the NCAA's March Madness. He was conference Coach of the Year three times and is now head coach of the USA U-19 National Team.

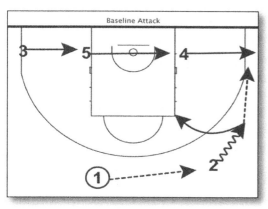

Diagram 11

Diagrams 11-13:

1. Attacking the baseline, point 1 swings ball to Player 2 as the front line shifts to the ball side and 2 dribbles down to stretch the defense. He delivers to Player 4 in the corner and cuts to the elbow (Diagram 11).

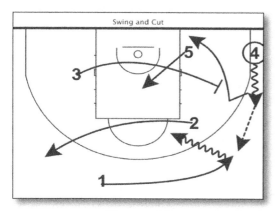

Diagram 12

2. Player 4 dribble pulls up and passes to 1, filling for 2. On the dribble move, Player 2 cuts to the weak wing and 3 starts his cut to pick the passer, Player 4. Point 1 dribbles to the middle to freeze the defense and has options for the lob to Player 4 first (Diagram 12).

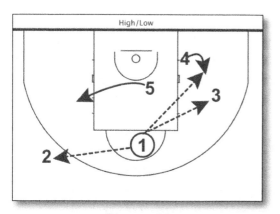

Diagram 13

3. If the lob is not there, he can pass to either wing for a shot with the board covered or for one of them to pass inside to Player 5 or 4 posted up (Diagram 13).

Diagrams 14 to 16 display an X-cutting action combined with pin-in screens for a possible 3 that can be run to either side, depending on whether the shot is for player 1 or 2. It can roll right into a high/low game as well.

1. If the shot is for Player 1, he gets the defense to shift on the pass to 4. Players 5 and 3 X-cut to the high/low spots. Wing 4 gives a look. Players 1 and 2 could even rotate if shot is for Player 2 (Diagram 14).

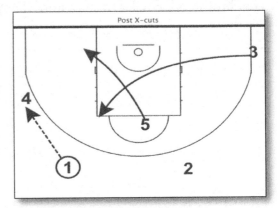

Diagram 14

2. The ball is reversed to Player 1 and then to 2 to get the defense to shift back. Player 3 cuts middle and 2 gives a look and a pass fake, as 5 and 4 seek to pin in the weak side high and low defenders (Diagram 15).

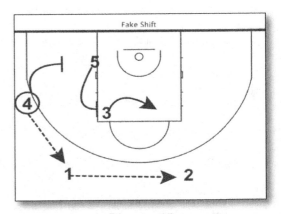

Diagram 15

3. Player 2 dribbles at the top defender as 1 drifts behind the screens for a look at a 3-point shot.

   a. If there is no shot, Player 3 will free up on the weak side high and can look for a high/low game (Diagram 16).

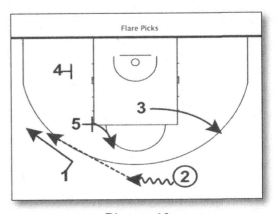

Diagram 16

Lorenzo Romar is a former NBA player who has had great success at his college alma mater, the University of Washington, as well as at Pepperdine and St. Louis University. He revived the UW program and has had nine post-season qualifiers with three Sweet Sixteen appearances and has been Coach of the Year Twice in the PAC 10/12.

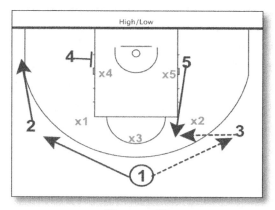

Diagram 17

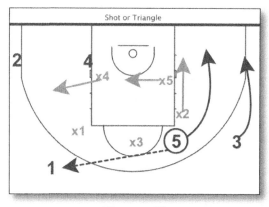

Diagram 18

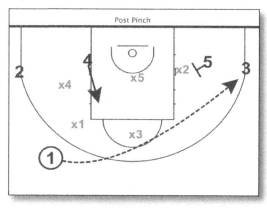

Diagram 19

Diagram 17:
1. The team lines up in a 1-2-2 offense. Point 1 passes to wing 3 and he and Player 2 slide away one slot, as 5 breaks up from the strong side low post to the high elbow area for a catch from 3.

Diagram 18:
1. Player 5 swings the ball to 1, and 4 pinches in on the low post as the ball is sent on down to 2 for a possible shot or feed to 4.
2. Player 5 dives to the weak side block for rebounding and to screen off the defender to help free up 3 in the weak side corner for a possible lob pass.

Diagram 19:
1. If Player 1 cannot make a play to 2 or 4, he fakes a pass there and looks for 3 in the corner, as 5 is hoping to screen off the defender who is sagging in with the ball on the opposite side.
2. If no quick pass to Player 3, 4 and 5 will move up to present themselves high and low. Player 5 can set a pick and roll if no easy play.

Bo Ryan has coached levels from Jr. High to the Final Four in his career and won every place in between. His teams won four NCAA D-III National Championships and he has won seven Big 10 championships in 14 years and made it to the Final Four in 2014 and the Final Two in 2015.

Much like what we are advocating in this book, Bo has invested in a basic motion type offense that has **continuity of action** with foci on **spacing and aggressive high/low action.** He emphasizes the strategic use of **shot and pass fakes** with good ball and player movement and backs up this strategy with special **set plays** to get the ball to certain players or positions on the court he calls "soft spots." We are going to include the first two sides of his continuity set and one special play here.

Diagram 20

1. Player 1 Dribble Rotates to the wing, pushing 3 down to flatten the defense. Player 3 can choose to go to the corner, short corner or even post if 5 flashes up us he does in this diagram. However Player 5 may stay in the low post, in which case 4 would not go to the low post on the weak side, but will always work opposite of 5.

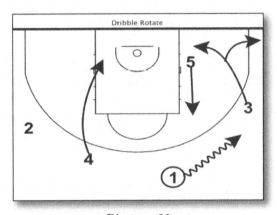

Diagram 20

Diagram 21:

1. Player 4 cuts to the post to overload the side and they can work the various triangles formed by 1-3-4 and 1-5-4, while Player 2 reads for the best openings on the weak side.

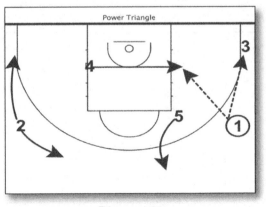

Diagram 21

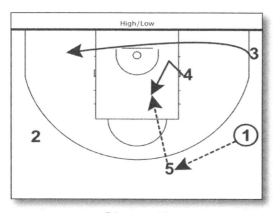

Diagram 22

Diagram 22:

1. If there is no easy play the ball is swung to the top to Player 5 for the high/low action as 3 cuts the baseline and 4 seals up down low. Player 3 will seek open spots on his move toward the corner, as there are sometimes gaps for easy passes from 5 or 2 on the wing.

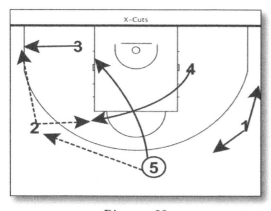

Diagram 23

Diagram 23:

1. After passing the ball on to Player 2, 3 may be open quickly in the short corner or the dead corner and 5 dives to the low block area. Player 4 flashes to the high post area on the X-cut with 5.

2. Again, the offense is in an overload and Player 1 is working the weak side for openings. The double triangle options are now the same on this side as were on the right.

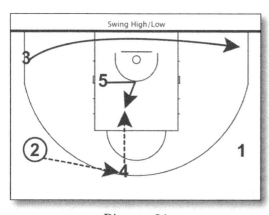

Diagram 24

Diagram 24:

1. If there is no easy play, Player 4 pops up to the top swing spot and the high/low action is in play again, as 3 runs the same cut and read action as before.

2. In the process there may be penetrating or screening options that can be utilized, but this is the basic movement.

Special set vs. 1-3-1

Diagram 25:

    1. Player 1 dribble rotates to the wing, pushing 3 down to flatten the zone to a 2-3. Player 2 cuts to the top for a swing pass option and 5 flashes up to the high post as the ball is passed from Player 1 to 2.

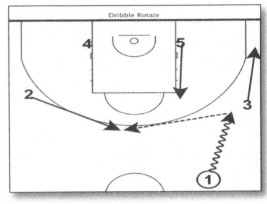

Diagram 25

Diagram 26:

    1. Player 2 passes back to 1 and stretches to the weak side wing. Player 4 cuts across the lane under the zone to complete the overload as the ball is passed to 3, who has the various passing options to 4, 5, 2 on the diagonal, or he can reverse it back to 1.

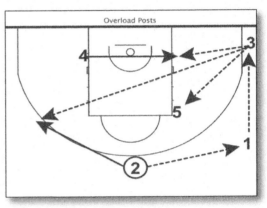

Diagram 26

Diagram 27:

    1. If there are no easy options, Player 3 reverses to 1 and 5 sets a pick for him. He may have a shot, or can pass ahead to 2 spotted up, or he may have 5 on a dive to the rim. Again, Player 3 may be open in the corner. Player 1 can continue to the corner and players 4 and 5 are set up for high low with 3 stretching the defense on the weak side.

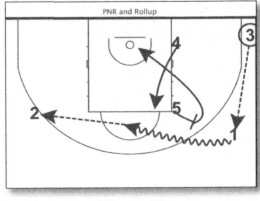

Diagram 27

Bill Self has had an incredible run of success at Oral Roberts, Tulsa, Illinois and Kansas in making it to the NCAA tournament 17 consecutive years, including 10 Sweet Sixteens, seven Elite Eights, a runner-up and one National Championship. His Jayhawks have won the tough Big 12 Conference an unprecedented 11 years in a row.

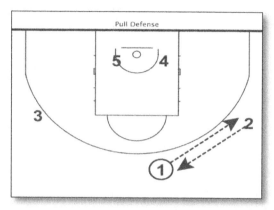

Diagram 28

From a 1-2-2 Set:

Diagram 28:

1. Point 1 passes to 2 and gets it back, pulling a defender to 2.

Diagram 29:

1. Point 1 dribble rotates down a slot, pushing Player 2 to the corner to flatten out the defense to a 2-3. Wing 3 rotates up to the guard slot directly above the lane line extended. At the same time Player 4 cuts to form a stack with 5, putting the better shooter of the two on the bottom of the stack.

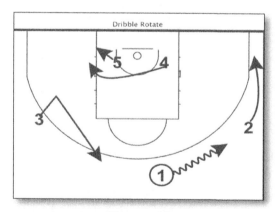

Diagram 29

Diagram 30:

1. Player 1 reverses the ball to 3 and 2 cuts hard on the baseline on the catch.

2. When Player 2 clears the stack, 4 screens the next man in the zone and 5 finds the open area in the middle.

3. Possible shot for Player 5 in the middle on high/low action or possible shot for 2. Obviously, the ball can be moved to Player 1 and any of various options can follow such as a penetration, a pick and roll or a second cut on the baseline by 2 as well as basic high/low play.

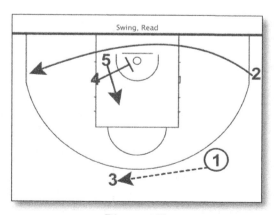

Diagram 30

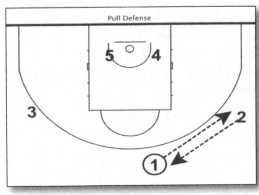

Diagram 31

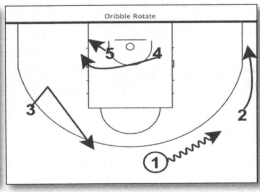

Diagram 32

Possible Lob Option play

Diagram 31:

1. To stir the defense and to make it easier to flatten the defense, Player 1 passes to 2 and gets it back.

Diagram 32:

1. Player 1 Dribble Rotates 2 down to the corner, as 3 fills behind him to the guard spot above the foul line extended and 4 cuts over the lane to form a stack with 5.

Diagram 33:

1. Player 1 swings the ball to 3 across the top and Player 2 runs the baseline on the catch.

Diagram 34:

1. Player 3 looks at 2 and may hit him if open, but will pass fake and throw to 1, if he is not. As the ball is thrown to Player 1, 5 sets a hard pick on the nearest defender and 1 looks to throw the high pass to 4 at the rim. If there is no play, they can finish off the set as noted in the previous play.

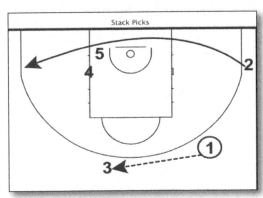

Diagram 33

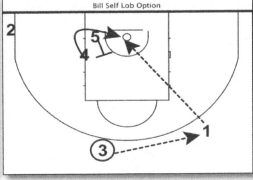

Diagram 34

A SELECTION OF PLAYS
FROM FIBA COACHES

As noted in the beginning of this chapter we both have been involved with FIBA basketball touching on six decades, beginning in the 1960's. As such, we have seen it grow from what one might call elementary school to graduate work. That is to say that there was no reason to scout Europe or South America for players in the beginning. But due to the passion for learning on the part of the world coaching community and the willingness of the athletes to commit to hard work and extended practices, the abilities of the coaches and athletes increased steadily. Italy and the Soviet Union were places that incubated a good bit of the early growth, but gradually the game became significant factors in Spain, what was Yugoslavia, Greece, Brazil and the smaller countries in Europe, South and Central America.

While many coaches in the United States thought they had a lock on the technical aspects of the game and often slacked off from seeking to progress once they had settled in on a comfortable spot in their coaching. Comments like, "it's a simple game," or "very little changes," were common phrases. At the same time international coaches were inviting top American coaches to come to participate in clinics and camps to help them learn. They read all the literature on the game they could find. Teams and players began to develop and the best performers began to show up on NBA rosters.

By 1991 there were already over 20 players in the NBA who were regarded as international players. In 1992 the US Dream Team helped promote basketball even further, along with the phenomenon of satellite television that has ultimately beamed NBA hoops to over 250 countries. Seeing these games around the world brought virtual clinics to every kid around the world who could get to a TV. When the NBA season opened up for the 2014-15 season, slightly over 100 of the NBA players were classified as international. San Antonio, the flagship franchise at the time for the NBA, had 10 such players out of 15 on their opening night roster.

With total respect we include some plays that some of the coaches we have coached against use, and there are many other great FIBA coaches that certainly qualify to be listed with top coaches in the world at this time.

A European Match-up Attack

Zeljko Obradovic is one of the most highly regarded European coaches. He has won eight European Cup titles with four different teams, and has coached five different Euro countries in the their top leagues with great success. In addition he led his home country to the World Championships of 1998. A method of attacking the match-up zone by Obradovic involves the high middle pick and roll. European position 4 players are, almost without exception, 3-point shooters. While they sometimes run the familiar "roll and replace" in their high pick and rolls, they routinely "pop" their 4 men out and thereby make the defense guard more space on the perimeter. This gives their ball handler and the picker more open room in the middle to operate.

Diagram 35:
1. Player 1 passes to 3 and cuts to the short corner.
2. Player 5 screens for 2 who cuts to the point.

Diagram 36:
1. Player 5 cuts in and seals X2 on his back.
2. Player 3 passes to 1 in the short corner forcing X5 to guard him, unless X1 bumped X3 down, in which case Player 1 can clear to the weak side corner and 5 would get open at the elbow between X1 and X2 for a shot or to make a play to 1 or 4 on the weak side who are 2 on 1 vs. X4.
3. On the pass down to Player 1, if X5 pulls to cover 1, post man 5 dives to the rim and 4 fill cuts up behind him. Player 1 hits 5 on the cut or 4 on the diagonal.

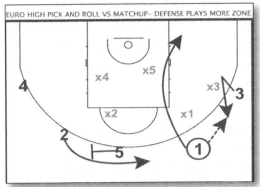

Diagram 35   Diagram 36

Note: The same set is used against a man defense as well as a zone. This is particularly good to use against teams that are changing up defenses on any of various keys during the game. In the play in Diagrams 35-36, if the point guard sees the defense is in a man-to-man this possession, he can pass to Player 3 and run to the weak side corner. As Player 2 comes off of 5's pick, 3 passes him the ball and 5 immediately turns and sets the pick and roll on 2. They then have various choices relative to the reading of the defense, an excellent option to have.

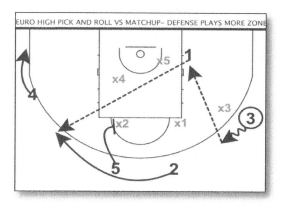

Diagram 37

Diagram 37 - **option**

1. This time Player 5 chooses the option of pin-screening X2 in when 3 passes to 1.

2. Player 2 cuts behind 5's screen and 4 drifts towards the baseline. Player 1 passes to Player 2.

3. If X2 battles to get to Player 2, 5 may be open on a slip cut or a pop at the foul line.

Before **Dave Blatt** became coach of the Cleveland Cavaliers, he had many years with great success as a coach in Europe with various teams in Israel, Turkey, Italy and particularly in Russia where he became the national coach and led them to a bronze medal in the 2012 London Olympics.

Diagram 38: The team lines up in a high double post with the corners filled.

1. Player 1 passes to 4 as he pops up to the 3-point spot above the elbow and cuts to the basket and hesitates there as 3 is cutting through the lane from the corner.

2. Player 4 reads X3's reaction and if he goes deep with 3 on the cut, he can be open in the corner vacated by 3. Otherwise, he will pull X3 off of Player 3 and that will free up 3 in the weak side corner.

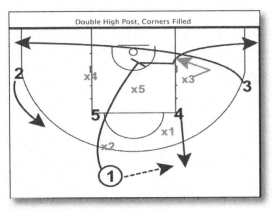

Diagram 38

Diagram 39:

1. Post man 4 reads X3 and knows he will have Player 1 open in the corner if X3 roves with 3. If X3 releases Player 3 and comes back to defend 1, 4 reverses the ball to 2, who has moved up to make room in the corner for Player 3.

2. Player 2 and 3 may have X4 in a bad situation, unless X2 is able to release X4 from 2 in time.

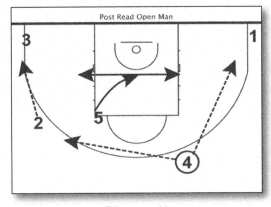

Diagram 39

3. Player 5 reads the defense as well. If X2 leaves his area to defend 2, he is open at the high elbow. Otherwise, he will cut into the low post area as the ball is thrown to either corner and will post up low.

Sergio Hernandez is a Spaniard by birth and established himself as one of the top international coaches as the national coach of Argentina from 2005-10. He continued the great success that had been established by Coach Ruben Magnano.

Diagram 40:

1. Out of a 1-3-1, Player 1 passes to wing 3, who passes the ball down to 4 who had lined up in a wide low post position and popped to the corner. High post 5 rolls down, looking for a catch in the low post.

2. Player 3 clears across under the foul line to the weak side wing after passing to 4. Player 1 fill cuts for 3 and wing 2 moves to a position in the guard slot above the elbow area behind the 3-point line.

Diagram 41:

1. Player 4 reverses the ball to 1, if he has no play and cuts hard on the baseline to the opposite corner.

2. The ball is reversed on to Player 2 and 3, as 4 cuts to the corner while 5 continues to seek the ball in the low post.

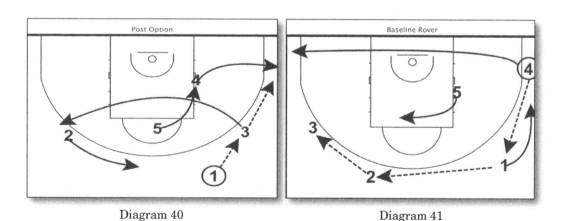

Diagram 40   Diagram 41

Diagram 42:

1. Player 3 can pass the ball early to 4 in the low post area or hit him when he gets to the corner.

2. Post 5 cuts to the high post to give room for Player 4 to post and may get a catch in the paint, but keeps on coming to set a pick on the ball, if 3 does not pass to 4. If the ball does go to 4, 5 seeks to get to rebound position on the weak side.

3. If the pick and roll is set, Players 1 and 2 quickly get into the proper space positions in front of the pick and roll. On the roll, Player 4 will curl up behind the action for a possible snap back pass from 3.

Diagram 43: **Quick hitter play**

1. Point 1 passes to Player 2 on the wing and steps in to get the ball back as 2 cuts hard on a loop to the weak side corner.

2. At the same time, as Player 2 passes the ball back to 1, 4 and 5 try to pin in the weak side zone players to clear space for 3 cutting up to the high guard spot for a shot or to send the ball on down to 2 in the corner, if he does not have a shot.

3. Player 5 can slip into the paint after trying to pin in and 4 will break up into the spot vacated by 5 looking for a high/low action.

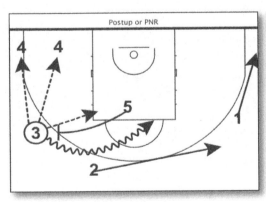

Diagram 42

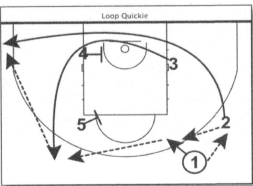

Diagram 43

Jonas Kaslauskas is a Lithuanian who has had a remarkable career in international basketball. He has been the head coach for two tenures of his native country where he is currently the coach, but has coached the national teams of China and Greece as well as the renowned Russia club team CSKA of Moscow.

Diagram 44:

1. Out of a 1-3-1 Player 1 passes to wing man 2 and makes a cut down the gut to the strong side corner.
2. At the same time high post 4 rolls down to the low post and Player 5 flashes into the high post.
3. Player 2 may hit 1 in the corner and there are various things that they can work with the high/low game on the strong side, if there is an opening.

Diagram 45:

1. If there is no easy play on the strong side, Player 2 will drag dribble up and swing the ball to 3 at the top weak side guard spot above the elbow and make a hard cut through the lane to the weak side corner. Player 1 lifts up out of the corner to the top guard spot opposite 3.
2. As Player 2 cuts through the lane, 5 rolls down to the low post and 4 flashes up into the paint and into the high post. Player 3 will hit any of those who are open for a productive catch.

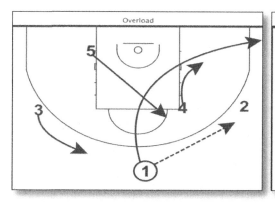

Diagram 44

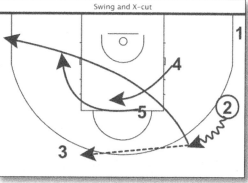

Diagram 45

Diagram 46:

1. If there is no play on the weak side, Player 3 reverses the ball to 1 at the top and makes the same cut that 2 had made initially, going to the weak side corner.

2. Again, the posts make their rotating action as Player 4 rolls down to the low post and 5 fills into the lane for a catch and on up to the high post. Again, if there is a good play to be made on the baseline or in the high/low action, they go for it.

Diagram 47: **Quick hitter moves he likes a lot.**

1. Like the corner cutback move shown before, he likes to use this as a quick play.

2. Player 1 passes to 3 on the wing and clears to the diagonal angle from the corner.

3. Player 3 passes to 4 who pops out to the corner from the short corner and starts a cut through.

4. Player 4 penetrates into the gap and 3 cuts back to the open corner instead of actually cutting through. At the same time Player 5 cuts from the weak side elbow and 4 makes the play.

5. Player 4 has excellent options: his shot, the kickback to 3 in the corner, the flip to 5 at the elbow, or the pass ahead to 1 at the diagonal or 2 in the corner.

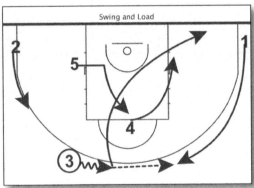
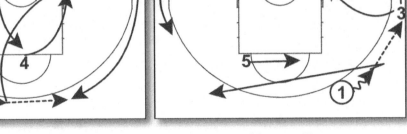

Diagram 46   Diagram 47

Ruben Magnano has been the national team coach of Puerto Rico, Argentina and Brazil among his many coaching assignments. His greatest accomplishment was winning the gold medal in the 2004 Athens Olympics, an event in which the USA won bronze. He established the Argentine Nationals as a world power in his years there, after which he became coach of the Brazil National team, leading them to the London Olympics.

Diagram 48:

1. Point 1 passes to Player 2 on the wing and cuts away to the opposite wing.

2. As Player 3 replaces 1 at the top, 4 sprints hard across the base to the weak side corner, rubbing off of 5, who tries to pin in any defender he can.

3. Player 1 will pass to 4 or to 5 in the post, if either is open.

Diagram 49:

1. If there is no play, the ball will be reversed from Player 4 or 1 on to 2 who has rotated with 3.

2. On the swing of the ball Player 4 cuts off of 5 again and looks for a pass from 3 on the wing either in the paint, low post or the corner area.

3. After Player 4 clears 5, player 5 will flash into the paint for a possible catch as well.

4. The team can repeat the cuts, looking for penetrations in the process of moving he ball, or Player 5 will come set a pick and roll at any time on the wing.

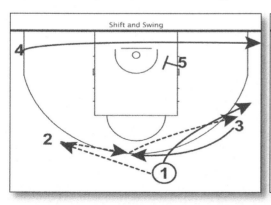

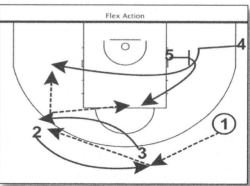

Diagram 48   Diagram 49

——————— CHAPTER 13 ———————

END OUT OF BOUNDS
AND
SIDE OUT OF BOUNDS
PLAYS

Out of bounds plays against zone defenses provide the offense with great opportunities to obtain a high percentage shot. Those who run inbound plays just to **"get the ball in-bounded safely"** are missing great opportunities for scores. It is very important to do that, of course, but that does not preclude creating high percentage scoring opportunities as well.

An under the basket OB is the only time that the defense has to face the baseline against cutters who receive the ball on a direct cut to the rim. Zones do not usually place a man guarding the in-bounder, who can take away vision and hinder the passing angle directly in line to the goal, as is generally done in man-to man. Against the zone we have a predictable alignment to exploit by moving defenders somewhat with cuts, while combining the cuts with screens to take advantage of gaps that open in the coverage. These gaps can be attacked for high percentage shots, whether they are on direct cuts to the rim, or short jump shots, or 3-point shots.

Good inbounds plays present a sequence of options that easily follow one another. It is a good policy to have three or four inbound plays for both man and zone defenses, where the details of each are thoroughly understood by your players. And it is likely a good team will need to change them during the season. There are literally hundreds of inbounds plays from which to choose. We have presented a sample selection here that we feel are "hard to guard," thereby creating opportunities for high percentage shots. Getting three or four scores on inbounds plays can often make the difference between a win and a loss.

End out of Bounds Plays. Against the man defense it is generally better to have a smaller player to inbound the ball since it puts a small defender on the baseline around the basket. This enhances the opportunities to attack the goal with a clever play action. However, against the zone defense it doesn't matter who inbounds, since the bigs will normally line up along the baseline regardless of who passes the ball from out of bounds.

Line Play

In Diagram 1 the ball is taken out by a good shooter, preferably a 2 or a 1. Player 3 cuts to the corner to draw X3 and Player 2 fakes a pass to him as 4 cuts inside of X5 to draw him. This leaves a slot for a big (5) to step into a gap for a possible short shot, assuming Player 4 was not open. The safety outlet is player Player 1.

In Diagram 2, if Player 4 or 5 were not open, 2 passes to 3 in the corner, if he can. After passing inbounds, Player 2 takes a couple steps toward the weak side and then sharply cuts back to the corner 3 has now vacated as he penetrates into the gap between X3 and X1. If Player 2 has a clear shot, 3 passes the ball, but if not, he sends it ahead to 1 at the top and both 3 and 2 sprint to the weak side wing and corner in that order. Player 4 tries to pin in the low weak side wing X4 and Player 1 freeze dribbles a bounce or two at X2 for timing and to occupy him so that the defense will have difficulty covering both shooters on the weak side. The rebounders are in place and Player 1 is back for defense.

Note: If Player 2 could not inbound to 3, he can pass deep to 1 and both he and 3 run the same cuts on the flight of the ball, with 3 going first, while 4 tries to pin in X4 and then seal and step to the ball.

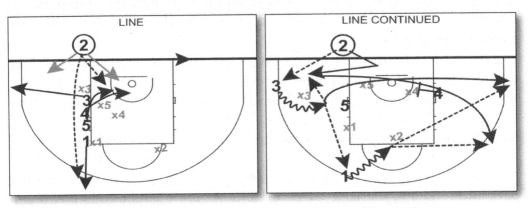

Diagram 1   Diagram 2

Stack Type Plays

In Diagram 3, Players 5 and 4 face the baseline to start and then face in to screen for 2 as the ref hands the ball to the in-bounder. The numbers will vary relative to your personnel. Assuming that Player 2 draws X4, 5 can screen in on X5 and free up 4 for a catch as shown, or 4 may be able to slip to rim over the top of 5, if X5 fights under. Player 5 may be open by sealing off and opening up to the ball late as well. Player 1 is the safety outlet. If there is no shot, Player 3 will cut up the lane to the top and the ball can be swung to 3 who can dribble over to the high wing as 2 roves back to the left corner and 4/5 get into a high/low (not shown).

In Diagram 4 we see a counter move to the previous play. Player 2 **fakes a cut** over the top and drops to the baseline looking for a catch that sometimes is available. Player 5 pins in on X5 and 4 tries to free up against X4 for a catch inside the 3-point line. If he gets the pass, Player 3 steps in to the corner for a pass back from 4. Player 1 is the safety and, if 4 is not open, he passes to 1 and 4 pins in X4 who denied him the ball and 3 steps in to the corner for a pass from 1. Once Player 2 sees he will not get the ball, he quickly cuts up to the top. Again, if there is no shot, the ball can be swung to 2 who can dribble over to the high wing on the left and 3 will rove the base to the corner. Players 4 and 5 will assume high/low spots and play will go on with the freelance principles.

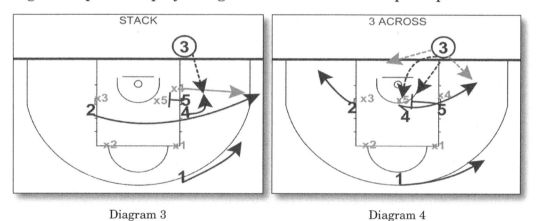

Diagram 3 Diagram 4

Quick option — with eye contact, sometimes the in-bounder can throw a direct lob pass to Player 4 over the defense, if the defender in the middle is looking sideways. Good try from time out. If it's not open, run the play as set.

Stack Gut action — Here we load up four players against three defenders on the baseline. Player 4
cuts out to draw X3 and 5 screens
across on X4 as a diversion and
should draw X5 and confuse X4 for
a second. At the same time player
3 screens the top and 2 hard cuts
to the baseline. Player 3 slips his
screen right away and is the main
target as he cuts into the gap that
is between X3 and X5. Player 2
may be open for an easy catch as
well, if X4 gets tricked into think-

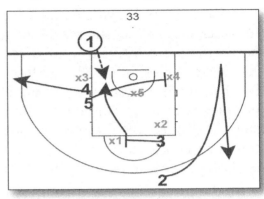

Diagram 5

ing he has to help with X5. If Player 2 doesn't get the pass right away, he
V-cuts back for safety outlet and defense.

Four Flat play — As simple as this play in Diagram 6 looks, it has
been effective. The baseline is loaded four against three. The defense will
usually drop one of the top players to help match the overload, but regardless, strong side player 5 crosses under the basket and 4 cuts over the top,
hesitating at the rim for a lob pass and then posting up where he can find
a spot, if he does not get the high pass. This is not a screening play so that
there is no natural switch. The better leaper will be in the 4 spot and the
better post player will be at the 5. Player 5 may get inside position on X3
and is the second look. Players 2 and 3 both read the defense and will
either body up to the nearest defender to catch or will fly back as safety
outlets.

In Diagram 7 the in-bounder 1 cuts into the open corner behind the man
he inbounds the ball to, if he makes the outlet to either Player 3 or 2 who
was able to pinch in for a semi-post up catch at 15-18 feet!

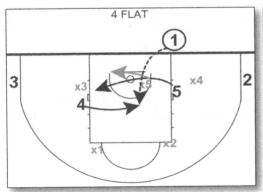

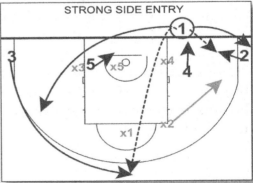

Diagram 6   Diagram 7

Some Majerus' favorites

Slash — In this action Player 5 occupies X5 by moving across the lane to re-locate. Player 3 lines up high enough that X2 will match to

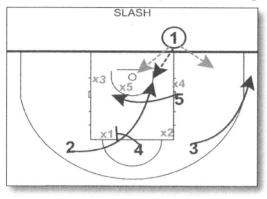

Diagram 8

him and cuts down to the corner to draw X4. At the same time Player 4 picks across on X1 and 2 cuts right into the gap for a catch in the paint or at the rim. Player 4 pops back for the safety outlet and 1 will read to cut into the open area, most likely on the weak side. Always note that the in-bounder must cut to become an option vs. any defense.

Rick loved attacking the slot between the wing and the top in the 2-3 Zone in his end out of bounds plays. He would cut one player into the bottom zone to occupy the wing, another player into the area covered by the top guard on the same side, and then slip a shooter into the gap between the occupied defenders. Rick used the following four actions to attack this spot.

In Diagram 9, Player 5 tries to attract X3 by putting a side or back screen on him if he cannot pin him in, which is unlikely since X3 has

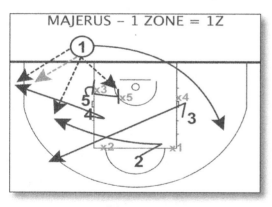

Diagram 9

to keep access open to the corner. Player 4 reads to get open as close to the corner as possible and then 5 looks to post up on X5 as an option. At the same time, Player 3 sets up his cut by jab stepping to the baseline and then cutting hard to the high wing area to draw X2. Player 2 jab-steps one step as if to screen for 3, but changes his direction and cuts behind 3 into the gap created between X3 and X2.

The jab-steps create the timing to allow Players 3 and 5 to be potential options. In-bounder 1 will look at Players 4 and 5 and either pass or pass fake to them, if not open, and then look for 2 in the slot, or 3 as the safety outlet. Then Player 1 will cut hard in bounds to the open area on the right side of the court.

In Diagram 10, Player 4 curl cuts up off of 5 to pin in X2 for player 2's cut, who has set his man up by jab-stepping away from his intended path over the double pick. Post 5 looks to slip in front of X5, to occupy X5 and pull him to the opposite side of the goal, hoping to get a short pass. Player 2 cuts to pull X3 to the corner, while 3 flares out to the wing to draw out X4. As Player 2 cuts off of the pick set by 4 that draws X3, 4 slips into the gap created between X5 and X3. If Player 2 or 5 were open, they would get the ball, but the crux of the play is to 4 in the gap. Player 3 may be open, but

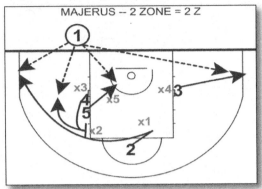

Diagram 10

if no early, easy catch for him, he rotates back for safety.

In Diagram 11. Players 4 and 5 are stacked to screen for 2 coming to the corner to get open for a shot or to draw X3. As Player 2 comes off the picks, 4 steps in to put his body on X5 and 5 looks to slip in to the goal for a short pass. Player 3 jab-steps away and cuts back to the high wing area just as 2 gets to the top of the stack. After picking X5, Player 4 steps into the space between X5 and X3. Either 3 or 4 should be open as X2 and X3 cannot cover all three men if they space properly in the overloaded area. In-bounder 1

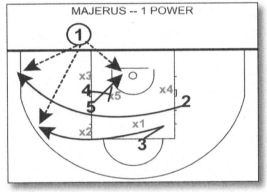

Diagram 11

will cut opposite his pass and seek an open spot on the weak side.

In Diagram 12 three players load up on the foul line with Player 4 on the low block. Player 4 initiates the action by looking to pin in X2. The pick on X2 may have to be either a ¾ angle or a back pick to deter X2. Player 3 will pop out first, which should draw X2 and 2 cuts off of 4, whether X2 is pinned in or has run out with 3. At that point X3 has to take Player 2 and 5 attacks X5 at the same time, looking for a short pass. This leaves a space between

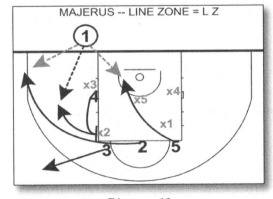

Diagram 12

X5 and X3 on the baseline and a space between X2 and X 3 in the pocket area about half way between the baseline and foul line as shown in the diagram. That is the slot Player 4 seeks to pop into for an easy catch. In-bounder 1 cuts quickly into the weak side area after passing.

3-Point End Out of Bounds Plays

In Diagrams 13 and 14 we have a potential quick 3-point option against the zone. In Diagram 13, Player 3 bodies up against X4 to seal off for a catch from 1, and 4 cuts out hard from the nail to catch from 3. After in-bounding the ball, Player 1, or a designated other shooter such as 2, cuts to the corner off of 5's pinch screen on X3. Note that Player 5 lines up inside to X3 to draw him inside to make it easier to slip around to set a pick on him. The first look for Player 4 in Diagram 14 is the skip pass to 1 for a 3-point shot, and 2 times his cut to be the second option, coming off of 3. It is important to note that Player 3 must release his initial pick on X4 to avoid tipping off the second option, and then quickly re-pick him. A last effort if there is no play, could be a dribble handoff from Player 4 to 2. As suggested, Players 2 and 1 can change roles if the play is run a second time.

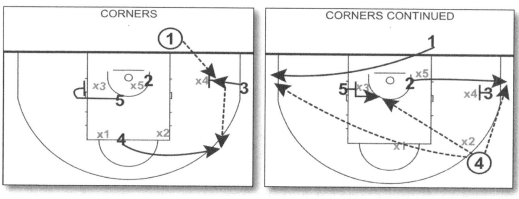

Diagram 13   Diagram 14

If Player 1 sees he could have an easy catch in the corner behind 3 on the initial pass to 4, he can go there. If nothing is open, he can pass deep to Player 4 and 2 can run the cut to the left corner off of 5's pin in screen and 1 can cut to the corner where 3 can pinch in again on X4 (Diagram 14).

Diagrams 15 and 16 show a play action that can be adjusted for three points. Player 4 rolls up out of the stack to put his body on X1 and player 3 comes up at the same time as 4 to offer a fake screen for 2. Player 2 jabs away and cuts toward the ball, and needs to hesitate if he does not

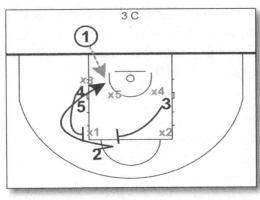

Diagram 15

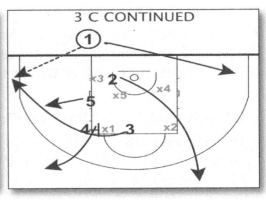

Diagram 16

get an easy, early catch — which he probably won't. But what he must do is draw X3 to him and then cut on under the goal to the weak side (Diagram 15).

Diagram 16 illustrates how the strong side gets flooded with players after 2 cuts out to the weak side. Player 3 cuts to the corner where X3 has at least temporarily vacated to tend to 2, and 3 may have a shot. The X3 defender will have a long run out to get to him, if Player 2 did a good job on his cut, possibly even bumping him a bit in the process without fouling.

Player 4 will pop out on the wing area to look for a catch and possible 3-point shot after 3 cuts off of him. Player 2 can in-bound to any of the first three cutters or late to 5 popping out to the gap/space between 3 and 4. Player 2 should have cut on up to the weak side wing by then and 1 bursts to the open corner beneath 2.

Player 5 may have a shot, if a 3-pointer is not needed, but if one is needed, he is in a good position to skip-pass out to 2 or 1 for a 3-pointer.

High 4-Up Set. Diagram 17 shows another set that involves over-loading the baseline with four players vs. three. Players 4 and 5 seek to put their bodies on X1 and X2 at the top, whether their positions allow side picks for a pin or a back pick. Player 2 and 3 jab to set up and then break out to the corners for a catch that may yield a 3-pointer. On their signal to one another, Players 2 and 3 can vary their cuts by crossing with one another and then cutting off of the picks and going to the opposite corners.

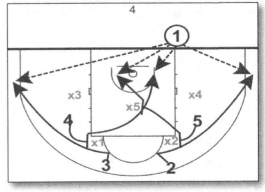

Diagram 17

As the smalls cut, the strong side post man will pick X5 as Player 5 does here and slips to the rim. Player 4 will cut off of 5 and look for the gap between X5 and X4 for a catch and shot. If nothing else, Player 2 or 3 nearest the player out of bounds may be able to seal off a defender for a catch along the baseline and pitch back to the inbounder like the play in the next diagram. If so, the other wing must run back to protect on defense, since all four players have cut to the baseline.

Pitch back quickie — Diagram 18 shows a common OB action that can be used against man and zone defenses. We have shown the action as an option a couple of times earlier as a bailout play when nothing else materializes, but here we

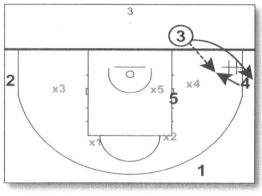

Diagram 18

have a short-second situation, or a time when we would like to get off a quick 3-pointer. The offense spreads and Player 4 cuts right at the baseline to seal off X4 in order to get a short pass from 3, who quickly steps in to the corner for a pitch back and a shot or a penetration into the X4/X2 slot and takes a shot or pass to 1 at the top, or 2 coming up out of the weak side corner or even to 4 popping back to the corner in a pitch back action.

Side Out of Bounds

The X-Series — Open. All these actions have 3- or 2-point potential. A pick and roll can be run to end a play, if no shot comes easily.

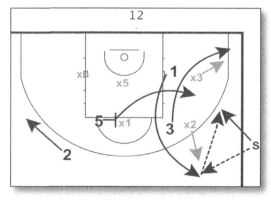

Diagram 19

Diagram 19 shows Players 3 and 1 looping in a crossing or X-action. If X2 and X3 make a mistake and simply match up and switch, shooter 4 can enter the ball to either one and step right in to a rhythm-up 3-point shot. If neither is open or if a 3-pointer is needed, Player 5 steps up off the elbow to set a pick on X1 to flare 2 out for a skip pass 3-point shot.

Player 2 must be careful not to drift too far because X4 can come up for a steal, so he has to create as much space from X4 as possible on his flare. If the pass does go to Player 2, 5 can follow to set a pick and roll if a 3-pointer is needed, or he can dive to the goal, if not. Player 5 flashes into the gap as shown after the flare pick, if no pass is thrown to 2.

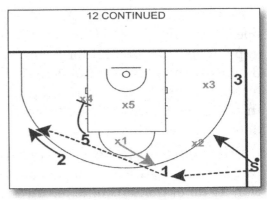

Diagram 20

In Diagram 20 the defense did match up to the ball and so 5 moves down on X4 to set up the flare out for player 2.

On both of the above plays, it is easy for Player 5 to end a play with a pick and roll, if needed.

Low post X-play

In Diagram 21 shooter 3 inbounds the ball. Player 5 is in the low post this time and Players 1 and 2 X-cut in front of 5 and he breaks out to the ball, just as they cross close in front of him. The ideal situation is for Player 3 to be able to pass to 5 who comes as far out as he must to get open, but hopes to catch within 15 feet of the goal. Assuming he catches, Player 2 cuts immediately out of the corner on a backdoor cut and 5 delivers the pass, if X3 does not drop with him enough to pre-

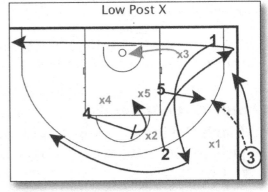

Diagram 21

vent it. Player 3 runs immediately to the open corner where he should be able to get a pass from 5 for an open shot.

In the event that X1 goes man-to-man with Player 3 to prevent the catch, Player 4 sets the flare pick on 1 and slides to the goal. Post 5 will have turned to face the basket at this time and can skip pass to Player 1 or 2 now in the weak side corner.

After setting the pick on X2, Player 4 slip-cuts to the basket where he may be open from 5 or either 1 or 2 as the defense scrambles to defend 1 and 2 on the weak side. This is a clever play action with great opportunities for smart players who can make reads. (Diagram 21)

Diagram 22 indicates that the opponent had the play very well-scouted and has managed to deny a catch to Player 5 as well as 1 and 2. Player 4 puts the flare pick on X3 anyway and rolls in to the goal, if the skip pass is made to 1 with a great chance to be open and to have good rebound position with 5 if 2 should shoot the 3-ball. If inbounder 3 determines not to make the dangerous skip pass, then Player 4 pops up to the 3-point line after setting the pick and should be open for an easy catch. If X1 attacks him he should be able to pass right back to Player 3 stepping in bounds for a rhythm-up 3-pointer or a penetration to make a shot or play.

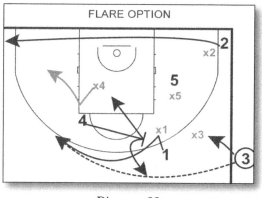

Diagram 22

Concept: in order to add to a coach's repertoire on side out of bounds plays, he can take his regular plays and assume the play is starting with the ball on the wing instead of out front, especially since plays normally do not really start until the ball is entered to a wing or high post. With the ball on the wing out of bounds and a regular half court play is called, you can have a lot more plays to use. That is how the standard "Zipper" play has become such as popular side out play action.

To use a Majerus play vs. zones called "Interior" as an example look at Diagrams 23 and 24.

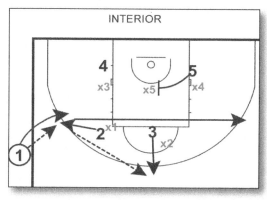

Diagram 23

Diagram 23 shows Player 1 inbounding the ball to 2, who must body up to his defender and pop out in a seal off position to catch the ball. Player 3 bumps his defender and releases to catch at the top as 1 steps inbounds and 2 cuts hard across the lane after his pass to 3 at the top.

In Diagram 24 the ball is passed from Player 3 to 2, and post 5 sets the interior screen on X5 while 4 cuts to the open corner. The X4 defender had to cover Player 2 on the low wing out option and that leaves 2 with the option to attack a big X4 or to pass to 4 or down into 5, sealing in the post. Of course, if Player 4 cannot deliver a shot when he gets it, he can feed 5 down low. In the event Player 2 passed to 4 in the corner, he would run the corner pass automatic and cut through to the weak side or could call out **"cutback"** and run the cutback move to the corner. Player 4 must then apply the **dribble up move** that is always good against zones as noted in **Chapter 4** and other places in the book.

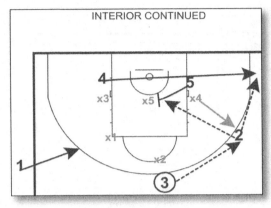

Diagram 24

Diagrams 25 and 26 illustrate another action that is effective as a half court play or as an OB action. Player 3 passes in to 2 on a hard cut to the ball off of the stack with 1 (that cut can be alternated to mix up the defense). After the catch by Player 2, or even to 1 if 2 is denied, 3 will dive for the weak side corner. Player 4 has cut hard up to the weak wing from the low post off of the pick by 5 on X5, as the ball is going to 1 at the top. Player 1 could possibly hit 5 inside, but normally passes on to 4 who has drawn the wing out and therefore can send the ball on down to the corner to 3 for a 3-pointer or to make a play to 5 on a pass or drive. Again, Player 4 will cut through or run a **"cutback"** as in the previous play.

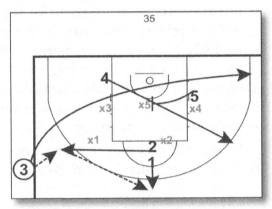

Diagram 25

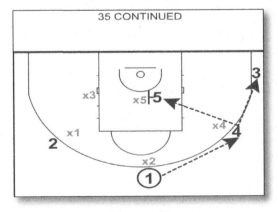

Diagram 26

In Diagram 27 the offense lines up in a box and Player 4 bumps down

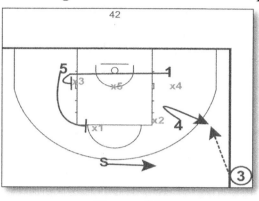

Diagram 27

on X2 and then flashes back to the ball to catch. On defense, they may stay in a box or, more likely, will match X2 to the ball out of bounds and move X4 up to 4 and keep X5 in the middle with X3 low on the weak side to start. Player 4 should be able to bump down and come to the ball to catch. Players 1 and 5 sneak up on the weak side to seal off X1 and X3.

After the catch in Diagram 28, Player 4 makes his **dribble rotate**

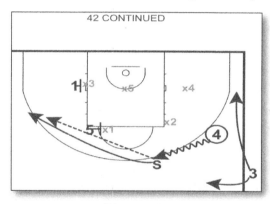

Diagram 28

over move and looks to hit Shooter 2 coming off the pinch picks. If not, he has a great counterflow, misdirection pass back to Player 3 cutting to the open corner after passing the ball inbounds. While not on the diagram due to limiting the amount of lines, note that Post 5, of course, slips down into the low box to follow the ball, regardless of whether the ball goes to the shooter or is snapped back to the weak side. Lot of good action in this play.

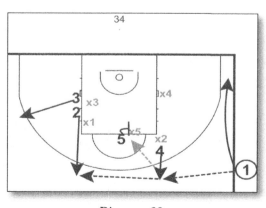

Diagram 29

In Diagram 29 player 4 bumps down to X2 and releases to catch. As he does 5 seals off X5 and 2 and 3 split off of the low stack. Players 2 and 3 may alternate who cuts up first, but the cutter must come up fast to catch and then quickly send the ball on to the wing as 2 does to 3 in the next diagram.

In Diagram 30, Player 4 cuts off of 5 and may have to go over or under,

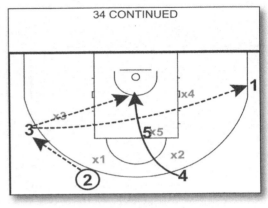

Diagram 30

depending on whether 5 is able to hold off X5. Either way, Player 3 has some good options: if 4 happens to get open on the cut to the goal, he will get it, but will pull X5 on out wide to the baseline area, if not. This may allow Player 5 to be open in the lane on a dive behind 4. Obviously, this action will free up Player 1 to be open in the weak side option for a skip pass from 3 as X4 and X5 will be tied up and X2 will be too far away to cover the corner.

Good Side Out when the opponent is changing defenses after timeouts or on dead balls.

A tactic that is good for a defensive team to use in tight situations is to change defenses from the style that was being used when the team called timeout, and then sometimes staying with the same defense to keep the opponent guessing as to whether to call a play that will be effective against a man defense or a zone. Another advantage to have in a team's repertoire is the high 1-4 offense that has options vs. man-to-man and zone. Following is a side out for both defenses, especially when the team has a full clock or near it.

Diagram 31:

1. Player 3 is a wing man and inbounder and will assume his wing position. Player 1 can cut off of 5 from the low position as shown or from a low position under 4.

2. Player 4 cuts low and 5 opens up as the safety in the middle if 1 and 4 are denied the ball. Player 5 will come as far as he has to toward 3 to get the ball inbounds.

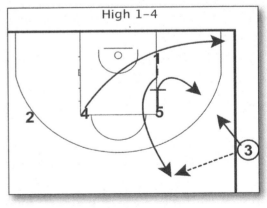

Diagram 31

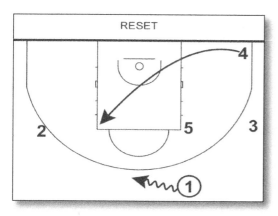

Diagram 32

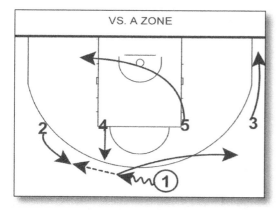

Diagram 33

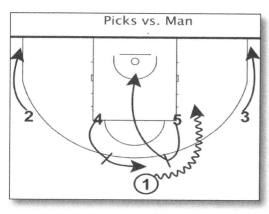

Diagram 34

Diagram 32:

1. The ball will usually be able to be inbounded to Player 1, if he rubs his man off of 5 when its man-to-man and should be able to find a slot if it's a zone.

2. Regardless the ball should be able to be passed into play even if just to the safety, Player 5. Then the ball should be passed to Player 1.

3. If it is a zone, the basic plays in play 14 described in **Chapter 5** and expanded upon in **Chapters 7-9** can be run with a pass to either post or wing or with the point cut options. If it is a man-to-man, the high double screen that is also effective vs. zones is an ideal play and Player 1 can use either one for a pick and roll or pop.

Diagram 33:

1. Here is the example of the wing pass option that turns into high/low action that can get right into pick and roll at any time as well, whether the defense is in man or zone.

Diagram 34:

1. **If it is a man defense,** the high double picks are offered and the play is made.

This play saves a lot of confusion on the part of the players against a team that is constantly changing defenses.

———————— **CHAPTER 14** ————————

ATTACKING THE BOX AND ONE AND THE TRIANGLE AND TWO

Sometimes the basketball purists treat what they call "Junk Defenses," such as the Box and One or the Triangle and Two, with measures of disdain. Some refuse to "Junk it Up" as they would say, since it is trickery or perhaps "not fundamental." However, these defenses have been used with great success at all levels of the game for short periods of time and, on occasion, for a full game. A classic example occurred in the 1998 NCAA Elite 8 when the underdog University of Utah team of Rick Majerus surprised, and defeated the number one seed Arizona, using the Triangle and Two Defense. Many other teams have used the Box and One and the Triangle and Two for short stints to stymie a more talented opponent for periods of time.

Without question these defenses can give opponents fits, if the element of surprise is used against a team that is unprepared. **Box and One** is an excellent weapon for teams going against an opponent with one superstar player, or in the case of the **Triangle and Two,** where a team has a pair of high-powered players. Del wrote on these in his 1971 book, ***Multiple Defenses for Winning Basketball***, as well as how to teach the match-up zone both in the half court and as a full court press. And it had been around for a few years prior to that, so it is not a new phenomenon by any means.

These defenses reappear every year and the ill-prepared coach is usually confused. It is good to work against it occasionally — and it might come in handy as a defense on a night you need a change of pace as an underdog team. "By failing to prepare, you are preparing to fail." This old adage is a truism in virtually all cases, and particularly true in the case of "Junk Defenses."

Defeating the Box and One Defense

Methods of playing the Box and One

There are two main methods that teams use to create the Box and One. The most frequent is to assign the best defender to the opponent's best player and the other defenders play in a box, typically with two "smalls" on the elbows and two "bigs" on the blocks. Similarly, the box may be turned into a 1-2-1 diamond shape to become a **Diamond and One.** Another method is assigning the biggest guard to the opponent's best player, while the other players line up with three bigs across the bottom and the other guard plays the top in a 1-3 set. The coverage is like that of a 2-3 zone, but the wings of the zone defense try to play the offensive wing players when possible. If a wing passes to a man in the corner, the post covers that pass or the weak side bottom defender would have to match with him on a baseline cut action. The guard on the top of the zone typically covers the same area that a point would play in a 3-2 zone, never going to the wing to play the ball is the plan. It is an effective way of playing a Box and One since it can be readily adapted if your team already plays a 2-3 zone. Against this type of defense, the best advice is to go with your zone offense. Some call this a "1-3 Chaser" since the wing defenders play any catch on the wing except to the man being defended by the man-to-man player. The post must cover the corner if the ball goes from the wing to the corner. Note that some of the plays will try to free up the star player and others will seek to make the zone players pay for attempting to defend the entire front court with a box or a triangle zone.

We begin with some sets versus the traditional Box and One that are also effective versus the Diamond and One. Understand that if the actions shown do not produce a good shot that the team can continue utilizing freelance options that will have been taught, if the coach has taught the principles of attacking zones. The various dribble moves, punching into the gaps, pick and rolls, handoffs and basic screening/cutting still will yield success, as opposed to standing around and giving in to the defense.

Simple Figure Eight Action

In Diagram 1 you see a simple attack against a Box and 1 involving a "figure 8" cutting motion by the man being defended 1-on-1. This play can be used by any level of team and can be inserted the day before the game in a high school or college situation as a quickie option. The other four players line up in a box with the bigs on the blocks and the smalls on top. Star player 3, being guarded 1-on-1, starts in the corner on the ball side.

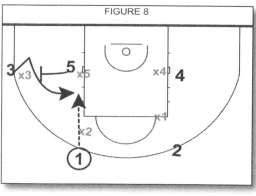

Diagram 1

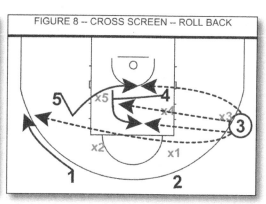

Diagram 2

In Diagram 1, Player 5 steps out and sets a flex back screen for 3. Player 3 may be open cutting into the middle and 5 will step back to the ball after the screen, looking for a catch. Ball handler 1 may hit Player 3 on his cut or 5 on the roll back.

In Diagram 2, Player 1 has reversed the ball to 2 and 2 has sent it on down to 3. Player 4 cross screens for 5 and either seals, if there is a switch, or he rolls back after screening for 5. Player 1 fades to the weak side to counter X2 sagging in on 4. If Player 3 has no shot or move, he looks for 5 on his cut, 4 on his roll back, or 1 on his fade behind the screening action.

Finally, if Player 3 still has no play, he passes the ball to 2, who then

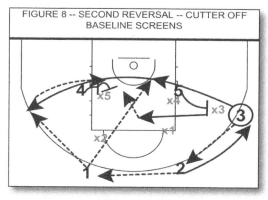

Diagram 3

reverses the ball to 1. After passing, Player 3 cuts to the ball side off of baseline screens set by 5 and 4 as in Diagram 3. Naturally, Player 5 rolls back to the ball after setting his screen and 4 seals his defender on the lane after 3 clears his screen. If Player 3 has no shot, he looks for 4 sealing or to 5 cutting high for the possible high/low game. Players 1 and 2 spread to the weak side wing when 3 gets the ball on the second wing, ready for a swing pass through 5 or for a skip-pass from 3 and continued action.

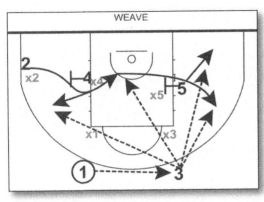

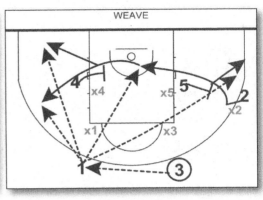

Diagram 4   Diagram 5

Baseline Weave

In Diagram 4, Players 1-3-4-5 start in a box set with 1 at the top with the ball. Player 2, being played 1-on-1 by X2, starts in the left corner. As Player 1 passes to 3, 4 sets a flex back screen on X2. Player 2 uses 4 and may cut over or under - or he may pop back off the screen, if his man tries to beat him over the pick. If he does not catch, he continues his cut as Player 5 screens in for him on the right side. Again, Player 2 uses 5 and may go over or under him. He may read to straight cut, curl or fade, depending on how X2 plays him. Player 3 hits him, if he gets open. If Player 2 catches, and does not have a shot, 5 may step up quickly and set a pick and roll for him.

Diagram 5 is a continuation of Diagram 4 as Player 2 has not been able to catch coming off of 5's screen, so 5 then turns and back screens for 2. Again, Player 2 uses 5's screen to cut to the rim, as 3 passes back to 1. After Player 5 picks, he rolls back toward the ball, looking to make a catch. Player 2 continues his cut off of 4, who screens in for him, as he returns to the left side. If Player 2 catches on the wing, 4 seals and 5 flashes high into the high low game. Then the read and react game takes over, unless the coach wants to reset, which is a possibility when there is no shot clock.

Single – Double

There are several ways that this play may be set up. **Single Double #1** has the player being played 1-on-1 starting at the foul line area, as illustrated in Diagram 6. Player 5 plays above the left block and 4 can line up on or off of the lane on the same side. Player 3 plays off the lane a little above the block on the right side.

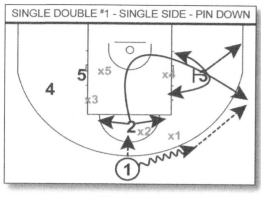

Diagram 6

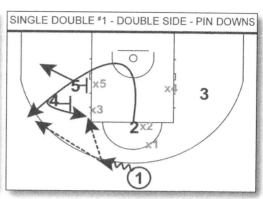

Diagram 7

In Diagram 6, Player 2 starts on the foul line and may elect to catch at either elbow to play against his man from time to time as a change up. In the principle action he cuts down the lane and decides whether to cut off of the double pick side or the single pick side. In the first diagram he decides to cut off the single side. He uses Player 3 as a screen where 3 has set up off the lane and above the level of the block. This gives Player 2 the ability to play against his man on the screen and to cut based on the defender's response. That is, he may cut to the corner or up to the wing area or curl. If he catches and has nothing, Player 3 may set a quick screen for him and roll or pop.

Diagram 7 shows Player 2 cutting off the double side. Players 5 and 4 screen in for 2 on his cut. Again, Player 5's screen is high enough that 2 may fade off toward the corner, if his defender goes over the top. Otherwise, he can cut out toward the wing, curl cut or even back cut to the basket and continue out off of the single pick side to get rid of his man.

In Diagram 8, on Player 2's catch, 1 fades to the wing while 5 sets a flare screen for 4, who is a good shooter. Player 4 can pop to the 3-point line, if he has that range, and 5 can post or slip to the basket. Player 3 flashes to the middle for the shot or to play high/low with 5, or can touch-pass to 1 behind him. Player 2 may pass to 4 on the pop, or he can pass to 5 at the rim, if he slip cuts, or directly to him if he posts up. He also has point 1 fading on the weak side as a skip pass option.

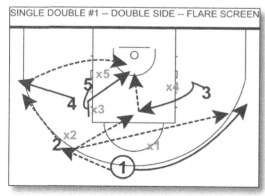

Diagram 6

The key consideration with this play and with the following **Single Double play** is, that **once the man being played 1-on-1 has the ball and does not have a score-threatening pass option in the action, he should be able to shoot, pass and cut, or receive a pick and roll, etc.** He is being played man-to-man for a reason.

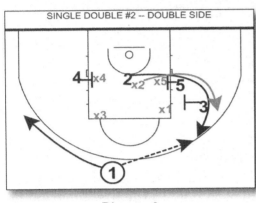

Diagram 9

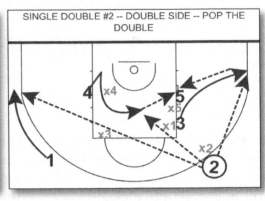

Diagram 10

Single Double #2

In Diagram 9 the point guard has the ball on the top with Players 3 and 5 on the right side and 4 on the left side above the block. Player 2, the player being played 1-on-1, takes his defender under the basket. He has the choice of coming off either side, although the double side is preferred. Players 3 and 5 screen in on the right side and 4 pinches in on the left side. Ball handler 1 passes to Player 2 as he cuts off the screens by 5 and 3 in Diagram 9.

In Diagram 10, Player 3 pops to the corner where 2 catches and 5 posts up hard above the block while player 4 flashes to the middle. Shooter 2 has the options of passing to 3 in the corner, the feed to 5 sealing, or hitting 4 flashing middle for the shot. He may also skip pass to Player 1, who may have the shot or a penetration opportunity. If Player 2 cannot make a play, 4 can come to set a screen for him as in Diagram 11. Player 2 can pass fake at 3 to send him through, as 4 comes to set the screen. Player 2 comes off of 4's screen looking to

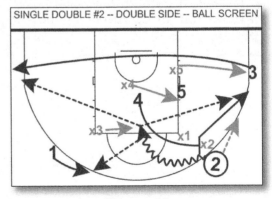

Diagram 11

attack and has play options to each teammate if he can't get off a shot.

Note in Diagram 11 that Player 1 must cut above the penetration angle by 2 to pull X3 up from helping on 2, though they likely will trap him due to his star ability. It also gives Player 1 a better angle for a possible jump shot and to be the safety as well. This also makes it easier for Player 1 to create a play of his own on a second penetration for a shot or a pass to 4.

Player 2 thus may have options to any of his four teammates, but will have to be ready for a possible trap anytime he penetrates against a combination defense. The objective for him against the combination defenses is to get a shot or a pass off before he takes the ball too deep and runs out of options when smothered by the defense. The negative on the pick and roll is that it is easily trapped, but that also creates openings for teammates, if the key player passes well and has teammates that can make enough shots when open.

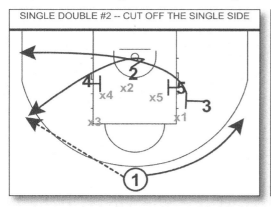

Diagram 12

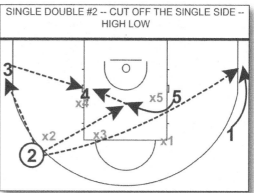

Diagram 13

Certainly, Player 2 may also choose to cut off the single side as in Diagram 12. He must have the option to use any angle off the single screen. Player 3 will break to the weak side corner below him to form the overload. Now they can keep the continuity that will be shown in Diagram 13, or posts 4 and 5 can get into a high/low action at that point and the team can continue to run the basic cuts of the Automatics in the high/low game presented earlier. (Diagram 12)

If the coach wants to stay with the continuity action to help free up the star player, he now has the same options in Diagram 13 that we showed when Player 2 cut off the double side in Diagrams 9 and 10. Player 2 may pass to 3 in the corner for a shot or a feed to 4 sealing, while 5 flashes to the middle for a shot or a dump down to 4, if 4 is fronted. Star Player 2 may also skip pass to 1 fading on the weak side. Again, all the previous options are open. Player 2 can cut on a corner pass Automatic as well. In that case, Player 3 can penetrate and 5 will cut up into the elbow to replace 2.

In Diagram 14 if Player 2 has no play, he pass fakes at 3 and send him through. Player 5 sets a screen for 2. Player 1 cuts to the weak side high elbow area. Player 2 drives off 5 who rolls and 4 lifts. Player 2 looks to go to the basket or to pull up. He may pass to Player 5, to 4 lifting or to 3 or 1 on the weak side.

In Diagram 15, Player 2 goes off the single side and curls to the middle off 4's screen, an option he is free to use anytime in all these Single-Double actions. That is why it is better to have the screens set wide enough to give room for a back cut to the basket against an overly aggressive defender, who has been assigned to deny him the ball. If he is not open initially, he continues on to use the screens of Players 5 and 3 and the play goes on.

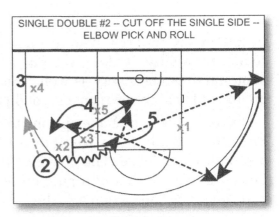

Diagram 14

Diagram 15

Play 31 — good quick hitter from time out to attack the zone part and involve other players

Diagram 16 illustrates a simple, but effective, play vs. the Box and One. In this attack Player 2 is being defended 1-on-1 and sets up in the left corner **as a decoy.** Player 4 starts above the left block and 5 is in the short corner on the right side. Player 3 starts on the right wing and screens in on X1 at the top of the box. Player 1 jukes a dribble toward 2 to get X1 to move in and then crosses over to use 3's screen, looking to attack for a score. Otherwise, he may be able to lay off a pass to Player 5, pass to 4 low on the weak side, or pass to 3 on his pop to the 3-point line on the wing to make it harder for X1 to reach him. Player 2 must roll up to the top.

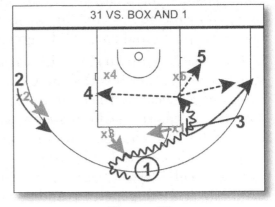

Diagram 16

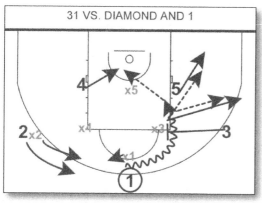

Diagram 17

In Diagram 17 we show **"31"** versus a Diamond and One. Again, Player 3 screens in on X3 and 1 drives off of 3, turning the corner to the rim, if possible. He may have a pull up jump shot, a drop off pass to Player 5 popping to the short corner, a pass to 3 popping behind him to the wing, or a pass to Player 4 going to the rim if X5 helps on him. Again, star man 2 needs to move to the top.

Triple — a system to use when your team sees a lot of combo defenses on your star player

As per the title, this play involves a triple screen for the player being played 1-on-1. In Diagram 18, Player 2 is being played man-to-man and starts on the left wing. Players 4 and 5 break up to the high elbows to set screens for him. At the same time, Player 3 loops under 5 and seeks 2's defender in the middle wherever he sees the defender on him.

Player 2 fakes away and cuts off 4, 3 and 5. Players 4 and 3 focus on pick-

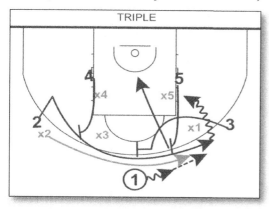

Diagram 18

ing the defender on the star player, while 5 hopes to get a piece of X1, if possible, and hopes to clean up anything 4 and 3 miss as well. The key player will usually be trailed because he is open behind the picks if his defender tries to go under. Thus, he <u>may</u> curl right off of Player 5 for a lob. But normally, he will get a catch in the high wing area coming off Player 5 and may be able to sweep and drive to the rim.

Continuing in Diagram 18, Player 1 with the ball has to be clever and should juke one bounce toward 2 to get the defense to shift left, so that the picks are more effective coming back to his right. He then bounces back to the right but **cannot penetrate,** as he must stay spaced enough from Player 2 in order to make a play to him. It is better to dribble slightly up and over, keeping an angle whereby he can pass to Player 2 as he clears 5's pick and can still have an angle to pass to 3 on the weak side, the

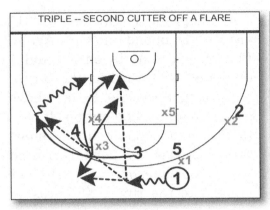

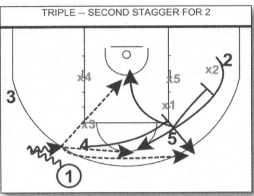

Diagram 19   Diagram 20

option in Diagram 19. It is essential that **point 1 keeps his dribble alive!**

In Diagram 19, Player 2 is not open on his cut so 3 waits for 1 to look at him to key him to cut off 4 who screens in for him. Again, Player 3 may curl, pop or straight cut off 4's screen as he reads the defenders and responds accordingly. Player 4 may slip to the rim at any time for a catch or to post up.

In Diagram 20 if Player 3 or 4 is not open, 4 and 5 stagger away for 2. Star player 2 should cut all the way to the low wing area after his initial cut to set up an angle for Players 4 and 5 to re-pick him. So Player 5 goes deep to get 2, who must set up his cut, while 4 sets his screen just below the elbow to give 2 good space to curl, pop or straight cut off his screen.

In Diagram 21, Player 2 catches, 4 down screens for 5 who curls to the rim. After the cut Player 4 pops back off of 5 for the outside shot. Another option, instead of Player 4 picking down on 5, is to have 5 set a flare screen for 4, to finish this action. That can be communicated between the two, by calling "flop" or "change," after they have run the play a couple of times.

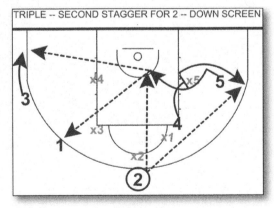

Diagram 21

Depending on how deeply one wants to get into it Diagrams 22 and 23 show counters to consider.

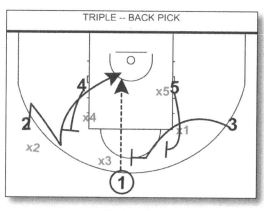

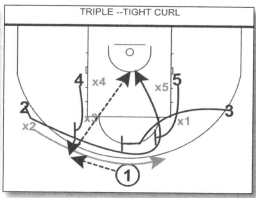

Diagram 22   Diagram 23

Diagram 22 shows a back screen by Player 4 on 2's usual cut. As star player 2 fakes up and cuts high, as if to cut off the triple, Player 4 changes his screen and sets a screen for 2 to back cut off to the rim. Diagram 23 shows another counter for Player 2. In this case, X2 is playing Player 2 extremely tight and cannot get an easy catch, so 1 makes a pass to 4 who steps up off his screen for 2. Player 2 curl's tightly off of 5 and 4 hits him on his cut with a high pass.

There are many actions designed for the Box and 1. We have just offered a taste or what there is. **A coach can take just the simpler ones shown at the start of this chapter, or can use only the first or second move from the more complex plays and then go to free lance motion to finish.** What we have shown are in some cases too extensive for what is an uncommon defense, so a coach can use any part as a play. Normally, a couple quick baskets are usually enough to get rid of the Box and One, but if they persist, continue to go with the easy ones you have and mix in your man-to-man offense is our advice. The same holds true for the following work on the Triangle and Two. We are giving more than anyone can ever need. **Just take what fits your team at any particular time and put in a couple moves.** Your team's knowledge of attacking defenses in general and zones in particular will help them finish off a play, if you **give them a couple quick hitters and have one or two in your pocket that you can draw up at halftime or in a huddle.**

Defeating the Triangle and Two Defense

Against a team with two dominant players and three others who are not nearly as good, the **Triangle and Two** can be extremely effective. Even in a scenario where one player is a great guard and the other is a tough forward, the Triangle and Two can be structured to make it very difficult for these two to operate as they normally would in a man-to-man situation. They are being denied the ball and screens may be switched into denials, or trapped, if the ball is involved. If they post up, they are fronted with help behind. This can create frustration and lead to hesitancy and confusion.

There are schools of thought that say taking the time to implement **special offenses or sets takes valuable time away from developing and refining your regular offensive systems and other areas that need work.** Thus, it is seen as being counterproductive. Their rationale is that if your offense has good spacing, ball and player movement as well as screening, it should be effective against junk defenses. Therefore, it makes more sense to practice just your regular offensive sets to go against the junk defenses, emphasizing the particular actions, which should be difficult for the defense to cope with. And that works in many cases, unless your team is structured in such a way that you see combination defenses game after game because you have only one or two highly talented players. If you have four or five, then this is probably good advice, along with having a couple quick hitters from timeouts. However, if that is your team makeup, you will not see the Box or the Triangle we would venture.

We, and many other coaches, believe that each coach needs some simple actions that take advantage of the fact that one or two players are being guarded man-to-man and the others are covered by a zone. At the high school level particularly, and at times even at the university level, it is not uncommon to have a really outstanding player or two and not much of a supporting cast, especially in smaller enrollment situations. We promise you, having been in that situation, that once a team in the league or district has success against your team with a combination defense, you will see it a lot by others in the league until you beat it. And that is when you will have to have more than just one or two moves. So, even in a lesser situation, you would be well advised to have one or two of them in your arsenal, for the occasions where you run into the junk defenses. Again, we refer to our great friend, Rick Majerus, and his experience with using these defenses. He had such success that he would use this type of defense for 20-30 minutes and one or two little moves were insufficient to beat his teams. The coaches had to come up with solutions and most failed to do it adequately.

Usually, however, the combination defenses are secondary defenses that will be used for short periods. If you have something that you can go to immediately when you recognize the junk defense, and can score against it with confidence through good execution, the defense will be short lived.

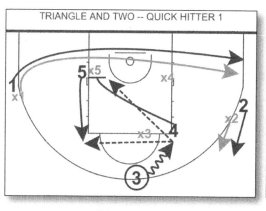

Diagram 24

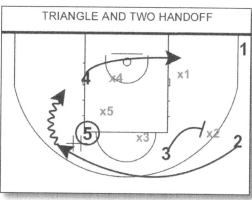

Diagram 25

Quick Hitter 1 — attacking from the elbow

The following diagrams show simple actions that can be effective against the Triangle and Two. They can also flow into a motion game, if you are not successful immediately. In the Diagrams, Players 1 and 2 are being guarded man-to-man.

In Diagram 24, Player 3 dribbles at 4 on the elbow as 4 vacates to screen down for 5, who cuts off the screen to the open elbow. Naturally, if Player 4 is a better shooter and 5 is a better post up man, these positions will be reversed. Player 1 clears to the ball-side corner, rubbing off of the action created by 4 and 5. Player 3 can pass to 4 or 5, who must be able to make that shot.

In Diagram 25, Player 5 has the ball and can shoot or pass down to 4 who may be able to post up, assuming X4 has to move to cover him, allowing X5 to move up to 5, after being delayed by 4's pick. Player 3 sets a pick on X2 to allow 2 to come right off of 5 for a handoff. Post 4 clears out and Player 2 has the side to make a play.

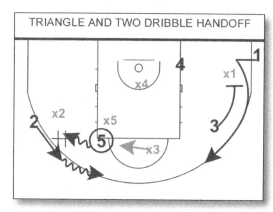

Diagram 26

However, if X2 prevents the handoff from Player 5, as in Diagram 26, 2 will go past 5 a couple steps and 5 can dribble at him for a dribble handoff or can dribble handoff the other direction to 1 who is coming off a second pick set by player 3.

Quick Hitter 2 — good overload action

In Diagram 27 the players set up stacks on the left and right sides above the blocks. Player 1 curls to the basket off of 5 and then clears to the weak side elbow. Player 5 pops to the wing off of 1's curl. As Player 1 clears, 2 curls to the rim off of 4 and 4 pops to the wing off of 2's curl. If either Player 1 or 2 gets free on their cuts, 3 will hit him with a pass. Both Player 2 and 1 finish their cuts to the elbows, if they do not catch deep, and either player may be able to catch on the elbow and go 1-on-1.

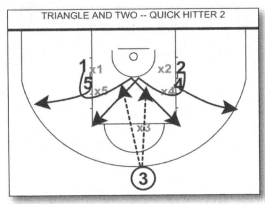

Diagram 27

Diagrams 28 and 29 show Player 3 passing to the big men to form a clever overload by making a strong side corner cut. It is hard for the back men X5 and X4 to cover both the wing and the corner on their side on the overload.

In Diagram 28, Players 1 and 2 have run their curls and 3 passes to 5, then cuts to the rim and on out to the strong side corner. Player 5 may hit 3 on his rim cut or he may pass to him in the corner for a shot there. Of course, Player 5 will cut to the goal after passing and look to post up. An <u>alternative move</u> is for Player 5 to set a pick right on X1 to free up 1 for a curl or pop cut and then 5 will continue on to the goal.

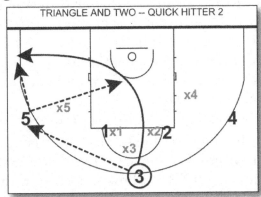

Diagram 28

In Diagram 29, Player 3 passes to 4 and cuts to the rim. If he doesn't catch, he continues to the corner. Player 4 passes to 3 on the rim cut or in the corner for a possible 3-point shot. Of course, Player 4 can dive to the goal after passing to the corner to post up. Alternatively, he can set a pick on X2 for

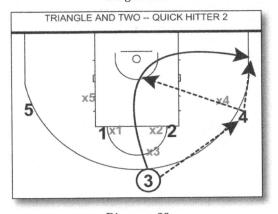

Diagram 29

a curl or pop cut, after which he will cut to the goal, as were the options for Player 5 in the previous diagram.

Note: if the two players being played man-to-man are a big and a small, they can help free up one another by cross-screening to create a mismatch when the ball is passed to the wing or corner. That can be an extra play call altogether.

Quick Hitter 3 — good play from a time out

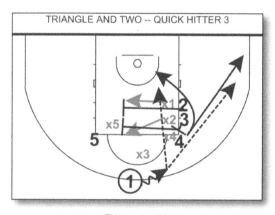

Diagram 30

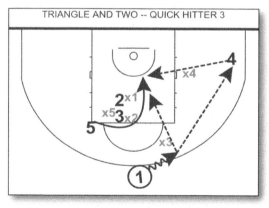

Diagram 31

In Diagrams 30 and 31, Players 2 and 3 are guarded man-to-man. In Diagram 30, the players line up in a triple stack on the right lane with Player 5 on the opposite elbow. Player 3 screens in on X4, and Player 4 may curl to the rim or cut to the corner. If open, Player 1 will hit 4 on either cut. Players 2 and 3 then set a double screen on X5 and 5 cuts off the double screen to the rim. If Player 4 had curled to the goal, he would continue on to the weak side block to clear space for 5's cut.

Diagram 31 shows that Player 1 may hit 5 directly or, if 1 had hit 4 going to the corner, 4 could hit 5 on the cut, if he has no shot of his own. Players 2 and 3 can pick for one another and split apart, looking to capitalize 1-on-1 on a mismatch with 4 and 5 in good rebound position.

Quick Hitter 4

In Diagram 32, Players 1 and 2 are being guarded 1-on-1, while 4 is in the left corner and 5 is on the left block. Player 1 spreads on the right wing and 2 is on the left elbow. Player 1 screens in on X4 and 5 cuts to the rim off 1's screen. Player 1 rolls back for a catch and then on out to make room for 4's cut off of 2's flex pick on X5.

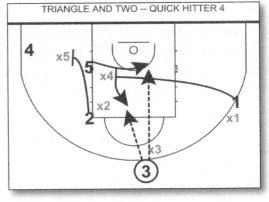

Diagram 32

In Diagram 33, Players 5 and 1 are not open and have spread on out to open up the area for the action by 2 and 4. Player 4 cuts to the rim off 2's flex screen and 2 rolls back off his screen while 1 clears to the corner. Player 3 may hit 4 on his rim cut or 2 rolling back on his screen.

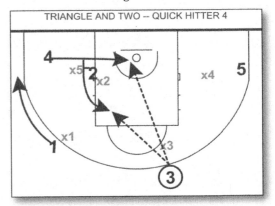

Diagram 33

If there is nothing at this point, Player 5 can lift up out of the corner to be an outlet and 4 can spread to the corner to overload that area against the triangle. To carry it even further though not in the diagram, they are now set up in positions whereby Player 3 can pass to 5 and set a good screen on one of the players, either 1 or 2, that is being guarded man-to-man for a cut to an open basket. Again, Players 1 and 2 are in good attack spots with 4 and 5 in rebound positions.

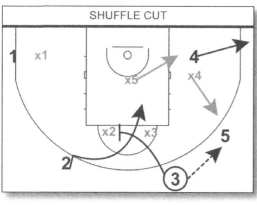

Diagram 34

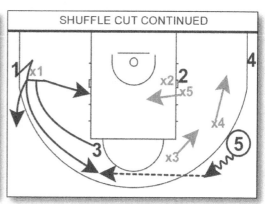

Diagram 35

Diagrams 34 and 35 show a **shuffle attack** that will tend to distort the defense, if Player 4 can shoot. The low wing man will normally move up to cover Player 5 and 4 pops to the corner to pull X5. These players may be exchanged to help draw out the bigs and play inside the 3-point line. Player 3 will pass to 5 and screen away for 2 to make a shuffle cut to the goal (Diagram 34).

In Diagram 35, Player 3 continues down to pick on X1 to help free up 1 for an elbow catch. Player 5 may need to dribble up a bounce or two to make a safer pass to 1. After Player 5 passes to 1, 4 and 5 may set a stagger screen down for 2. If Player 1 is not open he may find player 3 open after the second pick on a pop or a slip.

If you are unsure whether these more detailed offenses will be an effective use of time, select a couple of these specific plays versus the junk defenses and either way, you will be prepared. The main thing is not to be caught without a tool in your kit when a team throws one of these defenses at you. It is a quick way to lose the confidence of your players and the fans.

—————— **CHAPTER 15** ——————

A ZONE ATTACK
FOR
YOUTH BASKETBALL

The topic of zones in youth basketball has been long discussed and debated. We feel strongly that zones should not be allowed in youth basketball since it prevents the defense from learning the early concepts of defending against the ball and an individual, as well as the beginning principles of teamwork in man-to-man defense. Among many more reasons, the players on offense have their learning of the game stifled by looking at players clumped together in some form of zone. The reality is that coaches who use zones with young children usually do it because they may not be able to teach fundamental principles of man-to-man defense, or perhaps they have one big player who does not move well, but can be an effective defender in the middle of the key close to the basket. It really begs the question of whether the use is primarily to give the team an easier manner with which to win games, over teaching the youngsters how to play the game of basketball. It is the easy way out for the coach, but learning how to play the game well is never easy.

Regardless of the debate, it seems that it is unlikely that many organizations will ban zone defenses from youth basketball, so we will present some simple concepts that can be easily combined into a system of attack. Passing is the most basic fundamental used to attack zones. Players can pass a ball faster than a player can move, so we will deal with passing first in our simple attack. It is difficult to find a top level team that is not a good passing team. To be an outstanding all-round player, passing skills must be developed.

Alignment and Passing

Perimeter players start lined up in the gaps of the zone. The gaps are the spaces between two defensive players on the perimeter. Aligning in the gaps creates a situation where the defenders who form the gap must make a decision regarding which one of them will take the ball whenever it is passed to a player in the gap between them. Whichever defender takes him will be at the edge of his coverage area when he guards the ball and that creates space.

Diagram 1 demonstrates that ideally there are five perimeter spots versus a zone with a two-man front: the point, the wings and the corners (represented by two dots). The rectangles are the coverage areas of the perimeter defenders and the darker areas mark the middle man's (X5) coverage area. Aligning in the gaps forms good spacing between the perimeter players at the outset, but must be maintained throughout the possession.

In Diagram 1, offensive player 1 occupies the space between X1 and X2 and wants to make one of them guard him. **He then can pass to the wing on that side.** Players 2 and 3 operate in the gaps between the front and wing players, X1/X3 and X2/X4. Player 5 operates in the lane area between the basket and the high post always looking for a hole to cut into when it opens in front of the basket. Player 4 plays on the baseline position from sideline-to-sideline. He stays within his shooting range on the ball side and moves with the reversal of the ball.

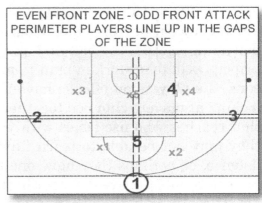

EVEN FRONT ZONE - ODD FRONT ATTACK PERIMETER PLAYERS LINE UP IN THE GAPS OF THE ZONE

Diagram 1

In Diagram 2 we see an odd, or one-man front zone: defense with X1 on the point, X2 and X3 at the wings and X4 and X5 are in the low spots along the baseline. This may be called either a 1-2-2 or a 3-2 zone, depending on how high the wing players play, the 3-2 indicating a higher wing positioning than the 1-2-2. Another zone using a one-man front would be a 1-3-1 zone. In the case of an "odd man" front, the offense would line up in a two-

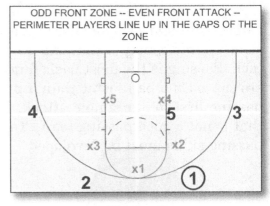

ODD FRONT ZONE -- EVEN FRONT ATTACK -- PERIMETER PLAYERS LINE UP IN THE GAPS OF THE ZONE

Diagram 2

guard or "even man" front. Player 1 lines up in the seam between X1 and X2, and 2 lines up in the seam between X1 and X3. Our wing players (3 and 4) line up in the gaps between the wing and back line players. Our post man 5 operates in the mid-post position, in the gaps formed between the front and back line players Again the colored rectangles indicate the coverage areas of the individual defenders in that area.

The wings play wide to create better passing lanes and to keep the middle open for cutters and penetration. They must maintain **"spacing"** of 15-18 feet from one another, in order to spread the defenders, though they may have to shorten the distance as they come to meet a pass. Each player must be taught to move so that they never line up **"three in a line with the ball."** Simple **"pig in the middle" drills** with three players can be used to explain that the receiver and the ball handler can work to break the **"three in a line"** in order to create a passing lane for the passer. When the ball is on the wing, the player on the point must play **high,** always giving the wing with the ball an open pass angle to reverse the ball. Many players at the top tend to move down too close to the foul circle and this creates flat pass angles from the wing and jams the middle of the offense.

In Diagram 3, Player 3 must ensure that X2 is not in the passing lane between himself and 1 in an even-front zone alignment. Player 2 on the other wing must ensure that X1 is not in the passing lane between 1 and himself as well. Any passer must **"see the defender"** responsible for the man he is passing to, and to **"pass away from the defender."** He can help create a better angle by utilizing a drag dribble in the direction of the receiver when necessary. The similar strategy of lining up in the gaps is shown vs. an odd-front zone in Diagram 4. The idea is to "create a pass lane to the ball."

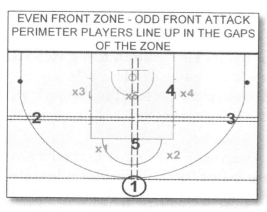

Diagram 3

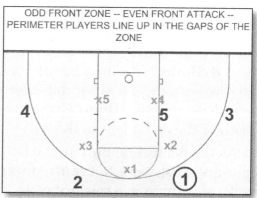

Diagram 4

Concurrently, it is important to teach players to prepare to be a receiver who is ready to catch and shoot. There are many theories relative to foot placement that shooting experts teach. As opposed to taking sides on such issues as having one foot pointing to the basket or readying to make a step to the ball or having the feet in the air when the ball is in the air, it is vital that a shooter be ready with his hands and feet to deliver the open shot before the defense closes on him.

Mental preparation is as important not only in terms of confidence, but in each receiver recognizing which defender is guarding him when he catches the ball. This allows him to know if he will have a shot, or whether to attack on the dribble, or where to pass to a teammate. We dealt with this skill in the early chapters.

Coaches may use cones as defenders changing them to the shape of the various zones to increase repetitions for players. The players then align in the seams. Skip passes can be taught when the players are strong enough to make that play. Technique is important and must be taught, because poorly executed skip passes lead to deadly turnovers. The proper technique produces low arcing, swift overhead or push passes. Passing with the left hand to the left side of the court and with the right hand to the right side of the court may be drilled along with the basic two-hand passes. Passes should not float, but be crisp to eliminate arc from passes around the perimeter and into the middle. "Pass fakes" should be introduced to move or to "freeze" a defender in the zone in ball movement drills as well. **The bottom line is to have the hands and feet ready to catch and shoot or make a play and to have in mind ahead of time where all the defenders and teammates are located. This teaching detail should not be overlooked at any level of play.**

Dribble Punch the Gaps

In the case where the perimeter defenders **"gap"** an offensive player, meaning that neither defender will commit to guarding the offensive player, this player must either shoot the ball or **"punch the gap with the dribble."** The ball handler takes one or two dribbles into the gap and will shoot, if neither defender comes to the ball and make a play if one does commit to him. The purpose of this maneuver is to draw one or both of the defenders to the ball.

As the defenders move to the ball (Diagram 5), the other four offensive players must move to **create passing lanes** for the dribbler, in keeping with our "three in a row principle." The offensive players on either side of the ball must quickly move to create easy passing lanes for the dribbler.

But every player needs to present himself as a possible outlet option in a perfect possession. A player should never assume he is not in play. It is important for the dribbler to pass the ball to one of his partners before the defender's smother him; he needs multiple targets to do that.

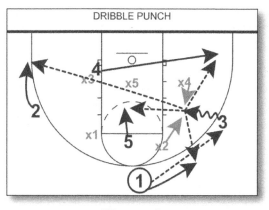

Diagram 5

As Player 1 passes to 3, neither X2 nor X4 go to guard 3, so he either shoots the ball, or takes one or two dribbles into the gap between X2 and X4 in order to draw one or both of them to him. Player 1 cuts behind 3 as a safety outlet and 4 cuts to an open spot on the baseline as shown. Player 5 steps into the middle for a short pass and 2 cuts to his diagonal spot as another outlet and to be in 3's vision.

Ten Basic Rules of Zone Offense

1. Perimeter players align themselves in the gaps of the zone.

2. Perimeter players must be taught to prepare for their catch by observing the positions of all the players on the court and to have hands, legs and feet ready to catch and shoot if open and to make the proper play, if not.

3. All players look to shoot, pass or dribble upon catching the ball, but it must be a high percentage play or move the ball on to a teammate.

4. Perimeter players must look to draw a defender to guard them before passing. Any time a guard covers the ball at the top, quickly pass to the wing on that side. **Any time a guard covers a wing on a pass, it is often a good time to look to reverse the ball quickly, since a low wing will likely have to move up to defend the weak-side wing.**

5. Ball handlers must see the defender(s) guarding the man that they are passing to before they pass.

6. If the defenders present gaps to the ball handler, he **"Punches the Gap"** and his teammates move to create open passing lanes for him.

7. Wing players on the weak side from the ball should move to create a diagonal passing opportunity for their partner, or be a baseline drifter option on a baseline drive.

8. Every third or fourth pass should go to a post player.

9. High post players must turn and face the basket when they catch the ball. They must see both corners when they face the basket. They look to shoot, pass to their post partner flashing to the rim, pass to an open corner player and look for driving opportunities as well.

10. Coaches designate offensive rebounders. Players 4 and 5 normally must aggressively rebound all shots and others need to put themselves in position to recover long rebounds and to see when there is a gap into which they can safely crash for an inside rebound as well. A strong rebound game is essential because many zone coaches fail to teach the specific rebound techniques zones require to be most effective.

Of course, you still emphasize defensive balance, since all good defense starts with a well-planned offense.

STARTING WITH SIMPLE ATTACKS

Once the concepts of spacing and aligning in the gaps has been explained along with the foundational work with the passing and shooting techniques that must continue throughout the learning process, it is good to put in simple ball and player movements even with kids that are in the 6- to 9-year-old range. This depends on the individual maturation level, of course, but there are kids at this age who have pretty well developed ball skills and are ready to learn the basics of ball and player movement to accompany their dribbling, driving and passing skill work.

To avoid being redundant, it is best to go to **Chapters 4 and 5** and look at some of the simple moves or sets described there once you go through this chapter. And, depending on the age group and the players development, **Chapters 7-9** have some simple plays, as well as quite complex ones, that may fit your particular program. Nonetheless, we will show some things in this chapter that we think are suited for young players who become gradually ready to take the next steps in team play. We suggest that the young ones learn early on the value of the high/low game and its automatic responses shown in **Chapter 2.** This single move will put most youth teams in a higher level of play immediately.

Diagram 6 shows a simple move from a 1-2-2 set against a 2-3 zone defense. In fact the alignment can be a 1-3-1 start by putting Player 4 in the high post to start. But here we start with both Players 4 and 5 low

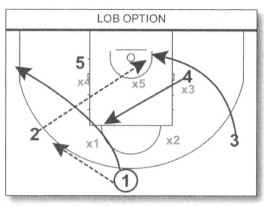

Diagram 6

and break the weak side low man to the high post. Players start in the gaps and Player 1 can throw to a wing on either side, who will move up a little to meet the pass and to shorten the angle. Here Player 1 passes to the left to 2 and cuts to the strong side corner. In youth ball probably both the front and the wing defenders will go to the ball, as the defenses will not normally be sophisticated. If just the low wing covers Player 2, 1 is open in the corner to start and may have a shot or a pass to 5 or 4.

The weak side low man, Player 4, breaks to the high post when 2 catches and has a choice to pass to 1, 5 or 4. This alone will be enough to get a shot for the youngest groups, especially if they have practiced the high/low automatic game. That is, if Player 5 gets the ball, he will try to score or can pass to 4 cutting to the goal or back out to 1, 2 or 3. If the pass goes to Player 4, he will look to shoot or pass under to 5 moving across the lane or swing it to Player 3.

In Diagram 6 we have Player 3 making a cut. Now that could be his move if the ball goes to Player 4 for younger kids, and for older kids it could be for a lob from 2 as is shown

Diagram 7 assumes the group is a little older and shows that either Player 3 cuts for the lob and didn't get it, or that he cut back door when

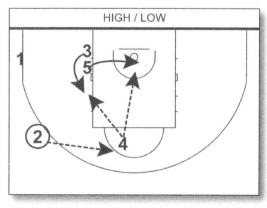

Diagram 7

4 got the ball and did not get it on that cut either and moves under 5. So, Player 5 flashes to the goal automatically, and 3 steps up in the open space between 5 and 1. If there is no play, Player 4 passes back to 2 and 3 continues to his spot on the original wing and they just keep playing. Generally kids can't take it any further until they get older, but obviously Player 4 can dive and X-cut with

Player 5 or could set a pick and roll.

In Diagram 8 the defense is in an odd-front alignment, the 1-2-2 or 3-2, so the offense lines up in those gaps. Here we <u>introduce the dribble rotate move</u> with Player 1 dribbling and pushing 3 down to the corner. Again, the weak side low post man cuts to the top, though he could have started there as well and popped to the top on Player 1's dribble down move. The 1-2-2 initial set is probably better as it gives them the idea of cutting and being in motion.

Player 1 could pass to 5 down low or to 3 in the corner, if open, or hit 4 for the high/low action. As the ball goes into Player 4 in the diagram, 5 moves to seal his man or at least to cut behind and look to be open. At the same time Player 2 cuts back door and 4 can shoot, pass low to 5, hit 2 on the back door on the weak side, pass to 3 in the corner or pass back to 1, who can start all over again by getting to the top and dribbling over to either wing.

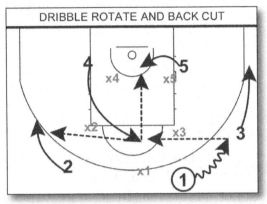

Diagram 8

Diagram 9 shows how ultimately, a team that knows just these two moves in these four diagrams would have a pretty good little offense at the middle levels. That is, they could start with the dribble move in Diagram 8 and pass to the middle, but if there were no play, Player 4 can pass it back to 1 who can move to the top and pass to the wing to player 2 and cut to the corner just as in Diagram 6.

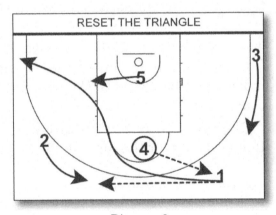

Diagram 9

The next steps with this progression could be to explain to the group old enough to handle it, two of the principles we have set forth in **Chapter 3.** That is, to show the **Corner Pass Automatic** when the ball is passed from the wing to the corner along with a fill cut behind the cut, and the **X-cuts** that the high and low posts can make when they pass the ball out from the middle to the perimeter.

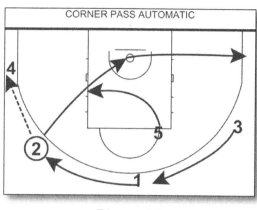

Diagram 10

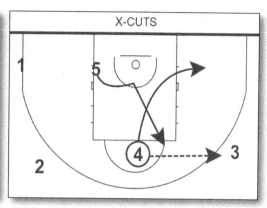

Diagram 11

Diagram 10 illustrates the simple **Corner Pass Automatic** that can be used anytime a wing passes the ball to the corner. The fill cut here is made by Player 1, but if 1 had already cut to the corner, the high post would move over to the wing in an inside fill cut. The ball then would be swung to the weak side, if there were no play by the corner player or the low post player.

In Diagram 11 there is a simple reverse pass from the high post out to the weak side wing that makes an easy **X-cut action** for post players 4 and 5. How posts may move in straight line cuts, circle cuts or the X-cut is described in **Chapter 2.**

Diagrams 12 and 13 demonstrate another simple, but effective, action for younger players at the zone offense game. This starts from a high 1-4 set, one that is a good basic set to have in the team arsenal against zones and changing defenses that is noted in **Chapter 3** that describes **play number 14.**

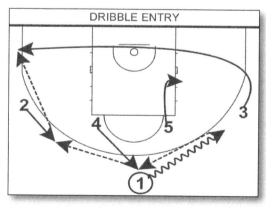

Diagram 12

Diagram 12 shows point 1 dribbling over to the wing on Player 3's side, but it can be run to either side. Weak side post 4 pops up to catch as Player 3 runs to the weak side corner. Player 1 could pass to 3 on the back cut or to 5 rolling down to the low post, but here he passes to 4. Player 4 passes to 2 moving to catch the ball, who may have a quick pass to 3 cutting to the corner.

ATTACKING THE ZONE DEFENSES

In Diagram 13, Player 1 has drifted to the weak side wing and 4 can pass to 2 or 3 in the corner and dive to the block for a catch from either. Low post 5 flashes to the high post. From there he can make a catch for a move of his own or to feed 4 down low or to pass to 1 on the weak side and dive to the basket himself. Player 4 would replace 5 at the top as a simple option. Of course, the coach could carry this out further whereby he would have Player 3 run the baseline off of picks by 4

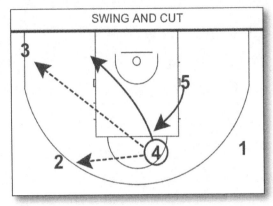

Diagram 13

and/or 5 and so on. The possibilities are almost limitless within reason.

We will now show more advanced moves for players that utilize some of our basic principles in simple alignments. Here a coach can pick from these actions to fit the team that will result in players being confident against zones. Since the 2-3 is the most commonly used zone, we will start with it by using the high/low attack.

2-1-2 Against an Odd-Front: 1-2-2, 3-2, or 1-3-1 Zone

As we follow the general rule that our perimeter players start in the gaps of the zone, we start in a 2-1-2 alignment in a simple attack vs. an odd-number front zone shown in Diagram 14.

In Diagram 15, Player 1 passes to 2 and 5 cuts to the basket. Player 3 will cut to an open spot behind 5 as he reads an opening under the zone, or just to the short corner. However, if he is a 3-point shooter, he can cut to the corner for the skip pass from Player 2. Player 2's first look is for 5, then for 3.

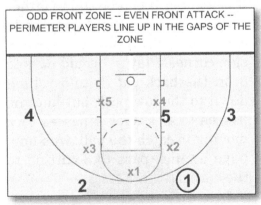

Diagram 14

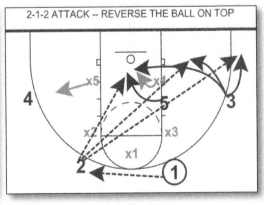

Diagram 15

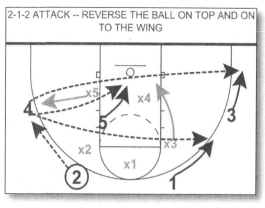

Diagram 16

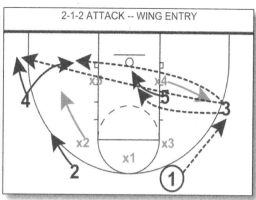

Diagram 17

Diagram 16 shows that Player 2 may also pass to 4, if X5 does not come out to guard him. On his catch, Player 4 may have a shot or he can pass to 5 posting or slipping to the rim. He may have Player 3 or 1 on the skip-pass to the weak side.

Diagram 17 shows the same action continuing on the other wing if the ball is passed to Player 3 instead of 2 in Diagram 15.

Diagram 18 shows **another option with the high post entry, the strong side lift.** When the ball is on top, Player 5 may flash the foul line area for a catch from 1 or 2. Here Player 5 catches and turns to face the

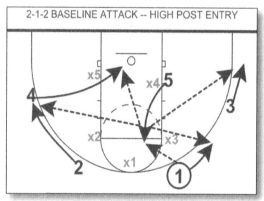

Diagram 18

basket as always in the high post. See **Chapter 2** on post play. He looks for his shot and then for his post partner flashing to the basket. The wings, 2 and 3, drop to the baseline and Player 1 spreads to the high wing area opposite the direction of his pass. Of course, Player 5 can pass to any of his teammates who may be open. Play can continue in the high/low game they must learn as a basic tool in zone play. As noted before, it's best to get the ball into the high post as often as possible because it is the best attack area against the zone and is tough to defend in any defense.

The passing options and player movements are simple. Quick ball movement along with simple reads will make it difficult for the zone. Players learn the basic principles to build on as they progress to the next levels. Although we have stated this previously, it bears repeating. It is better to teach players to play rather than to teach "plays." Whether you are teaching man-to-man or zone offense, you play against the actions of the defenders. By teaching the players to make plays against the defense, they learn the principles of play that help develop their basketball IQ.

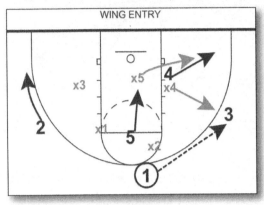

Diagram 19   Diagram 20

High Low Versus the 2-3 or 2-1-2 Zone

Three Perimeter players align as in Diagram 19 below in the 1-3-1 seams/gaps of the 2-3 zone. Post players start in a high/low alignment. The posts play as a two-man team in tandem with one another and in concert with the perimeter players as always. The simplest system of attacking the even front zone is to combine the perimeter passing with simple post movement. The best shooting forward, or it could be a smaller player, would play in 4's position in the low post.

Diagram 20 shows Player 4's operating area is roughly the small colored area along the baseline. He goes out to the limits of his shooting range on the ball side. The biggest player who is the best finisher inside will start in Player 5's position in the high post. His operating area is basically in the high, mid and low post area following the movement of the ball.

The point 1 engages either defensive guard and then passes to the wing on that player's side as in Diagram 19. This draws the defensive low wing player X4 out to guard our wing 3. On any pass from the point to the wing, Player 4 cuts to the edge of his shooting range in the short or medium corner below the ball upon the catch as in Diagram 20.

1. Player 3's first look is to shoot, if he is wide open. If Player 3 shoots, 1 and 3 are safeties and 2, 4 and 5 are offensive rebounders.

2. If X4 comes out to defend Player 3 in a "low wing out" move, 3 looks to 4 below him. If Player 4 is not open it will usually be X5 who is guarding him, keying 5 to dive to the basket. On the low/high action Player 4 must look to pass to 5, if he does not have an easy shot or a scoring move of his own.

3. If Player 3 sees that 4 is not open, 3 may pass-fake at 4 to induce X5 to move toward 4 to help 5 get more space to be open. He would look directly for Player 5 cutting into the hole left by X5. If Player 5 is not open in the lane, he exits to the hashmark above the ball side block.

4. If Player 3 cannot pass to 5 it will usually be because X3 has sagged in on him from the weak side. So, Player 3 may be able to skip pass to 2 on the weak side.

5. **KEY NOTE:** Any time that X2 comes to guard Player 3 instead of wing X4 or else comes to bump X4 back down to the baseline, wing 3 passes back to 1 to reverse the ball to 2, **which forces X3 to cover on a low wing out. See Diagram 21.** Player 4 roves the baseline when 3 swings to 1 and he may be open on the short corner on the weak side. Post 5 will slide across to post as well as in Diagram 22.

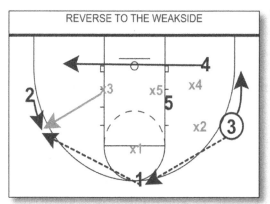 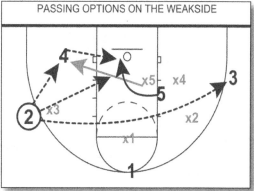

Diagram 21   Diagram 22

The youth team can simply swing the ball back to the top and over to the original side and repeat the process until someone gets open. The coach may want to teach the big men to offer a pick and roll after the ball has been swung two or three times as well. They can always rely on basic high/low post action learned in the section on post play in Chapter 2 or use some of the simpler of the plays in Chapters 5 through 12 for a little more advanced youth team. There are dozens from which to choose.

DRILLS FOR TEACHING ZONE OFFENSE

Passing and Execution Drills.

In Diagram 23, **Around the Horn Passing,** perimeter players present themselves ready to catch and shoot as instructed relative to feet, legs and hands positioning. The Post (P) is the only position that can move and step into the middle of the lane and come back into the high post area. Every third or fourth pass must go in to him. He must turn and look inside when he catches. On the catch, the weak side baseline player (4 or 5) must move toward the goal and the weak side wing (2 or 3) must move to the corner. There is no shot until the coach yells out "shot" and the next receiver shoots it.

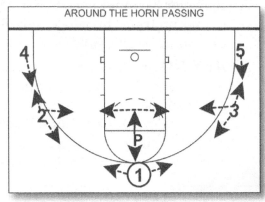

Diagram 23

Then the players form their rebound pattern with at least Players 4 and 5 going to rebound, as well as any other man down below the foul line in a position in which he thinks he can get the rebound. The other players check off for a long rebound, but must get in position to get back on defense as well. Perimeter players pass with their outside hands making one-hand push passes around the horn. Then they can change to two-hand and then to overhead passes around the horn and cross court. Receivers try to look at the middle of the floor and look at the basket when they receive a pass. Add a pass fake away before you make your pass to the drill as well. Use hard flat passes. You can have five, 10 or 15 players on a basket, and players rotate to the end of the next line after each shot.

Diagram 24 drills the **Diagonal Skip Passes** on the perimeter. Overhead passes with no wind up and limited arc. Start with the Player 1 to 3 pass and finish with the 2 to 5 pass, then change starting with the corner to high wing passes. Then incorporate pass fakes. Rotate positions after each series and continue.

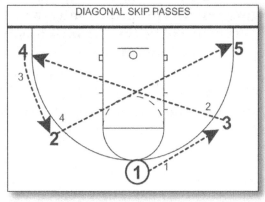

Diagram 24

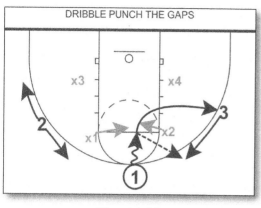

Diagram 25

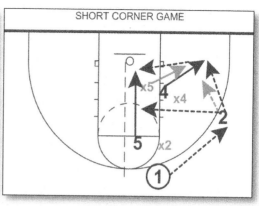

Diagram 26

In Diagram 25, three perimeter players work on **Punching the Gaps** with four perimeter defenders aligned in a box formation. Cones may be used instead, but at some point live defense is needed to prevent over-penetration and to develop the various abilities of passing and creating open pass lanes to the ball. Offense lines up in the gaps and dribble punch receivers create passing angles for the penetrator. Ball handlers pass before the defenders get to them and jump stop to pass to a partner. When the partner penetrates, the original penetrator fills behind the next penetration. Change after each offensive player has made two or three penetrations.

Diagram 26 shows the **Short Corner Game.** This drill is restricted to one side of the court working on Player 1 drawing X2 then passing to 2 forcing X4 out on the ball. Player 4 pops to the short corner. Everyone reads X5 to see if he will step out to take Player 4, which creates a hole for 5 to dive. At first this may be a coach playing at X5 to mix up the coverage.

Player 2 may pass to 4 who will shoot if he is open. If not he can pass to Player 5 diving if X5 has moved out to 4. If X5 has not moved to him, he may draw him with a shot fake and then pass to Player 5 on the dive or pass back to 3. Player 3 may also pass fake to 4 to draw X5 and then be able to pass to 5 directly on his dive. Everyone is keying on X5 while working with Player 5 on the timing of his dive. Move the ball until a good option occurs.

Diagram 27 (next page) shows a **High/low Game** set vs. a two-front defense and starts with Player 1 passing to 5 in the high post, then cutting away to the high wing, or high elbow, area. Player 5 turns and faces the basket, then 4 flashes in to seal, or can cut under the basket to the weak side block, as he reads the defense, which can be cones at first. Players 2 and 3 space to the corners. Player 5 looks for 4 on his flash and feeds him if he can get open. If Player 4 cannot catch, he clears to the opposite lane.

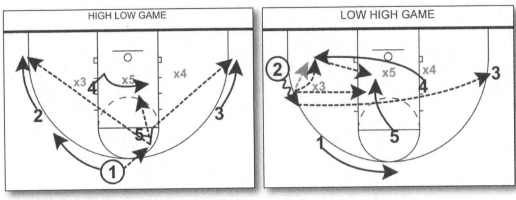

Diagram 27   Diagram 28

Diagram 28 shows that Player 5 has passed to 2 in the corner. Player 4 can straight line cut to the post. Player 2 dribbles up to the gap area bringing X3 with him, and 4 pops to the short corner. They all read X5 to attack what he leaves open. If Player 4 is open since X5 did not cover him, 2 passes to 4 for a shot, or for a pass to 5 diving to the rim if X5 comes late to 4. Player 2 may also pass fake at 4 to move X5 then pass to 5 directly as he cuts to the basket.

Then do the same drill working on the X-cut with the posts by having Player 5 dive when he passes to 2 and then 4 cuts to the rim and on up into the high post area looking for a catch.

A lot of 2-on-2 with the high posts working together on offense and defense while two wings pass to them or skip pass to one another with no defense on the wings is a must-do drill for post play excellence.

Drilling the Punch Game — executing the Bailouts

Working on the team response to penetrations will serve the team well against both the zone and man defenses. It is simple enough to drill progressively with two, three or four players against the cones and finally with all five. You can add defense to both, but in the drilling it is best to work on one move at a time to start.

We present eight simple drills that can be done with no defense to get habits to which defense can be added from time to time. The drilling of habits against no defense is important to form automatic responses. However, the reading of the defense cannot be learned unless defense is put in as the players get comfortable. Review on light days against no defense is still helpful, even in the last month of the season. The game is played 5-on-5 full court and practices must work that in a lot. But habits are learned in specific drill work at half and full court.

In Diagrams 29 and 30 there are three perimeter players drilling the penetration baseline in Diagram 29 and in the middle in Diagram 30.

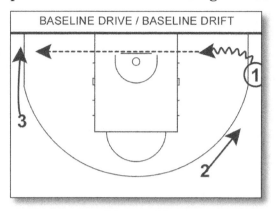

Diagram 29

Form lines behind the players and take a turn and rotate to the end of the line going around clockwise — you may have to explain in this digital age which way the clock runs. The drills are simple but need to be precise.

The first is the baseline drive with baseline drift with a safety follow-up (Diagram 29). Drill it from one side and then the other with the baseline pass being made for the score. Rebound it in and rotate. Use two balls to have the next players ready.

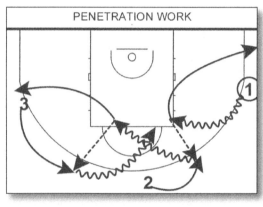

Diagram 30

Diagram 30 drills the **wing middle drive.** Player 1 penetrates in the middle and kicks back to 2 who must come toward the ball. Player 2 makes a second penetration across the top and 3 comes to the ball for a penetration shot. Rebound and rotate.

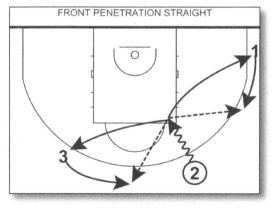

Diagram 31

The drill in Diagram 31 is for the **Direct Front Penetration.** Player 2 punches in from the top directly toward the strong side block. Player 1 is in the corner and 3 is in the other front spot, though you can alter the drill by putting him in the other corner. If he is out front, he follows the penetration as in this drill and gets the shot. If he is in the corner, he lifts up a couple steps and gets a cross court feed from Player 1 on the second penetration by 1. Note that Player 2 fills in behind 1 after passing to him. Rebound and rotate.

Diagram 32 illustrates the **Front Diagonal Penetration** toward the weak side elbow area. Player 2 drives it and kicks back to 3 after he is at least even with him, not in front of him, and it is good if he is a step past him. This stops the jump switch on defense. Player 3 makes the second penetration and 1 comes up out of the corner for a shot. Again, rebound and rotate.

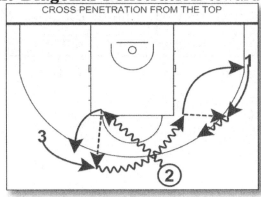

Diagram 32

Diagram 33 shows **the post men's responses to penetrations.** On the **Baseline Drive** strong side post man must move up to a spot that is a step or two up the lane from the block and a step or two out to the sideline as shown. He must present himself in a position to catch and shoot, if his man drops off to help the penetration, which he usually will do.

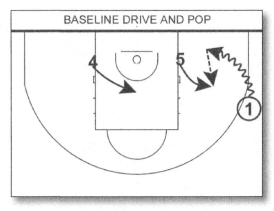

Diagram 33

The weak side post normally moves to the front of the rim, especially if there is a baseline drift. In fact, **if he sees there is no baseline drift cutter,** he can move to just under the goal and serve as a baseline pass outlet for the penetrator.

Diagram 34 illustrates the post movement on the **Wing Middle Penetration.** Again, the strong side post man **moves opposite the direction of the penetration.** The weak side post this time will read his defense and get to a spot where he creates an open pass lane wide or at the weak side of the rim for a high pass.

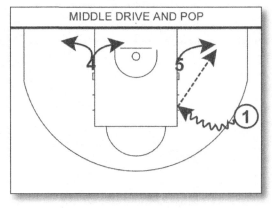

Diagram 34

A general concept of spacing has been to have options to the **front (down or forward pass), the middle, the reverse and to a wide diagonal angle.** This is true of offense in general as well as when there is a trap on the ball. We try to adhere to these principles in our sets as well as in press breakers. It is apparent in the five-man drills below relative to bailouts.

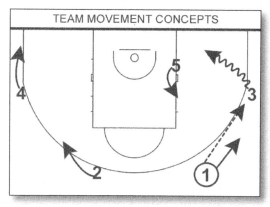
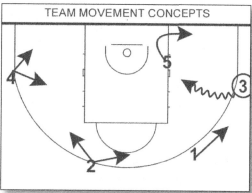

Diagram 35   Diagram 36

In Diagram 35 we have put together all five players to get them coordinated. Here we have the **baseline drive, baseline drift along with popping the low post.** Player 1 trails the drive for a safety outlet and player 2 gets into vision of the ball in the diagonal spot on the high weak side. The best way to drill this is to have Player 3 kick the ball back to 1, who will reverse it to 2. Player 4 will come back up to the wing area to catch and then he runs a **second baseline drive, baseline drift.** The coach can yell out how many passes he wants to see at that point and they make that number and shoot the ball.

Diagram 36 shows the **Middle Penetration** with the post pop to the baseline. The drill runs the same way as the baseline drift one on Diagram 35. The shot can be taken on the second middle penetration. Note that weak side players 2 and 4 have a choice of short steps to take to put themselves in positions for an open pass, what we call "breaking the three-in-a-row-line." They do not want to be in a position whereby their nearest defender is right in the middle of the pass lane from the ball.

In Diagram 37, Player 1 executes the **Direct Front Penetration.** Player 3 comes up a couple steps out of the corner and is ready to catch, if his man drops in to help on 1. Note that post 5 **relocates** to the opposite side. If he gets stuck, his alternate move is for Player 5 to pop to open up on the baseline, but that is not as good as when 5 gets to the weak side board for a lob (even off the glass) or a rebound. Player 2 follows the penetration for safety and 4 comes up a couple steps out of the weak side corner. On this drill, it is not as easy to run continuity, so the coach just yells out the number of

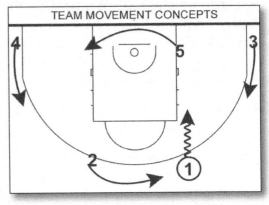

Diagram 37

passes that should be made and then they rotate. It is good for all players to get into every position on this. One never knows where a player will be when a drive is made.

Diagram 38 shows the **Cross Front Penetration.** Here is one where execution is very important. Player 2's natural tendency is to drift away from the drive, but that really puts the defense in a good position to steal that pass and turn it into a layup. By cutting toward the ball, but in a line above it, puts Player 2 in a position for defensive safety and takes his defender away from a help position on 1.

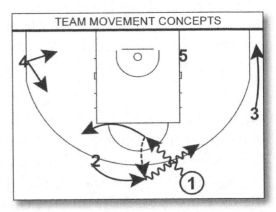

Diagram 38

Key Point is that the flip pass that can be made to Player 2 should be made after 2 has gotten even or just a step past the ball to keep the defender on 1 from jump switching. It also puts Player 2 in a position to turn the corner and drive downhill into the paint to make a play, if he gets the ball. Alternatively, Player 1 can pass ahead to 4 coming out of the corner. Player 4 can back cut, if his man tries to deny him instead of helping on 1's initial penetration. Also note that Player 5 holds position when 1 cross penetrates, but relocates when 2 penetrates directly down.

Competing in the Drills. In any of these drills you get a bit more out of them if you find ways to make them competitive, even if it is just seeing how many shots can be made in a row in the shooting drills. When there is an offense and a defense on the court, your team may play games to 3 or 5 with the defense swapping with the offense if they get a stop, or you may play games of five possessions and keep track of the number of scores out of five chances. Then switch from offense to defense and run five more possessions and see how many times the second group scores. The emphasis is on the defense if you play the game to count the stops, the **Stops Game.** If you count the scores, you are playing the **"O" Game.**

We have presented a very basic zone offense upon which a simple cutting game can be added as the players are able to learn more. However, what is here is a simple offense that is effective against zones and which has the players "read the defense," an important part of the game that will serve them well as they progress to higher levels. There is enough in the book to take the best ones to D-1 level as you add to their knowledge.

—————————— CHAPTER 16 ——————————

DRILLS FOR TEACHING ZONE OFFENSE

Good fundamentals remain the foundation of quality basketball regardless — from grade school to professional levels of play. As coaches we are entrusted with creating the best possible learning experiences for the athletes under our direction. Some call this a sacred trust. Not only must we teach them the skills of the game, but how to apply those skills in game situations or, "how to **play** the game." When players develop an understanding of the game, their basketball IQ grows commensurately, as does their sense of enjoyment and satisfaction. It is with this in mind that we offer this chapter on *Drills for Teaching Zone Defense*. The drills are simply "teaching tools" in which the whole is demonstrated so that the athletes get a mental image of the whole play and its sequences/actions. The skill or play is then broken down into its parts and the parts are focused on because they are simpler to deal with. Once the parts are understood they are then combined in the proper sequence to form the whole, and the learning process has been significantly enhanced. Focusing on the details of the action that are necessary for successful execution is obviously very important to the learning process. Most coaches have limited time, so it's important that any drills used relate very closely to what the athletes will perform in game situations. John Wooden often said "don't mistake activity for achievement." In other words, just because the players are moving and the ball is being passed etc., it is not necessarily true that much is being achieved. It is essential that all drills presented to the athletes contribute not only to the building of their skills and the timing of their movements, but to their understanding of how this relates to the game situation.

Passing Drills are essential. Passing and receiving are probably the most important skills required for attacking zone offenses. This is true whether it is quick passes around the perimeter to stretch and move the zone, or a post feed — a skill that is equally essential in attacking both man-to-man and zone defenses. The ball must be passed crisply, with no arc and with precise accuracy at the target. Shooters must be ready to get the pivot foot in position to be pointed to the target and hands ready, giving a target for the passer. All is affected by how much pressure the defense is applying, as opposed to standing wide open. There are various concepts on how best to do this, so coaches should examine these theories and present them to shooters. One method will be better for some, while another may be better for others. But teach technique options. Don't just assume that you cannot help shooters get better. That is the lazy person's way out.

Passers must read their own defender, certainly the defender guarding the receiver; and on post feeds they must note the position of the help side defender. Cross court/skip passes must also be practiced. See Diagrams 1 and 2 below.

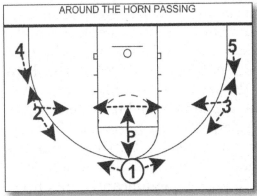 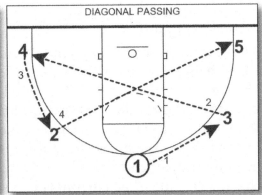

Diagram 1   Diagram 2

Diagram 1 shows a simple drill whereby the team will pass a designated number of passes and then take a shot. The ball must go into the high post every third or fourth pass. Twelve passes and a shot, then rotate is a good number to work with.. Weak side baseline players move toward the basket when the ball goes to the high post and weak side wings drop to the corner.

Diagram 2 drills the skip passing that is effective for varsity high school players on up. As shown Player 1 passes to 3, then 3 skips it to 4. Player 4 passes up to 2 who skips it to 5. Then Player 5 passes to 1 who starts it again with a pass to 3, but this time 3 passes to 5 and 5 skips to 2. Player 2 passes to 4 who skips to 3 and the ball goes back to 1. Rotate as desired.

This helps drill the concept of the "deep diagonal pass angle" that needs to be a part of offense. It is a spacing technique that lets a player know that he should have a player spaced from him at a diagonal angle from the ball when it is in his possession.

Post Feed Drills. Diagrams 3 and 4 help with understanding the **45-degree angle** or the **"Line of 45."** Feeding the post is vital to the development of inside players and fundamental to the inside game. Posts must learn to use their bodies to gain advantages for themselves as the basketball crosses the line of 45-degrees, either on the dribble or on the pass. In Diagram 3, Player 1 starts a step above the line of 45 and dribbles a bounce or two across the line as post 5 seals his defender off and provides a target hand for the passer with his baseline hand, while legally blocking the denial arm of the post defender. The passer makes the pass with his outside hand, passing into the body of the post player. The pass may be high pass or a bounce pass as determined by the post defender and where the post wants the pass. Start with no defense then progress to defense on the passer and the post player.

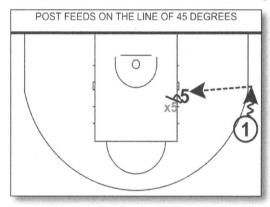

POST FEEDS ON THE LINE OF 45 DEGREES

Diagram 3

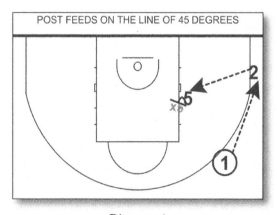

POST FEEDS ON THE LINE OF 45 DEGREES

Diagram 4

Diagram 4 adds another player below the 45-degree line with the passer significantly above the line of 45. Player 2 catches and sweeps the ball to the baseline side and passes the ball into the body of the sealing post man.

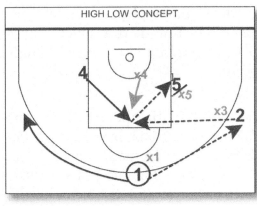

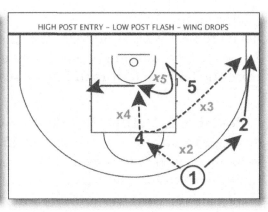

Diagram 5   Diagram 6

In Diagram 5, **we have added a weak side post player** in order to teach any player that, when he is on the weak side and his man is helping out against a post player, he must flash high to occupy his defender and to punish the post defender in the high/low game. It must be emphasized that Player 4 not break the split line on his cut, so that he does not destroy his passing angle to 5 on his cut high. He must read his defender and if he is below him he can "blast cut" directly to the nail at the free throw line. If his defender is closer to his cutting line, he then makes body contact with his man in an L-cut to get open at the free throw line. That is, contact the defender's body, then break to the ball as in a short phrase, "body — ball." So many players do not understand how to get open even at elite levels, unless someone screens for them. Unless the offensive player gets into the body of the defender and then starts the move to the ball on his own time, the defender has the advantage. He is running in the inside lane — the receiver is in the outside lane. Horses even understand that advantage. And once the offensive player has moved into the defender's body, he decides when the race to the ball starts — or whether the race is out the back door instead of the front. Common sense tells you this is a good plan for the offensive player.

In the drill in Diagram 5, if X4 does not play 4 but lags back to plug the area, Player 4 can shoot or sweep and drive to the basket. Make three or four passes into Player 5 then rotate positions with the outside players changing with one another and the posts doing the same. This teaches Player 2 to read the defense before his catch as well.

Diagram 6 is a drill to work on the passing and timing required in the high/low game. Player 1 passes to 4 and flares to the free throw line extended and 2 cuts to the corner. Post 4 faces the basket and Player 5 ducks in on X5 and 4 makes the pass to 5, if possible. If Player 5 cannot catch, he exits to the weak side lane. Player 4 may then pass to 2 in the corner and make his cut to the basket. (Not shown in the diagram) Player 2 works on passing to 4 for the layup. If no pass can be made, Player 5 can replace 4 in the high post and repeat the action with 4 and 5 changing roles. Make three or four scores and then rotate Player 1 with 2 and 4 with 5.

Post Entries off Skip-passes and Flash cuts. In a double low post set, when the ball is skip-passed to the weak side corner area, there is an **excellent chance to screen the middle man of the zone for a deep catch.** The concept here is that when a skip-pass is made to the weak side low area, the weak side post man should find the nearest man and screen him off at least momentarily on the flight of the ball. **Post 4 would pin X3 in, if possible, and release him when the ball is overhead to go seal off X5** for a deep post catch possibility.

In that case the post, who was on the strong side when the pass was thrown, becomes a flash cutter to an open high post gap, when the ball is caught on the weak side. Post 5 flashes up into an open gap in the middle as indicated (Diagram 7).

Diagram 8 shows a drill where we attack the bottom of a 2-3 from a 1-3-1 set that moves to a 1-2-2, when Player 5 dives to the strong side block. Player 1 passes to 2 and high post 5 dives to the goal. The weak side post 4 screens in on X3, the weak side wing defender, as the ball is passed to Player 2. Wing 3 drops to the area behind Player 4 as 2 pass fakes at 5 to draw X5, and then skip-passes to 3.

As the ball is overhead, Player 4 releases his screen and then seals X5 as deep as he can in the lane. Player 3 may shoot, or attack X3's closeout or pass to 4. Post 5 should move into a high post gap opening to pull out X4 or to get an open catch, if X4 helps on Player 4 (not shown).

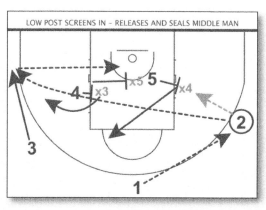

Diagram 7

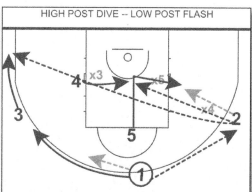

Diagram 8

Alternate sides and run three or four repetitions on each side. You may even add where Player 5 cuts to the ball off of 4's screen and 4 pops to the high post area. Coaches will adjust these drills to fit their offensive priorities, but in the course of play, players will find themselves in position to use these tactics to free up teammates, provided they know about them (Diagram 8).

DRILLING ON THE POSITIVE USE OF THE DRIBBLE

Our next drills focus on Dribble Pulls, Post Timing and Player Movement on Penetration. Diagram 9 illustrates the work on the timing of post movement. Point 1 takes one or two dribbles away from Player 4, the signal for 4 to pop opposite the dribble. Point 1 passes to Player 4 and clears to the high wing elbow area away from 4, who quickly turns to face the basket. Wings 2 and 3 drop to the corners while post 5 flashes to the front of the rim to seal the defender, and then exits to the opposite post above the block. For the purposes of the drill Player 4 pass fakes at 5 on the seal and then passes to 3 in the corner. Player 3's first look is for 5 now posted on the block. Assuming in the drill Player 5 is not open inside, 3 pass fakes and takes a couple dribbles into the gap, a dribble pull key for 5 to pop to the short corner area.

In Diagram 10, Player 3 pass fakes at 5, triggering 4 to dive to the rim. Player 3 pass fakes at 4 as well and skip-passes to 2 in the weak side corner. Post 4 posts above the block.

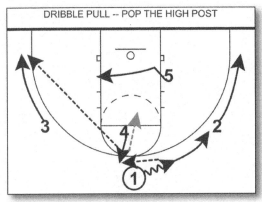

Diagram 9

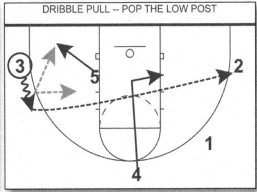

Diagram 10

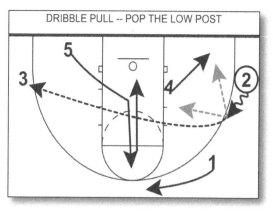

Diagram 11

Diagram 11 shows Player 5 flashing to the middle and up to the high post after 4's dive cut. Players 2 and 4 repeat the actions taken by 3 and 5 in Diagram 10. This can be run side-to-side for three or four times.

Punching the Gaps and Building Habits for Bailout positions on Penetration

Drawing two players to the ball and finding the open man is an offensive fundamental common to attacking both man-to-man and zone defenses.

The purpose of the drill is to "punch the ball into a gap in the zone," to draw two defenders to the ball and quickly pass to an open teammate, while the defenders are moving towards the ball handler. The ball handlers must avoid driving the ball too far up against the defense before making a pass.

Diagram 12, shows a drill that can be used to teach this aspect of the dribble attack. The drill is continuous as the passer goes behind the man he passes to after his pass; the receiver then attacks the next gap. It is a simple penetrate and go behind drill and after the third penetration the handler shoots. Rotate spots clockwise and repeat and with six players, of course have the next group go right behind the first. These are easily incorporated into the daily shooting drills.

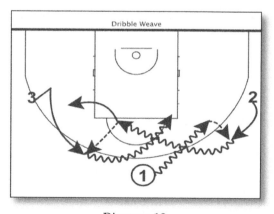

Diagram 12

Diagrams 13-17 show the various angles to work on in these drills. They are pretty self- explanatory and can be adjusted to fit any offense.

Diagram 13 shows a **front penetration** with two players in the corners. Each comes up a couple of steps on the penetration and Player 1 passes to 2 and replaces in the corner.

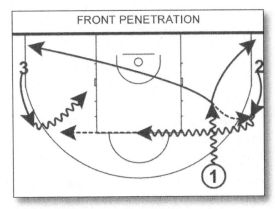

Diagram 13

1. Player 2 makes a **middle penetration** and passes to 3 now on the weak side wing and replaces him in the corner.

2. Player 3 **penetrates middle** and passes out to 1 who has moved up to the wing after 2 penetrated and passed to 3.

3. Not shown is that Player 1 **penetrates middle** and shoots. Then they rotate.

Diagram 14 shows Player 2 on a **front direct penetration** as in Diagram 13 but this time with the players behind him reacting. Player 3 is at the top and rotates behind the penetration as the safety. Player 1 rolls up to the top filling behind 3.

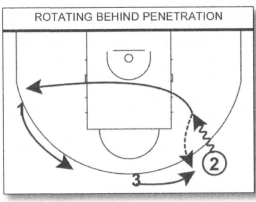

Diagram 14

1. **Player 2 pivots and passes back to 3** and rotates to the weak side wing to replace 1.

2. Player 1 rotates behind 3 and 3 penetrates the same way 2 did, pivots and passes back to 1 and rotates to the weak wing to replace 2.

3. Player 1 penetrates and shoots.

Diagram 15 shows a two-man drill for the **baseline drive-baseline drift** move.

1. Player 1 can drive and pass to 2 for a catch and shoot. Do this on both sides and change lines after each shot.

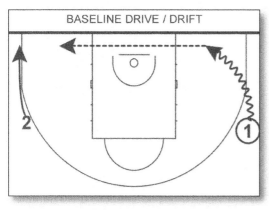

Diagram 15

2. To include a third player, one can start at the top and rotate behind the baseline penetration. The driver stops and pivots and passes back to the top, as if he had been stopped on the drive. Player 3 can then throw a skip pass to 2, or he could penetrate to the goal and pass out to 1 or 2 popping up from the corners — depends on what the coach wants to do with it.

Diagram 16 shows another two-man drill with a **front diagonal penetration.**

1. Player 1 dribble penetrates from the front to the inside, angling toward the weak side block.

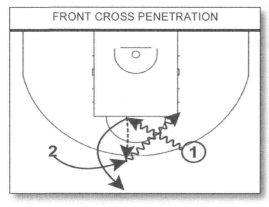

Diagram 16

2. Player 2 rotates behind the penetration instead of drifting away in order to be a safety and also to be able to make a second penetration.

3. Player 1 passes to 2 when he is even or, preferably, a step past him to prevent switching.

4. Player 2 catches, makes the second penetration and shoots.

5. Player 1 also **must cut** <u>behind</u> 2 after he passes to him.

6. A third player can be added in the corner to move for a catch and shoot after the second penetration.

Diagram 17 shows the **cutback drill** that can be an option when the ball is passed from the wing to the corner.

1. Player 1 passes to 2 in the corner and cuts to the lane and then cuts back as soon as he gets there.

2. Player 2 catches and pen-etrates two or three dribbles and kicks the ball back to 1 in the corner. While they could go around in a circle on this two or three times, it is OK to run it just once when there are four or more players in the drill and take the shot each time, then change lines.

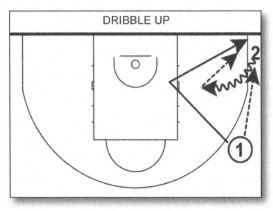

Diagram 17

3. The drill can be run with a player in the post who pops to the short corner — or 3-point line, if a shooter. In that drill, Player 1 would cut on through and go to the end of the post man's line.

Driving to the Basket — teaching and drilling the techniques of crossovers, change of pace, spins, etc. in 1-1, 2-2, and 3-3 drills with intent to get to the basket. It requires more than talk.

It is as important to drill driving to the basket versus zones as it is for man-to-man scenarios. We suggest that coaches may want to start teaching/drilling the principles of driving at the basket in a 2-on-2 situ-ation, then build to 3-on-3, 4-on-4 from the various spots on the floor. It is important to involve the bailout rules as you build your progressions. The principles and rules laid out in **Chapters 2 to 5** will prepare your athletes to understand what to do, how to do it, where to do it and when to do it. It will build your players' understanding of the game so that, when someone attacks the basket on the dribble, he has four passing outlets in predictable places whether you are facing a zone or man-to-man defense.

Drilling the Dribble Rotate move to distort the defense. This correlates to **Chapter 4** on the positive use of the dribble. One can get an idea of other things they can drill on if he likes one of the moves with the dribble in the chapter.

Diagram 18

1. Player 1 makes a Dribble Down move to push 2 to the corner and flatten the defense into a 2-3. Player 3 pops to the top and when 1 reverses the ball to 3, 2 cuts to the baseline and tries to find a gap where 3 can throw him a pass.

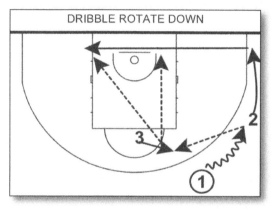

Diagram 18

2. In a game he would go on to the corner, if he did not get a pass. In this drill Player 3 will throw a pass to him as shown on one side of the goal or the other, and then the players rotate and do it again.

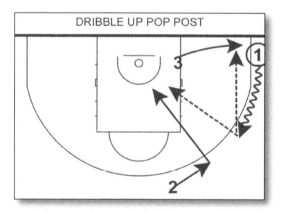

Diagram 19

Diagram 19

1. Player 1 runs a Dribble Up move out of the corner. Player 3 is in the low post or short corner and fills in behind in the open corner.

2. Player 2 takes a step or two toward the penetration and then back cuts to the goal. Player 1 can pass to either one and they rotate.

Screening Game Work — Drilling on some of the aspects presented in Chapter 6.

Flare Screens — many screening actions versus zones may be improved by drilling the exact actions. In Diagrams 20 and 21 we see flare screens used against the top a 2-3 zone.

Diagram 20

1. Point 1 passes to Player 2 as 3 sets a flare screen on X1. Player 1 cuts off the flare screen and 2 makes a skip pass to 1 for a possible shot.

2. Player 3 flashes to the ball as 1 clear's the screen then continues his cut up to the point. After passing to 1, 2 sets a flare screen on X2 for Player 3.

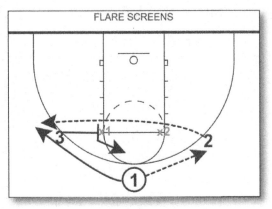

Diagram 20

Diagram 21

1. This shows the continuation as Player 3 cuts off 2's screen and 1 hit's him with a skip pass as 2 flashes up to the point. The drill can continue for three skip passes and the third man shoots the ball. Then rotate positions and repeat till each has had a shot.

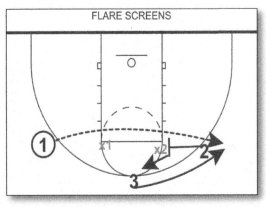

Diagram 21

Pin Screens — Diagrams 22 and 23 demonstrate a drill for simple **pin screens.**

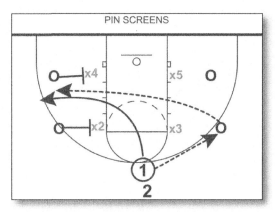

Diagram 22

Diagram 22

1. Player 1 passes to O on the right side as two O's on the left side pin in on X2 and X3.

2. Point 1 then cuts between the pin screens and O on the right side skip passes to Player 1 for the shot.

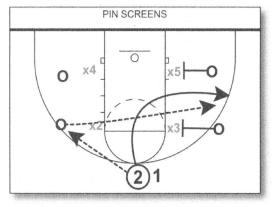

Diagram 23

Diagram 23

1. Player 2 passes to the O on the left side and cuts through two pin screens on X3 and X5 set on the right side.

2. O skip passes to Player 2 for the shot. The players can rotate spots so that all the potential shooters get shots and the logical pickers work on their slip cuts.

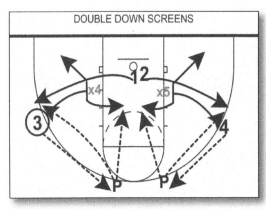 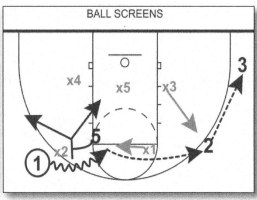

Diagram 24   Diagram 25

Down Screens and Ball Screens

Diagram 24

1. We present a drill for down screens. Players 3 and 4 screen down for 1 and 2, who cut off the screens. Players 1 and 2 read the defenders and may curl, fade or pop, depending on what the defenders do.

2. The two P's at the top have two balls each. With the first ball they pass to the cutter coming off the screens. With the second they pass to the screeners who flash to the ball as the cutter clears their screens.

3. Cutters and screeners can change positions and sides of the court. The coach decides how many shots must be taken or made before the drill is over. It is better if the P's are point guards instead of coaches or managers. Coaches may be good passers but that won't help win a game.

Diagram 25

1. Here is an example of a simple ball screen off the elbow versus a 2-3 zone. Player 5 sets a screen on X2 for 1. Player 1 uses the screen and tries to draw X1 to him. Player 5 may roll or pop.

2. If Player 1 draws X1 he makes the pass to 2 who is now 2 on 1 with 3 on X3. If X3 comes to him, he passes to Player 3 for the open shot.

3. If two more passers can be added to the drill in order to put up more shots, one would pass to Player 5 on the roll or pop, and the other pass would pass to 2, if he passed to 3 or he would pass to 3 if 2 shot.

4. This method allows three players to get shots on each rep. If you added three passers, Player 1 could be able to pull up and shoot if X1 does not take him, and the other three teammates would get a shot as well. This is not necessary but gets more shots up. The execution is the most important factor.

MORE ON PASSING DRILLS

The last two items here drill essential passing while also instilling some of the habits that fit many of the Automatics from Chapter 3 and the High/low Cutters game from Chapter 5 for those who wish to utilize them.

We have already addressed drills for the High/low Automatic, dribble moves and penetration responses. The following emphasize passing and reading the defense and making good player movement responses to ball movement instead of standing in the offense.

The Automatics as explained in Chapter 3 can be taught and drilled starting with four perimeter players and four defenders set in a box. The purpose of the drills is to teach the players to:

1. **Draw a top defender** then pass to that side to a high wing position. This **gets low wing defender out on the ball** far from the open corner below the ball.
2. **Cut to the open corner** below the wing with the ball to have an open shot or to force the zone to rotate.
3. **Cut to the opposite corner,** if you do not draw a back wing defender out.
4. **Cut through from the wing on a pass to the corner** and the corner man dribbles up. Learn the **cutback move** with that as well.
5. **Rove the baseline** when covered in the corner and the ball is reversed from the wing, usually after a pass fake to the man in the corner to key it.
6. **Fill cut the open space** left by a cutter to provide for ball reversal.

The first in a set of three passing drills will involve only 4-on-4 with a non-aggressive, yet moving 2-2 box defense, as it is a drill for passing and reading how the defense responds as opposed to having the defense get steals or to trap, though such features can be added.

Perimeter players passing and cutting. The first set is one to read the first defensive response on a wing entry pass, having already worked the high/low passing drill. The idea is to read if a **low wing defender** covers the wing, the X3 or X4 in a 2-3 or an X4 or X5 in a 1-2-2 set.

In the first set, we do not have a man in the high post, just perimeter players in the drill. Note that on the first side we try to get the low defender out to the wing on the first side and cut to the open corner. Players 3 and 4 line up in the gaps between X1/X3 and X2/X4 respectively.

Diagram 26: shows that the low wing had to come up to cover the wing.

1. Player 1 drag dribbles at X2 or even toward X1 to get X2 engaged in guarding him and then crosses over to pass to 3, so that X4 will come out to defend. He passes to Player 3 and cuts to the open corner. All players behind the cut move up to fill cut for reversal of the ball. A shot may be taken at the end or can continue on as in the next diagram.

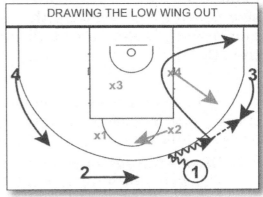

Diagram 26

Diagram 27:

1. Wing 3 passes to Player 1 in the corner, forcing X4 to chase down as X2 rotates in a bump down.

2. After passing, Player 3 cuts in the normal Corner Pass Automatic, and will move up to the weak side wing, since there will be no one on the wing. He would go to the corner, if a player were in the wing area.

3. The other perimeter players slide over to fill for the opening Player 3 left to allow ball reversal. The ball is totally

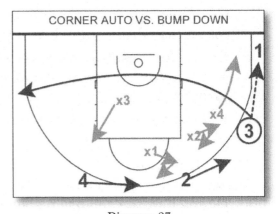

Diagram 27

reversed with Player 3 shooting. Rotate to the direction of the shooter, this time that is clockwise starting with Player 3's initial position on the right wing.

Diagrams 26 through 29 are team drills that can be run separately as individual drills especially at first, when they must be taught that way. Then Drills 26-27 can be put together in a pair with the shot being taken at the end of Drill 27 followed by rotating positions so that everyone gets a chance at each position. You can use 4 offensive lines with 2 or three players deep and rotate clockwise so that each gets a run at the separate spots. All players need to know each spot.

Drills in Diagrams 28-29 then can be taught as individual drills and then in pairs as well. Ultimately, it is possible to use all four drills in sequence before a shot is taken, if a coach cares to get a good run-through in a short time with a team that knows what it is doing.

Diagram 28:

1. In a game there **may** be a move for Player 1 for a shot or pass to the post. In the drill, he will dribble pull up to shorten the reverse pass while Players 2 and 4 slide over a slot to keep spacing for the swing of the ball.

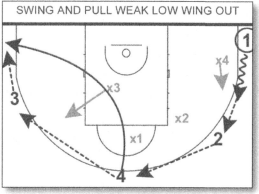

Diagram 28

2. The ball gets to Player 3 on the wing and inevitably this pulls X3 up off the baseline area, so 4 cuts to the open corner and Players 2 and 1 must slide over a slot toward the ball for spacing.

3. Player 4 shoots or goes 1-on-1 and rotates in the direction of the shot, clockwise again.

Diagram 29:

1. After passing to Player 4, 3 makes a cut to the basket and on up to the open weak side wing as he would do to continue the drill in Diagram 28.
2. Player 4 dribbles up out of the corner, as if there had been no shot or play and swings the ball to 2 and 1 and on to 3 as each moves into proper spacing.
3. Player 1 passes to 3 on the wing and reads that X4 has come off the baseline to cover the wing and so he cuts to the open corner. It is wise to end the drill with a shot or move by Player 1 out of the corner. Player 3 may need to cut to the basket to open up a gap lane for 1 to drive, if the ball has not beaten X4 to the

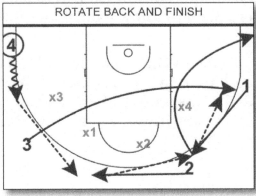

Diagram 29

corner, but in reality, the shot should be there vs. only four players.

Diagram 30: Quick recognition that front player will cover the wing; rapid reversal to force the low weak side wing out followed by a quick cut to the weak side corner.

1. Point 1 passes to Player 3 and sees front defender X1 run to cover him, drawing X2 over to defend 1. This tells the offense immediately that by reversing the ball quickly to the weak side wing that the low wing defender, X3, will have to come out off of the baseline to defend the weak wing.
2. Player 3 quickly reverses the ball to 1, who passes to 2 and cuts to the weak side corner.
3. Player 4 moves up to catch from 2 and looks to hit 1 on the way to the corner, or in the corner. It will be hard to bump X3 fast enough to cover Player 1, so X4 in the

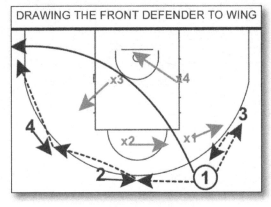

Diagram 30

drill may have to pull out to cover. In a game the middle defender, often X5, would have to come out as an alternative to the bump down.

Diagram 31:

1. Here Player 4 passes to 1 in the corner and runs the Corner Pass Automatic while Players 2 and 3 fill cut over to accommodate the swing of the ball after 1 penetrates and has no play.

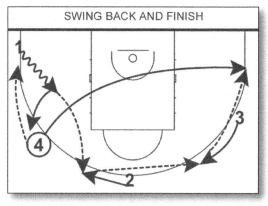

SWING BACK AND FINISH

Diagram 31

2. The shot can be taken on the second side by Player 4 and the drill ends and the rotation is the same pattern as before.

3. This drill can be run just to the second side and end with a shot as noted, or can be swung on to the third and then the fourth side for the shot to end it. The rotation will be the same, rotating to the area where the shot was taken in a clockwise manner.

Baseline Rover Drill

Diagram 32 assumes either Player 1 had passed to 3 to draw X4 and the defense had bumped 4 down quickly, or more likely, that a play has been broken up and the offense ends up in this overload.

1. Of course, Player 5 is not shown in the low post since this part is a four-man perimeter drill, but he would be in the low post in a regular 5-on-5 situation.

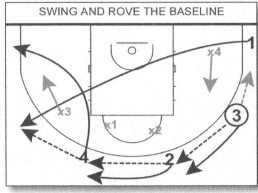

2. In this action, Player 3 does not pass to 1 either because he is not open, or because he wants to move the ball to stir the defense. So, he <u>pass fakes to Player 1</u> to key 1 to start his **Baseline Rover Automatic** cut and swings the ball quickly to 2 and on to 4.

Diagram 32

3. Player <u>1 reads that there is no wing player</u> since 2 and 4 are on top after 1's pass to 3 and corner cut, so he <u>cuts to the open wing area</u>.

4. Player 4 swings it on to 1 on the wing and that pulls the low wing X3 out, inviting 4 to pass to 1 and cut to the goal area and out to the corner as he looks for a return pass before X3 can rotate to him or a big man from the low post area can rotate out to him.

Diagram 33 shows a repeat action to the second side.

1. Player 1 sees 4 is not open for a good move and pass fakes to him to key the second Baseline Rover Automatic.

2. The ball is swung from Player 1 to 2 to 3 and on to 4 in the low wing area for the shot to end the drill. Rotate in the direction of the shot with Player 1 rotating to 4, 4 up to 3, etc. in a clockwise manner.

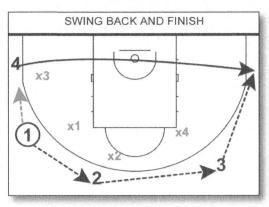

3. The drill can be run to the third and then the fourth side before the shot is allowed and then the rotation would occur as the coach desires.

Diagram 33

NOTE: Any time a wing does not cut on a pass to the corner to open up the gap for the corner player, or if the wing simply looks him off, the corner should run the Baseline Rover Automatic as opposed to having both players stand on the strong side, giving the zone a rest. The cut loads up the second side and forces adjustments.

In fact, it is better that BOTH cut than to have neither one. The first cutter would move to the weak wing and the second to the corner in that case. This assumes that there would be an open wing on the weak side.

Drilling with a high post player and three perimeter players.

Without going into quite as much detail here, the same drill can be run by drilling with the high post player to instill the habit of his being an **"inside fill"** cutter. This is vital to a successful high/low attack that allows the offense to have an open middle in which to attack instead of having three offensive players with their three defenders jamming the lane, preventing proper space for the posts to operate, while jamming up the lane to make it less profitable to make cuts or drives into the gaps in the area. As with drills 26 through 29, drills 34 to 37 can be combined as they are learned

Diagram 34:

1. In a 1-3 set against the box defense to start, Player 1 challenges X2 to defend him by using the dribble to draw him. He then crosses over to pass to Player 3, pulling X4 up.

Diagram 34

2. Alternatively, Player 1 can pass to 2, if X1 insists on matching to him, to pull low wing X3 up to defend 2. Then either Player 1 or 3 could cut to the corner under X3. This part can be added once the players learn the basic drill.

3. Having pulled up X4 in the drill, however, as shown in the diagram, Player 1 cuts to the corner, though a play can be set that would have any other player cut there as well, causing a rotation or distortion in the defense.

Diagram 35:

1. Player 3 passes down to 1 in the corner and <u>4 pops out</u> of the high post to be the <u>fill cutter</u>, moving on over to the sideline area to help 1's pass angle, once he sees 3 cut after the pass.

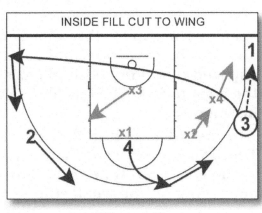

Diagram 35

2. Player 2 moves to the top guard spot above the foul lane line extended.

3. Player 3 sees the wing being open and cuts up to the wing area, if he had not seen that as being open before.

Diagram 36: continuation from Diagram 35. The drill can end when Player 1 shoots in Diagram 35, or can continue on to shoot it in the second rotation as in Diagram 37.

1. After Player 1 bounces up to shorten the pass to 4, Player 2 passes on to 3, pulling X3 out, and cuts a threatening cut to the goal area and on to the corner.

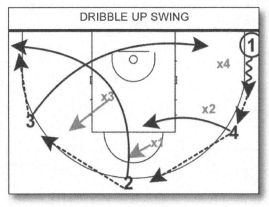

Diagram 36

2. <u>Post 4 gets</u> back into the high post area for a possible high/low that won't be there in this drill.

3. Player 3 cuts on through looking for a return pass and goes on to the weak side wing.

Diagram 37:

1. Post 4 again is the fill cutter when the wing cut is made by 3.

2. Player 2 dribbles up to make a safer pass and reverses the ball to Player 4 now on the wing.

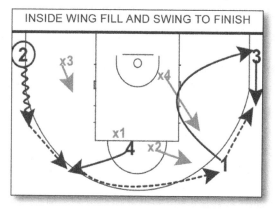

INSIDE WING FILL AND SWING TO FINISH

Diagram 37

3. The ball is swung on to Player 1 and 3.

4. Again, X4 has been pulled up to defend Player 3 on the wing, so 1 cuts to the open corner where the drill can end with a shot.

5. Rotations are as before, with the player behind the shooter rotating to that spot and all others moving ahead.

It is important that at least one of the players from the strong side cut on through to the weak side. Both of them can cut for that matter — **but they both should not stand on the strong side when the ball is rotated against the zone.** That can work in isolation moves for 1-on-1 and 2-on-2 plays against man-to-man, but not as well vs. zones normally.

Later, when the players know the concepts, the defense can mix up and refuse to allow the low wing to be pulled up on the first side with X1 sliding over to match to the ball and pushing X2 over to Player 3. In that case the ball will be reversed because this forces X3 to have to defend Player 4 on the weak side. On the read, Player 2 will pass to 3 on the wing and cut to the open corner. The drill then continues.

DRILLS FOR THE CUTTING GAME

We have shown a lot on ball movement, but that must be combines with excellent, meaningful player movement with spacing, as been said many times in this production. **Chapter 5** described an organized free-lance type of cutting game that has been very successful for Ken's teams over the years called **High/low Cutters** that can be taught and drilled starting with three perimeter players with no defense. Then you can add four defenders set in a box. Dels approach with the Basics, Automatics and Penetration bailout moves is a similar organized freelance approach.

Whether a coach chooses to use this particular program is not the point here. What this demonstrates is that a smart coach can set up a teaching system to teach through specific drilling exactly what and how to execute the individual aspects and then the entire part of an offense.

The objectives of the drilling is to teach the players to:

1. **Draw a top defender** then pass to that side to a high wing position. This **gets a low wing defender out on the ball** far from the open corner below the ball.

2. **Cut to the open corner** below the wing with the ball to have an open shot and to force the zone to rotate.

3. **Rove the baseline** to the high wing position if no one is on the wing, when you pass the ball out of the corner.

4. **Fill cut to the open space** left by a cutter to provide for ball reversal.

Perimeter players passing and cutting drills.

Diagram 38

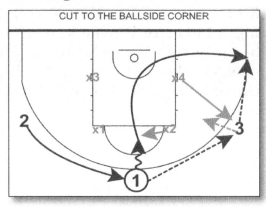

CUT TO THE BALLSIDE CORNER

Diagram 38

1. Point 1 freeze dribbles or dribble drags laterally to entice X2 to defend him and then passes to Player 3 to force the low wing player X4 to come out to guard him — the purpose being to get the wing or low defender out from the baseline corner area to expose it.

2. Player 1 then cuts to the open corner to force a bump down, or for a second low defender to leave the basket area. Player 2 fill cuts behind 1 to replace him.

Diagram 39

1. Player 1 passes the ball out of the corner to 3 and roves the baseline to the high wing spot on the weak side since the wing is open. When the wing is filled, the rover would go to the corner. This is a sprint cut so that we do not leave Player 2 holding the ball too long at the point.

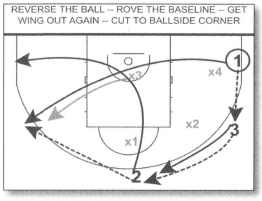

Diagram 39

2. Player 3 passes to 2 who engages X1, possibly with a freeze bounce for timing, if 1 is not nearing the wing area fast enough, and delivers the ball to 1 at the high wing.

3. This forces X3 to take Player 1, so 2 now cuts to the open corner and 1 passes to 2. Wing 3 fill-cuts to the point for Player 2.

The drills in Diagrams 38 and 39 can be run side-to-side twice and then go live, or as many times as the coach desires. Habits get formed through repetitions.

In Diagrams 40 and 41, the same drill is depicted; only this time guard X1 bumps X2 over, who takes the entry pass to Player 3, which keeps X4 inside.

Here the main teaching point is: If the guard (front defender) takes the first pass to the wing, the hole in the defense will be the weak side corner.

Note that in this drill when we only have three cutters as would be in a 1-2-2 formation, and no posts to fill cut to the perimeter, Player 1 must run a replacement cut for himself in which he cuts down a step, maybe two, then pops back for the pass from 3 when he sees X2 cover 3. You can add a post later to fill cut in a four-man drill as was done on the previous set of drills (34-37) that added a high post play to Players 1, 2 and 3.

Diagram 40

1. Player 3 cuts through to the weak side corner after he passes to 1. Wing 2 remains on the weak side wing to pass to Player 3 in the open corner below him.

2. Point 1 replaces himself and swings to Player 2, who sends the ball on down to 3 in the corner and holds. Low wing X3 had to lift to cover 2.

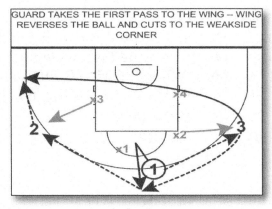

Diagram 40

Diagram 41

1. When Player 3 reverses the ball out of the corner to 2, he can cut baseline and on up to the wing, since the wing is open. After Player 2 reverses the ball to 1, he can cut to the weak side corner.

2. The drill can end with a shot in the corner by 2.

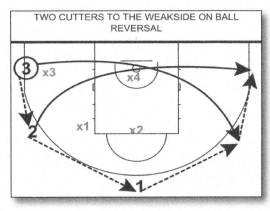

Diagram 41

Adding the Inside Players. Once the concepts of reading where to go on the cuts are understood, the posts can be added and "inside fill cuts" can be introduced to the same drill as was done in drills 34-37. Drills in Diagrams 42-43 pair up for a continued drill.

Diagram 42

1. Player 1 engages X2 with a freeze dribble or a pull laterally to force X4 out to cover 3 on the pass to 3.

2. Player 1 then fills the ball side corner, forcing the defense to decide whether to have X2 bump X4 down or to pull X3 away from the goal. Post 4 fill cuts for Player 1, and 3 passes to 1 in the corner.

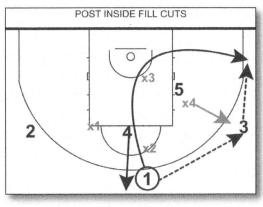

Diagram 42

Diagram 43

1. Player 1 in the corner passes back to 3 and roves the baseline. Player 3 may pass fake at 1, keying him to rove the baseline in this drill. The ball is sent on to 4 at the top.

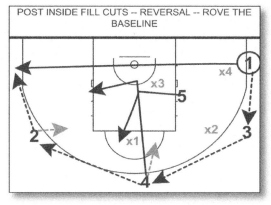

Diagram 43

2. Player 4 passes to 2 and dives to the basket. Player 2 pass fakes at 4, who then posts to a position above the block. As Player 4 exits the lane, 5 flashes into the middle in executing the **X-cut** and up to the high post.

3. Player 2 then passes to 1 in the corner.

Diagrams 45 and 45 show how the drill above can continue as well, though, like in previous drills can be done separately in breakdowns.

Diagram 44

1. The play continues as Player 2 cuts the Corner Pass Automatic after passing to 1 and goes on through to the high elbow/wing position on the weak side with an open corner.

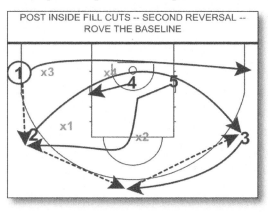

Diagram 44

2. Player 5, who flashed high in the **X-cut,** fill cuts for 2, and 3 fill cuts for 5 at the top. If no shot or pass inside is available, Player 1 then passes to 5 and roves the baseline. Post 5 reverses the ball to Player 3 and dives to the basket.

Diagram 45

1. The ball has been reversed from Player 5 in Diagram 44 with 5 and 4 making the **X-cut.** Player 3 has passed to 2 who pass fakes at 5 and looks at 4 flashing to the middle, when 5 exits the lane to post up.

2. Player 4 then fills to the high post. Best to finish here with a shot. **Use pass fakes to acknowledge all the options.**

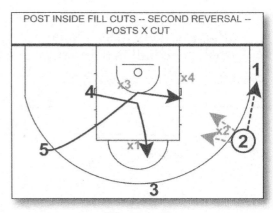

Diagram 45

The number of reversals is up to the coach, but two reversals seems to be plenty, focusing on quick cuts, properly timed along with pass fakes at the various options. If you follow this by going 5-on-5 and by focusing on forcing the middle man to guard one post player, while the partner post or another player challenges the opposite edge of his coverage, the action will be complete. The players will have learned to exploit the normal coverage seen in a 2-3 zone and you can try it vs. 1-2-2 and starting in a 2-1-2 and then in a 1-2-2 offense as well to see players make adjustments. Obviously, a key in the 1-2-2 set is to have the weak side low post have the chance to break hard up into the high post into a 1-3-1 set, although the strong side post may make this cut. In that case the weak side post has good low post options. It is a good change-up cut.

The drills that we have presented are ones that generally relate to our Principles, the Basic 5, the Automatics and the cutting game. There is no end to the drills that can be developed for teaching and refining zone attack actions. Use your imagination and you can develop breakdown drills for virtually any part of your offense(s) that you would like to simplify and refine.

ABOUT THE AUTHORS

Del Harris:

Del Harris coached basketball at every for 53 years, touching on seven decades. He started as a coach in junior high and coached four more years in public high schools followed by 10 successful years at the college level, nine years at Earlham College and one season as an assistant at the University of Utah. Del remains the winningest coach in Earlham College history, winning 15 different championships, and he was a finalist for NAIA National Coach of the Year in 1968

He been involved with the NBA at various levels for 40 years, including head coach of the Houston Rockets, Milwaukee Bucks and the Los Angeles Lakers, where he was NBA Coach of the Year in 1995. He became only the 19th NBA coach to win 500 regular season games in 1997. He was voted the top assistant coach in the league by the NBA general managers in the NBA.com poll three of his final four years on the bench, including the last two. He sat on the bench for over 200 NBA playoff games as a head or assistant coach, including trips to the finals in 1981 as head coach of the Rockets and 2006 as assistant coach of the Dallas Mavericks.

During the summers while coaching at Earlham College, Indiana, he coached in Puerto Rico where his Bayamon Vaqueros team won three consecutive PRBF National Championships and finished third in the World Club Championships in 1973. Filling in as the head coach of the Puerto Rico National team, his team won their first international gold medal at the CentroBasket Games, and a silver medal in the Tournament of the Americas and Europe, both in 1974.

Internationally he has coached with the national teams of Puerto Rico, Canada, the United States, the Dominican Republic and China in World competition. His teams won six medals —three bronze, silver and two golds. As the first foreign coach of the Chinese National team his team performed their greatest win in Olympic history when the eliminated the then World Champion Serbia/Montenegro in the 2004 Athens Olympics.

In 2014 he was honored with the Coach John Wooden "Keys to Life" Award for leadership at the NCAA Final Four. In 2010 he was honored with the Jerry Colangelo Award for character, leadership and faith in the home, community and on the court at the NBA All Star game.

ABOUT THE AUTHORS

Ken Shields:

Ken Shields began his coaching career in 1970, leading the UBC Women's Basketball Team to the National Senior Women's Basketball Championships that year. He went on to serve as the Head Men's Coach at Laurentian University and at the University of Victoria. At Victoria Ken's teams won seven consecutive National Championships. During his last 11 years at Victoria's his team made the finals nine times. By 1989, he accumulated more coaching victories than any man in Canadian inter-university sport and was honoured with four CIAU Coach of the Year awards.

Ken coached the BC Provincial Men's Team to a Gold Medal at the 1981 Canada Games. He also coached Canada's Junior National Team at the World Junior Championships. In 1989, Ken became the Head Coach of the Canadian Men's National Team and Program Director. He then led the team to a 7th place finish in the 1994 Men's World Championships

In 1994, Ken left coaching to take the position of President of the Commonwealth Center for Sport Development, a legacy of the Commonwealth Games. He served in this capacity until 1998 and returned to coaching when offered a position to coach the Daiwa Hot Bizzards of Japan for 2 seasons. Since coaching in Japan, Ken has continued in the sport as an advisor to Professional Basketball Teams in Japan as well as throughout the world. From 2002 through 2004 he served as an Assistant Coach with the Australian Men National Team through the 2004 Athens Olympic Games. In 2009, Ken was appointed as the Lead Assistant with Great Britain's National Women's Team and served in this capacity through the 2012 Summer Olympics in London.

Ken was appointed as a Member of the Order of Canada in 1999, the top honor to be bestowed upon a citizen of Canada for service and contribution to the country. In 2007, Ken received The Dr. James Naismith Award of Excellence for his contribution to Basketball in Canada. In the same year, the Competition court at the University of Victoria was named the Ken and Kathy Shields Court. In 2009, Ken was inducted into the Canadian Sports Hall of Fame. In 2015 Ken received an Honorary Doctorate from the University of Victoria.

Made in the USA
Columbia, SC
17 January 2020